DATE DUE

July 9, 2010

Becoming a Professional Life Coach

Becoming a
Professional Life Coach

Lessons from the Institute for Life Coach Training

Patrick Williams and Diane S. Menendez

W. W. Norton & Company
New York · London

Artwork, tables, worksheets, and exercises were created by the author unless credited otherwise.

For coach certification training and other courses and products, please visit www.lifecoachtraining.com.

For information about permission to reproduce selections from this book, write to Permissions, W. W. Norton & Company, Inc., 500 Fifth Avenue, New York, NY 10110

Composition by Paradigm Graphics
Manufacturing by Hamilton Printing
Production Manger: Leeann Graham

Library of Congress Cataloging-in-Publication Data

Williams, Patrick, 1950-
          Becoming a professional life coach : lessons from the Institute for Life
Coach Training / Patrick Williams and Diane S. Menendez.
          p. cm.— (A Norton professional book)
          Includes bibliographical references and index.
          ISBN-13: 978-0-393-70505-8
          ISBN-10: 0-393-70505-6
          1. Personal coaching. I. Menendez, Diane Susan. II. Title.

BF637.P36W54 2007
158'.3—dc22

                                                                                        2006046884

ISBN 13: 978-0-393-70505-8
ISBN 10: 0-393-70505-6

W. W. Norton & Company, Inc., 500 Fifth Avenue, New York, N.Y. 10110
www.wwnorton.com
W. W. Norton & Company Ltd., Castle House, 75/76 Wells St., London W1T 3QT
    3 4 5 6 7 8 9 0

Contents

Acknowledgments

Coaching continues to evolve as a profession that is changing the way people get help by improving their lives and their business. I am very proud of what we have created at the Institute for Life Coach Training (ILCT) and I thank my faculty, all the students who have learned with us, and all the coaches who have helped me to keep my vision alive and fun! I especially thank Diane Menendez and Sherry Lowry who helped craft the first coaching training manual in 1998, and Diane and other faculty—Lynn Meinke, Jim Vuocolo, Marilyn O'Hearne, Doug McKinley, John Bellanti, Lisa Kramer, Sherry Lowry, Christopher McCluskey, Judy Silverstein, and Judy Santos—who continually made rewrites and revisions. Thank you all for your professionalism and high-quality standards for coaching and for our teaching content. And to my personal assistant and operations manager, Edwina Adams. You have been with me from the beginning and all of this would be just a bunch of great ideas without your diligence, organization, and sense of humor.

—Patrick Williams, October 2006

I am deeply grateful to those who have given so much to me as a coach over the past 18 years. For Pat Williams and Sherry Lowry, colleagues *par excellence,* whose original commitment to creating a program for training professionals to become coaches led to a wonderful working relationship and a great curriculum for the Institute for Life Coach Training. To my husband, Lew Moores, who encouraged me to create a real voice for the writing of the ILCT manual during its three revisions. To the faculty of the Gestalt Institute of Cleveland, whose programs supported me to develop my first approach to coaching in 1988. And, to my clients, from whom I have learned so much about the challenges of leadership and life.

—Diane S. Menendez, October 2006

Becoming a Professional Life Coach

Introduction

Life Coaching as an Operating System

Personal and professional coaching, which has emerged as a powerful and personalized career in the last several years, has shifted the paradigm of how people who seek help with life transitions find a "helper" to partner with them in designing their desired future. No matter what kind of subspecialty a coach might have, life coaching is the basic operating system: a whole-person, client-centered approach. Coaching the client's whole life is the operating system working in the background. A client may seek creative or business coaching, leadership development, or a more balanced life, but all coaching is life coaching.

Before about 1990, there was little mention of coaching except in the corporate culture. Mentoring and executive coaching were resources that many top managers and CEOs utilized, either informally from a colleague or formally by hiring a consultant or psychologist who became their executive coach, as we often did. We will elaborate on the history of coaching but, for now, let us examine why life coaching is becoming more popular and prevalent.

The International Coach Federation (ICF) was founded in 1992 but did not have a real presence until its first convention in 1996. The ICF has kept detailed archives of media coverage on coaching since the early 1990s. Two newspaper articles appeared in 1993, four in 1994 (including one from Australia), and seven in 1995. The majority of articles appeared in publications in the United States. Then, in 1996, a huge increase in publicity occurred, with more than 60 articles, television interviews, and radio shows on the topic of coaching. Every year since, media coverage has increased to hundreds of articles as well as live media coverage in the United States, Europe, Australia, Canada, Japan, Singapore, and other countries. This coverage has comprised both national and local radio and television, including *Good Morning America, Today,* CNBC, BBC radio and TV, and other outlets around the globe. In print, the only books written about coaching before the 1990s were geared to corporate and performance coaching. Good, solid books about life coaching are now becoming numerous, and a few recent ones are national best sellers.

Life coaching as a phenomenon originated in the United States and has spread worldwide rather rapidly. Coaching will soon reach a critical mass in society—people will have heard of coaching, know when they need a coach, know how to find a coach, and know the difference between partnering with a life coach and seeking the services of a therapist or counselor.

Understanding the history of coaching provides current and prospective life coaches with both a framework for understanding their profession and insight into future opportunities. This framework also helps life coaches to place themselves squarely within the larger context of a profession that is still evolving. Casting our eyes across the diverse threads of the past can assist us in understanding the present more accurately and better prepare us as life coaching expands in the 21st century. We believe an examination of the evolution of life coaching also helps counselors and others from helping professions to make the transition to life coaching by clarifying the similarities to and differences between life coaching and other helping professions.

When Pat Williams first founded the Institute for Life Coach Training (ILCT) in 1998, then called Therapist University, only half a dozen coach training schools existed, and the profession of coaching was in its infancy. Diane and I had both been executive coaches since the 1980s and were expanding our practices to include life coaching. We both saw that psychologically trained professionals would have unique skills to transition into coaching, and we had begun to work independently with a few individuals and small groups mentoring therapists who were intrigued by this new profession of coaching. At the second ICF conference in Houston, in 1997, Diane, Sherry Lowry, and I met for the first time and discovered our common passion and interest in teaching coaching skills to therapists, psychologists, and counselors. Given our reverence for the theoretical foundations of our own training, we realized that much of coach training was borrowing theory and technique from psychology, philosophy, and organizational development. It was natural for us to join. I shared my vision of creating a curriculum uniquely designed to train therapists and psychologists to add coaching to their current businesses. After having a few phone calls with other therapists who had entered the coaching profession, I invited Sherry and Diane to help in writing the curriculum. Part of my vision for training was that a complete curriculum would include the coach's personal development because coaching requires that coaches live their life in as fulfilled and purposeful a way as possible. Sherry and Diane got excited because they had just completed about half of just such a series of articles for an e-zine called *The Seamless Life,* housed at www.sideroad.com. In the fall of 1998, as Sherry and Diane were meeting to develop the content for the early training manual, they were looking for texts that would complement and offer outside reading for students. One week, Diane and I both received an e-mail announcing the publication of a three-ring binder manual by Dave Ellis titled *Life Coaching: A New Career for Helping Professionals* (Ellis, 1998). I immediately called Dave, told him that we noticed his manual, described the development of our curriculum, and asked if we could use his book as one of our texts. Dave had written a book and didn't know what he was going to do with it. He was thrilled that we had developed our training and he invited me to a life coaching think tank at his ranch in South Dakota in March 1999. During this conversation, I learned about Dave's previous book, coauthored with Stan Lankowitz, *Human Being: A Manual for Happiness, Health, Love, and Wealth* (Ellis & Lankowitz, 1995), which became (and still is) the supporting text resource guide for "Coaching from the Inside Out," the personal development portion of our curriculum (Part III of this book). Many of the ILCT students over the years have told us that this portion of the curriculum has been transformational for them, offering unique methodology for working with clients. This initially surprised us because helping professionals are expected to have done a great deal of inner work as part of their training. We came to realize that the "Inside Out" topics were unique in that they are more about designing one's life rather than cleaning up and completing old issues.

    With our texts chosen and ordered, Sherry, Diane, and I outlined a curriculum, wrote a very basic training manual, shared chapters back and forth, and looked for a couple of texts to accompany the manual so that the course would take the shape of a graduate program. We felt that this was important because our students were primarily doctoral level and master's level practitioners. We wanted them to both bring the best of what they knew and leave behind what was specific to therapy and psychological treatment. So our curriculum—but not this book—included discussions, exercises, and specifics about what needed to be learned for coaching and what needed to be unlearned from therapeutic training and practice. Our students brought quite a bit of knowledge and experience, and they also had much to leave behind as they transitioned from therapist to coach.

The first class was held in February 1999. It included 20 students, several of whom would go on to become ILCT faculty. We were all pleasantly surprised at the students who were attracted to our training. We thought we would be getting a lot of burned-out therapists. Instead, we got the cream of the crop. We drew therapists who, for the most part, were already coachlike in their orientation: they were future-oriented, most were trained in solution-focused methods, and they were ready to work with high-functioning clients who wanted to live their lives beyond mediocrity. This first crop of students was also excited about working by phone and expanding their client base.

After the class, Sherry, Diane, and I gathered our feedback, listened to student comments, and refined the curriculum design and execution for the second class, which began in April 1999. At that time, the basic curriculum was 30 hours of foundational training. Today the foundational training is 40 hours, and it is the first course in an accredited coach training program (ACTP) leading to the Professional Certified Coach designation by the ICF. Currently the basic foundational texts include *Therapist as Life Coach* (Williams & Davis, 2002), *Co-Active Coaching,* (Whitworth, Kinsey-House, & Sandahl, 1998), and *Human Being* (Ellis & Lankowitz, 1995). We continue to use these texts because together they encompass the basics of life coaching and provide what we believe to be a solid foundation, despite the great number of coaching texts that have been published in recent years.

Since our first program in 1998, we have learned a great deal from our students, from the ILCT faculty, and from our work with clients. The feedback received from students is that they are extremely thankful that the content, and the research on which it is drawn, are so rich in theoretical foundation.

Readers of this book should be aware that it covers much of what is taught in the ILCT foundational course (the first 40 hours of the 130-hour ACTP). Those wanting a deeper and richer experience of becoming a coach will want to consider taking the live training, where learners are able to experience the power of group learning, modeling from the instructors, and the opportunity to practice coaching and get feedback. The full ILCT program consists of 90 additional hours that go into depth in specialty areas of coaching (relationship coaching, executive coaching, emotional intelligence applied to coaching, and many other areas such as coaching ethics, evidence-based coaching research, use of assessments in coaching, practice development, advanced practice, and other graduate-level courses.

Anyone who reads a book with this much content is well aware that to put it into practical use often requires a more formal learning structure. Explore the ILCT Web site and discover the options available to you at www.lifecoachtraining.com.

THE ROOTS OF LIFE COACHING

Coaching has a unique paradigm, but it's not new in its sources, theory, and strategies. Much of the foundation of coaching goes back many decades and even centuries. The draw of pursuing life improvement, personal development, and the exploration of meaning began with early Greek society. This is reflected in Socrates' famous quote, "The unexamined life is not worth living." Since then we have developed many ways of examining our lives, some useful and some not; some are grounded in theory and are evidence-based, while others are made up and useless. What persists, however, is that people who are not in pursuit of basic human needs such as food and shelter do begin to pay attention to higher needs such as self-actualization, fulfillment, and spiritual connection. In Greece, as now, people have always had an intense desire to explore and find personal meaning.

Coaching today is seen as a new phenomenon, yet its foundations can be found in modern psychology and philosophy. Coaching is a new field that borrows from and builds on theories and research from related fields that have come before it. As such, coaching is a multidisciplinary, multitheory synthesis and application of applied behavioral change.

Coach training schools today, both private and academic, must be clear about their theoretical underpinnings and the philosophy that supports what they teach. From its inception, ILCT declared that their intention was to have a content-rich, theoretically based curriculum equivalent to a graduate-level education. Because the original participant base consisted of helping professionals—therapists, counselors, psychologists, industrial-organizational practitioners, and psychiatrists—they knew that they needed to discuss participants' common and varied education, the impact of psychology and philosophy on coaching practice, and coaching's use of adult learning models. The curriculum that emerged was written *by* therapists and *for* therapists transitioning into coaching. It has since expanded in its reach to other aligned helping professionals who have a similar educational background and a psychological orientation for achieving greater human potential.

Contributions from Psychology

So what has the field of psychology brought to coaching, and what are the major influences?

There have been four major forces in psychological theory since the emergence of psychology as a social science in 1879. These four forces are Freudian, behavioral, humanistic, and transpersonal. In recent years there have been three other major forces at work, which we believe are adaptations or evolutions of these four. Cognitive-behavioral psychology grew from a mix of the behavioral and humanistic schools. Positive psychology utilizes cognitive-behavioral approaches and repositions many of the theories that humanistic psychology emphasizes: a nonmechanistic view and a view of possibility as opposed to pathology as an essential approach to the client.

Along with each revolution in psychology, a changing image of human nature has also evolved.

Psychology began as the investigation of consciousness and mental functions such as sensation and perception. *Webster's New World Dictionary* defines psychology as (a) the science dealing with the mind and with mental and emotional processes, and (b) the science of human and animal behavior." Much of the early influence on psychology came from the philosophical tradition, and early psychologists adopted the practice of introspection used by philosophers. The practice of introspection into one's desires, as well as noticing and observing behaviors, thoughts, and emotions, are core practices for increasing client awareness and, as such, are cornerstones of ILCT's approach to coaching.

Introspectionists were an early force in psychology. Wilhelm Wundt in Germany and Edward Titchener in the United States were two of the early defenders of introspection as a method of understanding the workings of the human mind. But they soon realized the inadequacies of introspection for the validation of the young science of psychology. Consciousness and mental functioning were difficult to study objectively. Psychology was experiencing growing pains then, much as coaching is today.

Psychology's Major Theorists
What follows is a quick tour of the growth of psychology and how its major thinkers set the stage for the coaching revolution.

Williams James was the father of American psychology. James preferred ideas to laboratory results and is best known for his writing on consciousness and his view that humans can experience higher states of consciousness. He wrote on such diverse topics as functions of the brain, perception of space, psychic and paranormal faculties, religious ecstasy, will, attention, and habit. Because of his orientation, he gradually drifted away from psychology and in his later life emphasized philosophy, changing his title at Harvard to "professor of philosophy." Nevertheless, James had a tremendous influence on the growth of the psychology profession, and he is still widely read today. One of his most historic books, *The Varieties of Religious Experience* (1994), is a treatise that offers much to us today on the topics of spirituality and transpersonal consciousness.

Sigmund Freud influenced the first force in psychology. While psychology in the United States was struggling for an identity and striving for recognition by the scientific community, European psychology was being reshaped by the theories of Freud. Freud created a stir in the medical community with his ideas and theories, but he finally gained acceptance in psychiatry with the "talking cure" breakthrough—psycho-analysis. Freud brought us such terms as *unconscious, id, ego,* and *superego,* and ideas such as the unconscious, transference, countertrans-ference, defense mechanisms, and resistance. His theories, although strongly based in pathology, did allow the pursuit of our unconscious desires and subconscious mechanisms that influenced behavior, and soon began to gain acceptance in the United States as well.

As Freudian thought was taking shape in Europe and the United States, William James and others began to focus on measurable behavior. Many American psychologists began to combat Freudian theories as another nonverifiable, subjective pseudoscience of the mind.

The time was ripe for the emergence of behaviorism as the second major force in psychology, led by *B. F. Skinner* and *John Watson.* Hundreds of years previously, Shakespeare had commented, "What a piece of work is man?" The behaviorists took this literally and looked upon humans in the early twentieth century as *Homo mechanicus,* an object to be studied as any machine. *Homo mechanicus* was a machine whose mind was ignored.

In the 1950s, *Abraham Maslow* and *Carl Rogers* initiated the third force in psychology, humanistic psychology, which focused on the personal, ontological, and phenomenological aspects of human experi-ence, as opposed to the mechanistic and reductionist theories of Freudianism and behaviorism.

Maslow eventually posited the fourth force, transpersonal psychology, which included mind, body, and spirit. It delved into altered states of consciousness that were both naturally induced by esoteric practices and drug induced by LSD (Stan Grof, Timothy Leary, and Richard Alpert, aka Baba Ram Dass) and other hallucinogens as a way to explore the transpersonal realm. This research began to open up our knowledge of the human mind and expand our windows of perception and possibility.

Carl Jung introduced symbolism, ancient wisdom, the spiritual arche-types, life reviews, synchronicity, transpersonal consciousness, stages of life, individuation, the shadow (both good and bad), and spiritual quests. Jung broke away from Freud in pursuing a more holistic, spiritual under-standing of human motivation. He is quoted as saying, "Who looks outside dreams . . . who looks inside awakens." That is a powerful quote for coaching today. ILCT emphasizes an approach to clients that must include examining their developmental stage or orientation as part of the coach's working alliance with the client.

Alfred Adler worked on social connections, humans as social beings, the importance of relationships, family-of-origin themes, significance and belonging, lifestyle assessment, the big question ("What if?"), and "acting as if."

Roberto Assagioli, the father of psychosynthesis, wrote about our ability to synthesize our various aspects in order to function at higher levels of consciousness. He introduced such terms as *subpersonalities, wisdom of the inner self, higher self,* and the *observing self.*

Karen Horney was an early, influential feminist psychiatrist. Her key theories involved irrational beliefs, the need for security, early influences on rational-emotive theory, and modeling the goal of "self help." She was a contemporary of Adler's and an early influence on Carl Rogers.

Fritz Perls, founder of gestalt therapy, worked with personality problems involving the inner conflict between values and behavior (desires), introducing terms such as *topdog, underdog, polarity* (black-and-white thinking), *the empty chair technique,* and *awareness in the moment.* Gestalt theory also valued the whole-person experience of the client, including mind, emotions, physicality, and spirituality. Perls was influenced by Kurt Lewin's change theory and his work in figure-ground perspectives.

Carl Rogers developed a client-centered approach that suggested clients have the answers within them. He brought us the terms *unconditional positive regard* and *humanistic psychology.* He introduced the practice of listening, reflecting, and paraphrasing, and the value of silence and sacred space.

Abraham Maslow introduced his hierarchy of needs and values. He reflected on being needs versus deficiency needs, the higher self, and our transpersonal potential. He is considered the father of humanistic psychology and also transpersonal psychology.

Virginia Satir was the mother of family therapy, sometimes called the Columbus of family therapy. She believed that a healthy family life involved an open and reciprocal sharing of affection, feelings, and love. She was well-known for describing family roles—such as *the rescuer, the*

xix

victim, and *the placater*—that function to constrain relationships and interactions in families. Her work was an early systemic look at relationships and one that has had a strong influence on coaching in the business context.

Viktor Frankl developed logotherapy out of his personal experience during World War II. Influenced by existential philosophy and his own existential crisis, Frankl wrote *Man's Search for Meaning* while in a Nazi prison camp and later published it from the notes he had made on toilet paper. He is quoted as saying that the one freedom that could not be taken from him while in prison was his mind and his freedom to think, dream, and create. Frankl introduced paradoxical intent into psychology—"what you resist persists" or "what you give energy to is what you manifest." Coaches today help their clients to focus on what they want and on creating desired outcomes. Frankl is cited today by coaches as an exemplar of the importance of intention as well as the necessity of finding meaning in work and life.

Milton Erickson investigated hypnotherapy, as well as languaging and the double-binding of the client. From his work we learn to focus on possibility and looking for the uncommon approach to change, including paradoxical behaviors. Erickson is the father of American hypnotherapy and, along with Gregory Bateson, an early influencer of neuro-linguistic programming (NLP) created by Richard Bandler and John Grinder and popularized by Tony Robbins.

Jeffrey Zeig and *Bill O'Hanlon,* students of Milton Erickson, introduced pattern interruption, the confusion technique, forced choice, assumption of the positive path, nontrance hypnosis, and unconscious competence. Reframing is another important coaching tool based in their work. We're certain that most coaches today use reframing to shift a client's view of a situation.

In the 1970s, solution-focused approaches emerged that emphasized putting less focus on the problem and instead putting energy into discovering what works. Three well-known practitioners in this arena are the late *Insoo Kim Berg,* her husband, the late *Steve de Shazer,* and *Bill O'Hanlon.* O'Hanlon developed solution-oriented therapy, which has now been reframed as solution-focused coaching. Berg, along with Peter

Szabó, wrote *Brief Coaching for Lasting Solutions,* which blends solution-focused theory and brief, short-term coaching sessions.

Fernando Flores is a philosopher who took J. L. Austin and John Searle's work on speech act theory and applied it to human interaction through conversations. By exploring how language really brings action into being, Flores inadvertently devised one of the most useful coaching tools—making requests. Flores was the early influencer of Werner Erhard and the EST training, which later became Landmark Education and influenced Thomas Leonard's early curriculum at Coach University.

Martin Seligman promoted positive psychology as a strength-based approach to human fulfillment. Positive psychology is applied to therapy as well as coaching and education. Its consistent focus is on building and utilizing strengths rather than weaknesses. Seligman's work is highly useful to coaches, as he focused on intense use of current academic research to back up the theories. Positive psychology has evolved today as an entire movement. Life coaching can be viewed as applied positive psychology.

In addition to the theorists discussed above, a vast array of research into life-span developmental psychology has created an understanding of particular developmental trajectories that can be helpful to coaches. *Daniel Levinson's* early work on the life development of Harvard graduates over their 50-year life span (*Seasons of a Man's Life,* 1986) yielded great insight into men's development within that age cohort. *Carol Gilligan's* work on girls and women created insights into the ways in which women's thinking and behavior differs from men's over the life span. *Robert Kegan* developed theories and methods for assessing the development of levels of consciousness in human life-span development.

Ken Wilber's integral approaches to psychology and life built upon and went beyond the transpersonal approaches. In essence, Wilber's integral psychology (IP) examines all the various therapies that exist and then plugs them into the developmental levels for which they are most appropriate. For example, Freudian psychology is most relevant to disorders that occur in early childhood (ages 2 to 7). Jungian psychology is best suited to existential issues of early adulthood, most of which are seldom addressed until midlife. Transpersonal therapies are best with people who have healthy ego structures but sense the absence of higher meaning in their lives.

Wilber synthesized the developmental models of several leading psychologists, including Freud, Piaget, Erikson, Kohlberg, and Bandura for early development, and then added Jung, Gilligan, Aurobindo, Washburn, Kegan, Fowler, Underhill, and dozens of others to produce a developmental model that incorporates every stage from birth up to total, nondual enlightenment. For each of Wilber's basic 13 fulcrums of development, different pathologies develop as a result of the challenges of that particular stage. IP attempts to match the most appropriate therapy for each developmental challenge at any given stage.

These and other amazing tools that have grown out of modern psychology support coaches in assisting clients to change directions as desired. As research in positive psychology shows, new developments become available every day.

The hallmark of coaching is its synthesis of tools from other fields, as well as its proclivity for innovation. With all the research going on today, coaching is developing its own evidence-based theories. It has borrowed from what has gone before, much as psychologists borrowed from philosophers. As coaching grows as a profession, it is developing its own focused research base of effective strategies and tools within the unique relationship that is the coaching alliance.

Our profession is strongly grounded in sound academic and scholarly theories that preceded coaching, and it will be strengthened by the validation of theories and evidence-based research as we move forward.

THE FUTURE OF COACHING

The future belongs to those who believe in the beauty of their dreams. —Eleanor Roosevelt

Is coaching a passing fancy, or is it the true evolution of a new profession? Several indicators point to coaching being a new profession that is establishing itself within the framework of existing helping professions. First, the establishment of a professional organization—ICF—and associated ethical standards and minimal competencies predict the continuation of this profession. Second, the number of practicing coaches is growing rapidly and is clearly responding to the needs and demands of our fast-paced, disconnected society. Third, there is evidence of an increasing number of recognized coach-training organizations and a growing number of college courses on coaching, which further establishes the profession within the mainstream of continuing education for professionals.

Pat Williams predicted that with the evolution of the coaching profession and the proliferation of coach-training organizations, the next logical step would be graduate degrees in coaching (Williams & Davis, 2002). George Washington University offered the first ICF ACTP after starting as a certificate program within the organization development department. The University of Sydney (Australia), spearheaded by Dr. Anthony Grant, launched the first M.A. program in coaching psychology in the late 1990s. Those were soon followed by other colleges offering classes in coaching, some of them leading to certificates in coaching as part of a degree in a related field, such as organizational development, management, or leadership.

As of 2007, over four dozen colleges and universities offer either a certificate program in coaching or a full graduate degree in coaching. The valuable addition of academic institutions in the growth of the coaching profession is very welcome. This trend adds courses of study that underpin the actual coaching relationship, such as personality development, developmental psychology, theories of human change, research methodology, organizational development, and cross-cultural issues.

A powerful attraction of life coaching is having a partner who is committed to helping people develop and implement their ideal life. Life coaching also provides a sense of connection, belonging, and significance in a world that can sometimes seem isolating, overwhelming, or both. Coaches also keep people focused, challenged, and motivated for living their personal and professional lives *on purpose.*

Hopefully life coaching in all its various forms (retirement coaching, career coaching, relationship coaching, parent coaching, and so on) will permeate society at all levels. In reality, this has already begun to happen. Coaches are now in schools, probation departments, churches, nonprofit corporations, and other community agencies. Coaching is a combination of communication and empowerment that is becoming ingrained in our entire cultural fabric so that relationships at all levels can implement the coaching paradigm as a new and effective way to bring out the best in people and create solutions to complex problems. An entire company trained in basic coaching concepts and skills could become a "completely coachable company," one in which every employee has learned and practices a coaching approach. For example, in the lunchroom, imagine two people are having lunch. One complains about a coworker and catches himself: "Oh, here I go again. Can you give me some coaching about this?" Or the coworker could initiate, saying, "I think this might be an opportunity for coaching. Would you like me to coach you?" In so doing, they would eliminate many costs and empower employees at all levels to coach each other at times of stress, change, or need.

Any profession that wants to be recognized by the public as credible and ethical needs to have those who "belong" to the profession participate in coach-specific training as they build their career. Additionally, those who are well established and experienced need to participate in training to update and refine their skills on a regular basis. Every profession worth being recognized has requirements for continuing education. More important, those who call themselves coaches owe it to themselves and the profession to regularly learn new skills, as well as availing themselves of coaching as a client, and to move toward ICF certification and upgrading skills and status as desired. These are ways we "sharpen our saw," as Stephen Covey, author and speaker, has stated. A good example of professions that have done this well are certified financial planners (CFPs) and certified public accountants (CPAs). Most citizens now know that you can hire a financial planner or accountant who is not certified, and that awareness leads consumers to make an informed decision about who they hire and the level of expertise they can expect.

As people enter into our profession, many think that a one-day workshop or reading a book makes them a professional coach. Ask yourself, does taking a first aid course or learning CPR make one an emergency medical technician? Of course not. It's possible to learn coaching methodology in a quick manner and be effective, but that doesn't make someone a professional coach. Training and coaching are the two ingredients that ensure the success of the coaching profession. As you meet colleagues and people who call themselves coaches, be curious about where they received their training. If they have not received professional training, please encourage them both to get coach-specific training and to join the ICF. We need one organization that stands for the entire profession. Other organizations will also thrive that support coaching specializations, such as executive coaching, business coaching, life coaching, relationship coaching, and career coaching. Still, all coaches should be trained in similar foundational skills and be members of the global association that the ICF aspires to be. This is how people can participate in the evolution and acceptance of our growing profession. We can all be stewards of our profession and models of excellence for those who are in the stands instead of on the playing field.

One other thought. We have noticed that as we gain more training and gain more experience in working with clients, it is not so much that our skills and competencies change. But our "beingness" and our spirits as coaches are at a different level. Mastery is more about who you are than what you do or say. Research in the field of psychotherapy has repeatedly found that the relationship between the therapist and client is the most important ingredient in client success. The therapeutic approach or technique is less important than the ability of the therapist to create and maintain a strong relationship and an environment of trust and confidence.

That is mastery! Where could you use some training? What new skill, technique, or personal strength would you like to master? Go get it. We all will benefit.

We are on the verge of a fundamental shift in how and why people seek helpers. We believe psychotherapy has played an important role in the lives of many clients and that psychotherapy will still be needed in our society, especially for the seriously mentally ill. We also believe coaching will become the prevailing strategy for personal development—the most common way to learn to identify strengths and use them to overcome obstacles and challenges while pursuing possibilities.

People today need connection with a mentor, coach, or guide more than ever before due to the rapid pace of change, the difficulty of sustaining relationships, and the desire to fulfill one's life purpose. We believe this is what the human potential movement of the 1970s intended. Psychological research and theory over the last several decades has contributed much to our understanding of how people change, how they adjust to life's struggles, and how they develop into self-actualized human beings. That knowledge now lends itself to this new field of life coaching, without the medical model stigma and diagnosis labeling that often comes with psychological counseling or therapy. Being able to receive coaching and have a personal coach, whether privately hired or provided by your company or community agency, is a service we hope becomes ubiquitous and transformational to individuals and our culture as a whole.

We believe that the profession of coaching will soon be bigger than psychotherapy. The general public will know the distinction between therapy and coaching, and will be clear on when to seek a therapist and when to seek a coach. Coaches will refer to therapists and therapists will refer to coaches. Coaching will permeate society and be available to everyone, not just executives and high-powered professionals. We expect to see a variety of specialized coaches, such as relationship coaches, parenting and family coaches, wellness and health coaches, spiritual development coaches, career coaches, and many others.

The entire profession will foster the idea of life coaching as the umbrella under which all coaching rests. Whether a client seeks specific coaching for business or job challenges, coaching for a life transition (such as a career change, relationship change, or health issues), or for pure life-design coaching, it is all life coaching. A coach may also serve as a referral source for specialty coaching as needed or requested by their client.

The coaching profession is experiencing dynamic growth and change. It will no doubt continue to interact developmentally with social, economic, and political processes; draw on the knowledge base of diverse disciplines; enhance its intellectual and professional maturity; and proceed to establish itself internationally as well as in mainstream North America. If these actions represent the future of coaching, then the profession will change in ways that support viability and growth. Life coaching exists because it is helpful, and it will prosper because it can be transformational.

In the chapters that follow, we share the specific ways that coaching can bring about transformation in the lives of clients, as we have been teaching them at ILCT since 1998. As you read, you will be joining the several thousand ILCT coaches now coaching on every continent (except Antarctica) around the world.

Coaching Fundamentals

The three chapters included in Part I, "Coaching Fundamentals," lay the groundwork for an understanding of coaching as a profession and as a process of growth and change.

Our working definitions are as follows:

Professional Coaching: Professional coaches provide an ongoing partnership designed to help clients produce fulfilling results in their personal and professional lives. Coaches help people improve their performances and enhance the quality of their lives. Coaches are trained to listen, observe, and customize their approach to individual client needs. They seek to elicit solutions and strategies from the client, and they believe the client is naturally creative and resourceful. The coach's job is to provide support to enhance the skills, resources, and creativity that the client already has (International Coach Federation, 2007).

Life Coaching As an Operating System: Life coaching is a powerful human relationship in which trained coaches assist people to design their future rather than get over their past. Through a typically long-term relationship, coaches aid clients in creating visions and goals for all aspects of their lives, as well as multiple strategies to support achieving those goals. Coaches recognize the brilliance of each client and their personal power to discover their own solutions when provided with support, accountablility, and unconditional positive regard (Williams & Davis, 2002).

Part I includes an in-depth discussion of "Listening as a Coach," a discussion of the language specific to coaching, and the human developmental theories that underpin the coach's understanding of clients at various phases and stages of development. These sections offer general principles that apply to most coaching situations and approaches.

If you are familiar with coaching, you are likely to reencounter here the basic principles that you are already aware of. We hope that you also discover something new that will enrich your way of thinking about and practicing coaching. For us, the usefulness of human developmental theories as a way of informing the context of coaching has been a more recent area of discovery, one that we have added in the last 5 years.

Chapter 1

Listening as a Coach

Kafka understood the value of paying close attention. Listening is a deceptively simple skill that's often overlooked in its power. Listening as a coach is very different from normal, everyday listening. Even when done extraordinarily well, common conversational listening lacks the intentional focus the coach brings to the coaching conversation. The coach listens with a very different quality of attention that includes an impulse to be of service (without having an agenda aside from listening carefully for what "wants" to happen).

As Carl Rogers demonstrated, active listening, accompanied by unconditional positive regard, supports clients in making tremendous positive changes. The coach's ability to be fully present to the client, *patiently* listening, communicates fundamental acceptance of the client. This quality of listening and acceptance allows the client to be vulnerable in sessions. Clients seldom experience the patient listening from others that they receive from their coaches. This explains why coaching can feel *therapeutic,* even though coaching definitely is not *therapy.* Coaches often refer to this as creating a *sacred space* or an *inspiring space* in which the client experiences the impact of powerful listening. This space supports the client's personal unfolding. If lapses occur in the coach's ability to listen with patience and undeniable focus, or to create an inspiring space, the client's trust will erode.

Lapses in being present and patiently listening can take these forms:

- Interrupting clients or speaking as soon as clients finish a sentence; allowing no space for clients to hear themselves, to feel the impact of what they have said
- Beginning to speak while clients finish the last few words of a sentence—this doesn't allow clients the choice to continue and elaborate.

You need not leave your room. Remain sitting at your table and listen. You need not even listen—simply wait. You need not even wait. Just learn to become quiet, and still and solitary. The world will freely offer itself to you to be unmasked. It has no choice. It will roll in ecstasy at your feet.

—Franz Kafka

- Attending superficially, missing signals provided by the clients' tone of voice or body language
- Breaking eye contact or doodling during a face-to-face session
- Multitasking, with sounds clients hear during phone coaching
- Random or fidgety movements unrelated to clients' statements that grow out of the coaches' interior thoughts or feelings

Helping professionals in a wide variety of fields use listening skills as an integral aspect of their work. Helping professionals know how valuable it can be to simply listen and focus their attention on a client. However, coaches listen in unique ways that support the goals of the coaching relationship and maximize opportunities for achieving those goals.

Listening forms the cornerstone of coaching, just as it remains the bedrock for every human relationship. Like every professional with extensive education, training, and experience, we develop habits as listeners. Most helping professionals listen instinctively for the client's feelings, and just as instinctively they reflect, probe, and work with the client toward therapeutic change. As coaches, we listen for the client's feelings, too. However, we pay equal attention to other domains of the client's life.

THREE KINDS OF LISTENING AS A COACH

Coaches use three main kinds of listening skills: listening *to,* listening *for,* and listening *with* (Whitworth, Kinsey-House, & Sandahl, 1998, pp. 9, 257).

Listening To

Listening to is what many people call active listening. Listen to what the client says—and does not say. Listen to the content and to what is beyond the words. This is the kind of listening that most of us learn readily to do as students, as parents, and as partners.

A basic skill in active listening includes knowing when and how to mirror back to the client what was heard. When mirroring, the coach repeats back to the client what he said so that he feels fully heard. Artful mirroring allows the client to hear himself. However, masterful coaches go beyond elementary mirroring. People new to practicing mirroring sometimes make the mistake of parroting back what they heard, rather than offering a nuanced interpretation that captures the client's attention. New coaches sometimes mirror too often, interrupting the client's flow.

Coaches also *listen to* by observing the client's body movements, gestures, tone of voice, speech pacing, pauses, and eye movements. Paying attention to the congruence of words and nonverbal behavior, the coach can begin to sense dimensions of the experience that clients may not fully have brought into their consciousness.

Listening For

A second kind of listening we do as coaches is *listening for.* Laura Whitworth describes this well: "The coach listens for clients' vision, values, commitment, and purpose in their words and demeanor" (Whitworth, Kinsey-House, & Sandahl, 1998, p. 257).

To *listen for* is to listen in search of something. The coach listens with a consciousness, with a purpose and focus that come from the alliance that was designed with the client. The alliance includes the client's goals and desires, what many coaches refer to as "the client's agenda." The coach listens to forward the client's agenda, not the coach's agenda.

We sometimes call this *listening for the large life.* For example, a particular client's agenda includes improving work–life balance. His coach listens for expanding the possibilities beyond just having balance, instead creating the most authentic and designed life that the client can imagine. The coach listens for the bigger picture, the richer possibilities available, beyond just the obvious improvements like reprioritizing time, focusing on time for self, and so on. What life can the client create so that balance would simply be a "given"? The coach listens as if asking, "What crucible can contain the presenting goal, providing an expanded container to support the client's unfolding?"

One kind of *listening for* that is not useful, however, is listening for "the solution." As coaches, we do not need to be the expert.

People who enter professions such as coaching, counseling, and consulting are often under the impression that they need to know or are expected to know what's best for other people. Their impulse to make a

3

difference can get confused with an inclination to impose their own values on their clients. Novice coaches, as well as coaches who have not devoted much attention to their own development and inner life, are especially prone to overlay their values onto clients. More seasoned coaches with firsthand experience of how this orientation can distort or derail a coach–client relationship are clearer about the need to release their conviction that they know what's best for a client. Coaches learn to observe their own process and let go of their investment in being the expert and having the answer.

Coaching is not about listening for problems, pathologies, history, pain, and blocks—instead, it's about listening for possibilities, goals, dreams, and aspirations. It's about discovering, harnessing, and expanding on strengths and tools clients have, not about rooting out problems and tackling them (which, in addition to being disempowering, is not an appropriate focus in the coaching relationship). Listening for solutions is, in fact, a block to the coaching process: it distorts the process by superimposing an artificial agenda onto it. The agenda might be:

- To advise or teach something the coach is passionate about. While coaching sometimes includes brief moments of teaching, these need to be labeled as such and used at a minimum. A coach who has expertise in a domain needs to be vigilant about not listening for opportunities in this area. One new coach we worked with was passionate about nutrition and tended to insert his knowledge in coaching conversations where it didn't belong. In general we recommend that coaches steer clients to resources when the client needs to learn something. The new coach could easily have recommended specific texts or Web sites to clients who needed to learn more about nutrition. He didn't need to use the coaching time for teaching.
- To find answers (often too quickly). The coach needs to avoid pushing for answers. New coaches can find it hard to not be hooked into a client's urgency around finding answers.
- To have the coach feel successful (fulfilling the coach's need, not the client's). This is a definite mistake. The coach in this case is listening to her internal dialogue or to her own needs, not the client's.

A metaphor we use with clients is to explore the difference between flying from L.A. to New York and driving there. Driving allows for adventures, unexpected insights and meetings. Flying is more predictable and efficient. However, "flying" a client to his or her goal skips important steps and reduces the possibility that the growth will become grounded or rooted in the client's life.

When we coach clients in the domain of work, *listening for* includes paying attention to the particular interdependence of the fundamental results of the client's work. Michael O'Brien (personal communication, April 10, 2002) describes this as "The Work Triangle" (Figure 1.1).

Figure 1.1
The work triangle

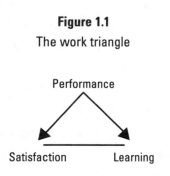

Most conversations people have *at work* focus on performance. Clients can bring this habit to coaching. Coaches listen for how the clients' satisfaction and learning grow from their work because these are critical to maintaining performance. If individuals are not learning, their performance will decline over time. If the clients' predominant experience of work is boredom or stress, both learning and performance will suffer.

Listening With

Coaches do a third kind of listening—*listening with.* There are many ways to *listen with.* The best way we have found is to consider listening with the whole self. This includes *listening with heart, listening with intuition,* and *listening with the body.*

Listening with heart, coaches notice what emotions are emerging as they resonate with clients. Listening with intuition, coaches pay attention to the images, metaphors, and internal words or phrases that emerge from within as an intuitive connection. Listening with the body, coaches notice where in their body they are reacting to what they are hearing or sensing from the presence of the client. An everyday example occurs when people say they have a "gut feeling." That's a somatic response to a situation or conversation that lacks a logical explanation. However, the coach's "gut reaction" or "intuitive hit" needs to be checked out for accuracy. Oftentimes physical or intuitive reactions lead to an understanding that neither coach nor client had before. A coach might say to the client, "I just had this sense that you may be ambivalent and I want to check out whether that's on target or not. You say you want to start this new business, and yet I don't sense that your energy or excitement is present or convincing as you speak about it." Sharing the intuition might lead to a deepening or a shift in the coaching conversation.

Skillful coaches listen and resonate with clients' words, meanings, and tones. They listen consciously to what is evoked in them by clients. They listen deeply from the heart and attend to the images, feelings, and senses that arise. These are sources of insight and resources for both coach and client.

Coaches are careful to avoid "me, too" listening. We see this kind of listening every day, when one person shares a thought or feeling, and the other replies, "Gee, that happened to me, too!" That kind of listening shifts the focus away from the client's experience.

However, a unique feature of the coaching relationship is appropriate use of self-disclosure by the coach. A masterful coach must know the difference between self-disclosure to enhance the client's learning and disclosure that interferes. Self-disclosure must serve one of two purposes: to increase the connection with the client or to function as a learning point. For example, a coach might say to a client that she, too, had jitters about leaving a full-time job to start a business. Through coaching many other clients who are starting businesses, she's learned how normal that is in the situation. That enables the client to put his own jitters into perspective.

For therapists becoming coaches, learning to self-disclose at all can be difficult. Most therapists were taught *not* to do any self-disclosure with clients because it interferes with the clients' healing and shifts the relationship out of the professional role. Since coaches work with clients who are not emotionally fragile, occasional self-disclosure deepens the relationship as clients see coaches as fully human.

The great gift of coaching is that we can freely share our intuition with clients because the relationship is one of partnership. Often, how freely we share what we hear is one of the key differences between the kind of listening we do as therapists and the kind of listening we do as coaches.

Coaches need to be cautious about what psychologists know as *transference* and *countertransference*. In simple terms, transference means that a person is unconsciously bringing their experience and feelings from another situation into a current one.

Clients may bring into coaching the unconscious expectation that coaches will solve their life issues for them, thereby hooking a natural tendency coaches may have to rescue or fix. Countertransference can happen to coaches when clients' conversations evoke in them an unconscious reaction based on something in their own life. Coaches, for example, may be listening to clients talk about the desire to have another child or to live on a Caribbean island. That story might evoke in coaches their own longings, and their internal reactions are transferred to the coaching conversation. This is likely to get in the way of powerful listening.

Coaching relationships have a quality of intimacy about them that makes it critical for coaches to commit to reflecting on any leaks of their own "stuff" into the coaching relationship. To be effective and powerful, coaches at their best must recognize what might trigger or hook them when it occurs, and let it go.

A USEFUL LISTENING TEMPLATE

Just as maps help travelers find their way, listening templates help coaches pay attention to what can be listened for by providing a structure to guide their attention. Templates help coaches see gaps that might lend themselves to the starting points for the coaching conversation.

Listening for the "Big Five"

One powerful tool ILCT-trained coaches use is the ability to *listen for* the "Big Five." In early coaching sessions with clients, the focus is on understanding the clients' goals and discovering what needs to shift so the clients can create what they most want. Once clients have articulated the goals for change, it is time to start listening for the clients' strengths and any potential blocks they may encounter in achieving their goals. Discovering potential blocks helps both coaches and clients identify what the clients will need to do—or become—to achieve their goal.

The Big Five provides a generic listening template that helps coaches to discern what is currently in place and what needs to be added to the clients' repertoire. The Big Five are frequently the source of guidance about the specific fieldwork and coaching coaches will do with clients. These five factors are drawn from sports psychology and personal coaching experiences (Coffey, 1997; to order a copy of this audiotape, go to www.lifecoachtraining.com/resources).

Focus

Clients' focuses are the characteristic parts of their work and life that draw their attention at the current time. An ideal focus is appropriate, steady, flexible, able to be maintained, and related to goals that foster the clients' well-being. Clients may come into coaching with a "fuzzy focus." They come to coaching with a sense that they want to do something different. They are not happy in their current situation, but they are not clear on what needs to be different or what they want to create. That's a common coaching conversation. Coaching takes the sense of something missing or something desired and assists clients in gaining clarity and choice by asking powerful questions, working with clients on their vision—how they want life to be. Through powerful questions, journal exercises, and reflections, clients will gain more clarity of focus and be able to move toward what they want.

A metaphor we use with clients is that clarifying their focus is like charting a course on a sailboat. They know they want to get there, and they have many choices about how to get there. But they can't start sailing until they know what island they want to visit. Coaching helps clients determine the destination so that the coaching can move ahead to exploring the various routes clients can choose to get there. Knowing the routes helps, and successful sailors also need to be able to adjust to various circumstances, such as wind shifts, and storms.

One of coaches' tasks is to work with clients to assess whether the clients' goals are feasible—whether they are appropriate and achievable for the clients at this time. One of our faculty worked with a client who wanted to open a new business, a retail outlet, at the same time when she was three months pregnant with her third child. While this isn't something that we would want to do under the circumstances, the coaching conversation helped the client determine that yes, she could do this, and helped her strategize how to open the business as well as support the upcoming birth.

So if your client has a goal of expanding his business, and that's his reason for seeking coaching, you will ask yourself, "Does he have a focus? Is the focus clear?" If the focus seems fuzzy, that may be a starting point for coaching. For example, he may talk about expanding but not be clear about how he would measure the expansion. Would it be numbers of clients? Bottom line revenue? New markets? New products? If he isn't clear, the coach needs to help him explore and gain clarity about the focus for expansion—in other words, what expansion really means to him. If he holds his focus too generally, he will not be able to achieve his goals.

It is, of course, possible to be *over focused.* Over focusing does not allow clients to discover options because they are so focused on just one direction. Being highly motivated isn't the same as being overfocused, which is like having tunnel vision. Clients can overfocus on work achievements, ignoring other aspects of their lives. Coaches support the clients in exploring this by bringing a broad perspective to the clients' lives. Another benefit of coaching is that it expands the view and puts goals in the context of the rest of clients' lives.

The client who wants to expand his business may be overfocused on that goal and may almost obsessively focus all his attention and energy on it. That could lead to coaching conversations about work–life balance, the needs of other people in his life, and how he will maintain

9

his health and physical well-being during the expansion. Life coaching—unlike pure business coaching—takes a whole-person perspective on any client who comes for coaching.

Mind-set/Attitude

Coaches consider the clients' mind-set by observing and listening to the clients. How do the clients tend to interpret their experiences—negatively, seeing only problems? Positively, seeing possibilities? Is the clients' mind-set helpful, or is it limiting? The coaching conversations can help clients shift away from limiting beliefs and toward powerful possibilities and a more "can do" attitude.

Mind-set and attitude are the characteristic or current mental and emotional positions from which clients view themselves, other people, events, and the world. Mind-set and attitude can often be the source of—or have significant impact on—clients' motivational patterns. For example, if clients are frequently fear-driven, it is hard to move toward things—including goals clients have set. The key factor is whether the clients are aware of their mind-set and attitude. Are the mind-set and attitude appropriate? Do they support the clients to reach the goal?

Mind-set includes the characteristic ways clients view themselves and the world. As a coach listens, over time clients will reveal mind-set through:

- The ways they characteristically approach people and relationships
- The ways they define success and themselves in relationship to people, events, and circumstances
- Whether they tend to see themselves as actors, participants, or victims
- How they draw conclusions about events, experiences, and why they have unfolded as they have
- How they think about their ability to create and to influence
- How they evaluate the importance and value of people, situations, experiences, and results

For our client who is interested in expanding his business, the coach will look for whether he holds a positive attitude about the opportunity.

10

Does he want to expand his business but describes that process pessimistically? Does he say things like, "I have a great idea but I'm not a businessman. I don't know what to do. I can't afford to hire the right people." In this case, the coach would notice that working on mind-set will be important. This client seems to have limiting beliefs: he is focused on what can't happen, what limits him, what he can't afford. If this is a habitual way of thinking, he could end up inadvertently sabotaging his goal by not directing his efforts appropriately. In Chapter 14, "Mind-set Is Causative," we focus extensively on ways of noticing and working with mind-set.

With corporate clients, mind-set quickly shows up when clients describe conflicts with others. Clients often focus outside of themselves in conflicts, which shows up as blaming others and the situation, and not noticing or claiming what the clients themselves are doing to perpetuate the situation. The coach's role is to listen and notice to what extent clients see and claim their role and will accept accountability for taking actions to change what is going on.

Skills and Capacities

Given the clients' goals, the key question is whether they have the necessary skills and capabilities required for success. Skills tend to be learnable and teachable. Capacities, on the other hand, can be developed but generally are not things we expect to build through teaching. An example of a capacity might be a client's ability to tolerate ambiguity without rushing to action. Capacities can be found by discovering what the client has patience for and can tolerate, or what the client has impatience for and can't tolerate. Clients may need to develop, for example, their capacity for staying engaged when conflict occurs, instead of retreating or running away because they don't have the capacity to stay calm in conflict. Coaches can help clients develop their capacities, as we describe later in Chapter 6 when we discuss assigning practices as field-work in coaching.

First, coaches and clients identify current skills and capacities the clients have that will support the coaching goals. These are the resources the clients can draw upon. The coaching helps the clients determine whether to learn other needed skills or to delegate or hire someone. For

11

example, a client starting a new business will need some basic skills to run a business: bookkeeping, marketing, staffing, Web site development, and so on. As we know, he doesn't need to be hands-on with all of these, but he does need to identify who can assist him or provide the service. The key questions are: What are the gaps between what he currently can do or acquire and what is needed? What is the most effective way to fill these gaps?

This assessment can also help the client determine whether the goal he has set is feasible within the time he wants to achieve it. Assessing skills and capabilities sometimes becomes an entry point back to examining the goal, as well as to other areas within the Big Five.

For the client wanting to expand his business, you may begin to notice skills and capabilities such as time management, networking (or the lack thereof), marketing knowledge, follow-through, and project management. Does the client complete things on time? Take on too many requests from others? Can the client work satisfactorily with the level of detail required to manage the business as well as expand it? If any of these are not current capabilities, the client will need to develop them or delegate them to others. Many business owners discover that to expand their business, they need to engage more support staff or outsource things they have been doing themselves.

Habits, Practices, and Patterns

These are what clients do automatically—without thinking or planning. These can be habits, practices, and patterns in the physical, emotional, mental, and spiritual realms. Key questions are: "Are the clients' habits, practices, and patterns supporting them in achieving the goal? Do they need to be shifted in some way? Can they be unlearned, noticed, or developed into new patterns?

Note: *This is not an invitation to judge clients.* Avoid labeling the habits as bad or good. Simply discover whether they are useful or not—whether they support the clients in effectively attaining their goals.

A common example is time management, especially if clients move into a home-based business, a romantic notion for many people. The good news is that they are working from home. The bad news is that they are working from home. Time management as a habit becomes crucial in how they organize their work time versus play time amid the distractions from family and pets, and the temptation to go outside and sit in the sun. Can they set the boundaries they will need to do their work? Coaches will help them explore their time management habits and determine whether they are sufficient.

Clients may have a pattern of thinking that they need to do all the work themselves. They may be reluctant to delegate and then get overwhelmed with administrivia. If they want to start a business, they must develop new patterns. They will need to find people who can support their business; otherwise they risk not launching it successfully. A common goal clients set in a case like this would be to gradually move from working *in the business* (providing direct service) to working *on the business* (leading, strategizing, and so on).

This may be where you assess whether clients habitually overpromise and underdeliver. Clients who want to expand their business may need to have a deliberate habit or practice of regularly contacting current and former customers, which is an accepted business strategy, sometimes describes as TOMA, "top of mind awareness." Keeping the business in the forefront of the customer's mind often leads to repeat business or the willingness to buy new products or services. TOMA also creates referrals. If clients lack these habits, coaches need to move back to examining skills and capabilities: what would the client need to learn in order to have TOMA become a new business practice?

In the corporate environment, a pattern could show up as a boss paging an employee at all hours of the evening and expecting the employee to respond. Unless they have an agreement that the employee is to be "on call," the client will begin to experience demotivated employees. In a case like this, the coach would explore the source of the after-hours calls. Are they occurring because the client doesn't plan? Does this client make a distinction between home and work life? Does the client treat situations as crises and initiate a reactive pattern, so that every crisis the client experiences becomes a crisis for his people?

13

Attending to Clients' Energy

This factor is the clients' ability to bring forth, as needed, an appropriate amount of physical/emotional/mental/spiritual *energy* in a timely and appropriate way. Energy serves as a gateway into clients' health, motivation, commitment, and way of being in the world. Energy may be either sourced or blocked by the previous four factors. A good coach will notice regularly how clients motivate themselves and generate energy, as well as whether their physical well-being impacts their energy. For example, aging, menopause, illness, and parenting or caregiving all can have an impact on available energy.

Even when coaching by phone, coaches can sense clients' energy. It is critical for coaches to have a sense of their clients' energy through the enthusiasm they express about the goal. Are they excited about the goal? Does the energy they communicate to coaches dissipate after the coaching conversation? Can clients maintain their energy level?

On the other hand, this might be the entry point for coaching: the clients' goals are valid, but they have so many energy drainers in other places in their lives that they are unable to move forward as they want to. They simply don't have the required energy available. Their intentions are great, and the prospects of growing the business are solid. But the coaches notice that they need to have more energy available consistently in order to make progress.

WHAT LISTENING IS NOT

1. Coaching is not about listening for problems, pathologies, history, pain, and blocks—instead, it's about listening for possibilities, goals, dreams, aspirations. Coaching is about discovering, harnessing, and expanding on strengths and tools clients have, not about rooting out problems and tackling them (which, in addition to being disempowering, is not an appropriate focus in the coaching relationship).

2. Coaching is not about listening for solutions. We distinguish *possibilities* from *solutions,* and encourage coaches to begin listening for possibilities from the beginning of their work. Coaches need to

remain open to clients' creativity in generating solutions. Listening for solutions is a block to coaching because it distorts the process by superimposing an artificial agenda onto it. The agenda might be:

- to find answers (often too quickly)—coaches need to not push for this and also need to not be hooked into clients' urgency around coming to conclusions.
- for the coach to feel successful. This fulfills coaches' needs, not the clients'.

3. Coaching is not advising or training. Sometimes coaches do need to teach their clients something briefly in order to help them build a skill or capability. A coach, for example, may take 15 minutes of a coaching session to teach a stressed client how to do breath-counting meditation. The coach would ask the client's permission to teach and would label the work as such.

CONCLUSION

We begin this book with a focus on listening because listening creates the foundation for great coaching. One of our colleagues, Dave Ellis, believes that coaches should spend 80 percent of their time simply listening and nondirectively working with what the client says. In terms of what an observer would notice, the coach would be doing any of the following (Ellis, 2006, pp. 54–56):

- *Listening fully and then affirming the client.* This would involve feeding back to clients what seems to be inspiring to them, which helps the clients feel affirmed as well as hear themselves. Coaches acknowledge the goals and help the clients feel heard.
- *Listening fully and then feeding back clients' desires.* Coaches feed back what the clients want in a way that clarifies and focuses the clients' attention. This helps clients notice the "key points" that the coaches create out of what could have been a sustained description by the clients.

15

- *Listen fully and ask the client to generate a few new possibilities.* This might involve a question such as: "What can you think of that would help you take the first steps toward this goal?"

Later on in the coaching relationship, coaches may offer possibilities to clients or teach a skill on a limited basis. But early in the relationship, coaches focus on listening to the clients and helping the clients discover what they want, what they believe, and what is possible. The coaches' responses as listeners focus on clarifying and magnifying the clients' desires.

Chapter 2

The Language of Coaching

THE BASIC COACHING MODEL

Our program is based on a blend of many of the theories from humanistic psychology (Maslow, Rogers, and others), the recent research in
positive psychology and its strength-based approach, and the early theories of Jung, Adler, and Assagioli. We also believe, like speech-act
theorists Searles and Fernando Flores, that conversations create action.
And, through coaching, as narrative therapy describes, clients rewrite old
stories and create new stories of their lives and possibilities.

When coaches work with clients, they simultaneously attend to three
aspects of coaching: the *relationship* with the clients, the overall *process*
of coaching (its goals, framework, and expectations), and the coaching
conversations that occur.

In this chapter, we refer to the *coaching conversation* as a template
for a specific type of dialogue, which has a beginning, a middle, and an
end. Within one coaching session, several cycles of the coaching conversation may occur. Or a coaching session may focus only on the first parts
of the conversation, depending on the depth. But the steps or phases all
will be repeated throughout each session. What makes the coaching
conversation differ from a nice chat is that it has a beginning, a middle,
and an end, which results in movement on the part of clients toward
insight or action. Coaching engages clients in commitment and action of
some kind.

Coaching is, above all, a conversation. A coaching relationship
begins when coaches engage clients in a conversation around their
visions, goals, wants, and desires. Like all good conversations, coaching
requires us to listen, to pace the conversations, and to genuinely enter
into a dialogue with clients. This creates what in coaching we call the
sacred or inspiring space. David Bohm's work on dialogue (1996)
provides a good model for coaches to follow in attending to the client.

*I believe we can
change the world if
we start listening
to one another
again. Simple,
honest, human
conversation.*

—Margaret J. Wheatly,
Turning to One Another

However, the coaching conversation is special because clients grant coaches permission to challenge and support. There is an *agreement* in place that enables the coaching conversation to occur. Without that agreement, you can have a great conversation, but it will not necessarily lead to the kind of change that coaching can facilitate.

In the coaching conversation, the dialogue between coaches and clients is designed to further the clients' growth, learning, and action toward their desires and intentions. It is a creative conversation where coaches dance with clients, intuitively following their pace and style while at the same time adding to and elaborating on what is unfolding in the moment. Moore and colleagues (2006) have researched this phenomenon and written an excellent description of this process.

The magic of coaching conversations is that they are conversations that would not take place within the clients' usual lives. As our friend and colleague Dave Ellis says when he teaches, coaching gives clients the opportunity to think what they've not thought, say what they've not said, dream what they've not dreamt, and create what they've not created. No two coaching conversations are alike, but there is a basic flow to the conversation that we repeat again and again. This flow is the framework for a coaching session. This chapter describes the components of a coaching conversation—its beginning, middle, and end. You can have good conversations with a lot of people, but it's not a coaching conversation until it's purposefully directed to the client's agenda and has all the components delineated in this chapter.

The coaching conversation impacts clients because it takes a whole-person approach. Tim Gallwey (2000) articulated this in his groundbreaking books, where he used the metaphor of the *inner game,* the internal world of clients. He described three critical conversations that need to occur for clients to be successful in making a change. Each of these pays attention to both the inner and outer world of clients. Gallwey said that coaching includes three levels of conversation:

> *A conversation for awareness (getting the clearest possible picture of current reality), a conversation for choice (getting the clearest possible picture of the desired future outcome), and a conversation for trust (in*

which the client gains greater access to internal and external resources in order to move from current reality to the desired future). (pp. 188–189)

Increasing clients' awareness is key because with awareness comes choice. Clients must become aware of their current situational reality— what's true, what is so, and what is available to them. Increased choice comes when clients become aware that they can *respond creatively* to life rather than just *reacting* to it. Our normal stance as human beings is to react, particularly to challenges. When even the smallest portions of fear or anxiety arise, the human brain and nervous system are programmed to react with the fight, flight, or freeze reaction. Increased awareness through coaching allows clients to see that they always have choices available to them. As they increase their awareness, their choices become more evident, allowing them to respond to life rather than react. As Candide said at the end of Voltaire's book *Candide,* "We must cultivate our garden."

As clients' awareness expands to include greater choice, they learn to trust themselves and trust the coaching process as great support that allows them to step outside their comfort zone. Clients come to coaching because they want to make change. What holds most people back from changing is self-doubt, fear, distraction, or busyness. Coaching helps people focus on what they want and increases their awareness, choice, and trust in their ability to create. One only need look at Olympic athletes or people at the top of their field in any game. Most of them would say they engage with a coach to bring out their best. Lance Armstrong and Tiger Woods are two recent examples of high-profile athletes who always make use of coaches, for both their skill development and for personal coaching.

In the description below of the flow of the coaching conversation, you'll see that the clients' *awareness, choices,* and *trust* in themselves are all intentionally engaged by coaches.

THE FLOW OF COACHING CONVERSATIONS

Clients typically hire coaches because they want to achieve something or enhance something in their lives. The results they want to create in their lives generally fall into three areas:

- Performance goals (for example, improving results as a business owner, eliminating clutter, or meeting daily standards for numbers of contacts with potential clients). These goals usually can be measured objectively, such as by examining the balance sheet of a business, measuring business processes, or tracking sales contacts.
- Learning goals (for example, improving public speaking, becoming a parent who is patient with one's children, or learning how to meditate and to do it consistently). The measurement standards for these goals may be either external or internal to clients. External measures for public speaking could come from observers' feedback. Parents might use both external and internal measures by keeping a log of daily interactions with children and rating themselves on their patience in each, as well as seeking feedback from their spouses and their children.
- Fulfillment goals (for example, achieving work–life balance, a satisfying relationship with a spouse, or the ability to work from the heart as well as from the head, which is a common issue for corporate leaders). The determination of whether these goals have been achieved rests with the clients' *sense* of fulfillment. Clients can track their felt sense of fulfillment on a daily or weekly basis. Then they can judge subjectively whether they are feeling more fulfilled. Clients can also create measures for themselves: time at work, time with family, time for fun, and so on, to provide an external source of learning for themselves. Generally fulfillment goals may also bring clients in tune with their life purpose. This is the central focus of the chapters in Part III, "Coaching From the Inside Out."

In the real world of coaching, most of the time a coach works with the client in all three of these areas during the time they coach together. For example, a client comes in wanting to improve her small business results (a *performance goal*), as measured by the number of sales per customer. In the process of identifying what needs to happen to create that result, the client discovers that she needs to be able to make contact with more potential customers. In order to do that, she realizes that she needs to become a better networker (*learning goal*). As she begins to attend more networking organization meetings, she discovers that she is spending less time at home with her children. She sets a new goal: to spend quality time with her children that is mutually enjoyable, because she deeply desires to be a caring and loving parent to them (*fulfillment goal*).

Our clients bring with them their goals and desires. They also bring the *stories* they tell themselves (and others) about those goals and desires—why they are attainable or not, what it will take to achieve them, and more. To paraphrase Bill O'Hanlon (O'Hanlon & Hudson, 1995), a well-known speaker and author in the field of solution-oriented therapy, every human being gets "lost in storyland."

> *Each of us has our own point of view about things that happen [in our lives]. We call these explanations* stories *to emphasize the fact that our points of view are not The Truth. Facts are different from stories. Facts are things we can all agree upon, what we can all verify with our senses. Stories involve opinions, interpretations, theories and explanations. Facts are the "what"; stories are the "why." Most of us are caught up in the stories we believe about ourselves, other people, our relationships; we have forgotten that these stories* are *stories and that we made them up. We are convinced that our stories contain The Truth.* (p. 19)

As you engage in a coaching conversation with clients, you bring this awareness to the conversation: to assist clients in getting what they want, you will be working with their stories about the goals, themselves, and what is possible. Clients may or may not recognize that their stories aren't the truth. As the coach, you will need to discover how tightly clients are bound to any confusion about the stories actually being the reality. The more the clients confuse stories with truth, the more difficult it will be for clients to make changes. Sometimes the first piece of work in coaching is to help clients be able to reflect on how they created and continue to create the stories, so that they can rewrite them.

As you read the description of the coaching conversation, refer to the transcript of a session, which follows on pages 28–35. As we describe

21

the structure of this conversation, we will do so from the coach's perspective because the coach is responsible for structuring the conversation. The 5 steps of our coaching model are presented below.

The Situation and the Desire

Step 1: Ask, What do you want from coaching?

Coaching sessions usually start with a minute or two of small talk and check-in. Then the coach begins the session. The flow of the coaching conversation begins when the coaches inquire into the clients' desires. The coaches ask open-ended questions—some version of "What do you want?" which starts the conversation—to engage the clients in articulating what they want and in clarifying the meaning of that desire. Subsequent questions will probe for more specific aspects of the current situation or the desire. These initial questions can be about a specific situation or about the entirety of the clients' life (for example, "What do you want from your vacation?" or "What legacy do you want to leave?").

In either case, a powerful question engages the clients in identifying more clearly what they want because, without that, the clients will continue to think, act, and live no differently than they have been to date.

The coaches' questions initiate a process of discovery and awareness for both clients and coaches. The coaches ask powerful questions, inquiring into the depths of the desire, the vision the clients have for what is desired, the subtleties of the situation, and why the desire is important to the client. Powerful questioning is a hallmark of life coaching and is explored later in this chapter.

Enter the Flow of the Coaching Conversation

Step 2: Listen and Clarify

Like any great conversationalist, coaches pay exquisitely close attention to what the clients say, as discussed in Chapter 1. As Dave Ellis often says in his workshops, listening fully is about softness, yielding, openness, and willingness to receive. When you pay attention, your world gets bigger. The coaches' ability to listen and reflect back helps the clients' world seem more spacious, more alive, and more vibrant.

As coaches listen and clarify, they may reframe what the clients see by providing perspective and creating possibilities that mirror or build on the clients' statements.

Coaches sometimes say that they *coach to the gap.* This means that the coaches help the clients identify wants and wishes, and compare them to what currently exists. The coaches help clients examine the present situation. The gap is the difference between the two. Once the gap is identified, coaches can help the clients find ways to close it.

In listening and clarifying, coaches ask questions to discover what *is,* what is wanted, and gaps that exist. While the intention first is to help the clients clarify, coaches are examining whether or not they fully understand what the clients are communicating. That is done by checking in with the clients. Coaches summarize and ask questions that verify their understanding: "Am I understanding you fully? Do I seem to have it all? Am I hearing you clearly? What else is there for you? Is there anything I'm missing?" An important point of this step is for the coaches to not own or be attached to their perception of what the clients are saying. Masterful coaches always check in with the clients and are willing to be wrong. Good coaching is about helping the clients get very clear, and not tainting the conversation by coloring what the clients meant in a way that doesn't reflect the clients' intentions. The importance of gaining this level of clarity is that, once clear, the conversation can move forward. "Okay, we're both clear about what you want. Now, what can you do about it?" The coaching can move to creating new strategies for the clients to get what they want.

Giving Honest Feedback and Observation

Step 3: Say What Is So

Once coaches are clear and reflect back to the clients their understanding, they can add perspective by sharing what they see. This can be the point of most potency and the highest leverage for change because the coaches' perspectives shed a powerful floodlight on the story the clients tell about their goals and motivation. Coaches are truth tellers, sharing the truth of the client's situation *as they see it.* They bring clarity to the clients' situation by articulating what they see, from their perspective—the gaps, the opportunities, the strengths, and the possibilities—in a way that is clear, respectful, and communicated in a manner that is heard by the clients as the coaches' best understanding in the moment. It is never meant to be *the truth*—only the coaches' perspective. It is offered as the coaches' observation of the situation. Masterful coaches do not think they know something the clients do not, but they respect the fact that power to change comes from being able to see circumstances from more than one perspective.

Coaches say what is so by sharing their perception of the truth in a way that is respectful, warm, and inviting. The coaches' language needs to be attractive and intriguing to clients, capturing their attention. Coaches share intuitions about possibilities and obstacles. Coaches share the truth about themselves, as well as about the clients. Since our coaching clients are not fragile, we do not need to withhold information from them.

One meaning of happiness is living in tune with the way things are. When coaches share *what is so,* they are also humbly aware that it is just one version of the way things are—their version. When coaches share what is so, clients gain another perspective on the way things are. When someone recognizes what is so, the transformation can begin.

At this point coaches often share their assessment of the situation— the coaches' take on what's going on. (For example, a coach might say, "My take is that right now exercising at the health club every day is more of a 'should' than a 'want to.'") The assessment might be a suggestion, from the coach's point of view, of what is keeping the gap in place. It might be a metaphor the coach offers.

Coaches assist clients in seeing the situation more fully in order to evoke fresh insights about both the situations and the clients in general. Ideally, these insights also shed light on factors that contribute to stagnating the situation.

Return to Listening

Step 4: Listen More

Once coaches have acknowledged the reality, it is time to listen again. They may find themselves asking clarifying questions to deepen the clients' ability to listen to themselves fully. A skilled coach allows the client time and space to examine *what is so,* to play with it, to explore it, and to discover its possibilities. Through the quality of the coaches' work during this step, they are inviting the clients to listen to themselves, too. Giving clients the time and space to respond can create new possibilities by legitimizing the process of listening to oneself deeply and honoring what one hears.

Insight occurs when clients begin to see the situation in a fresh way. They may reshape the story they tell themselves about what is possible. Seeing the situation in a new way will likely free them to take new action.

Create Accountability

Step 5: Request Action
The action the coaches request, although definitely a change of some kind, is not necessarily a performance goal. It could be a change in behavior, a change in a way of being, or a change in a thought pattern or mind-set—any change that creates momentum. In this step, coaches challenge clients to do what they perhaps had been wanting to do, but had never before had the push to do. Coaches ask for a new way; the old way has not helped the clients create what they want. A request for action may sound like this: "What will you do as your first step?"

At this time, the coaches needs to assess whether the clients are committed to the actions they identify. In other words, it's important to make sure that the clients own the action and are not doing it for the sake of their coach. Skilled coaches are aware of pacing and check in with the clients to ensure that the goals and the actions are in line with their desired outcomes and fit with what is possible, given the rest of their life. Appropriate action combined with the clients' willingness furthers the clients' agenda. Actions that are too big or too small may derail the clients' motivation. The coaches need to check in with the clients to determine whether the clients own the action: Are they excited? Do they show excitement and commitment through their voice, their energy, and their statements? The Big Five, which we discussed in Chapter 1, is a useful method for discernment here.

Don't underestimate the importance of discernment. There are experienced clients who get pumped up by declaring that they're committed to some big goal that, although in line with their life path, seems to coaches

25

to be too big or too soon. When clients declare their commitment, they can be fueled by the excitement of the adrenaline rush that comes with having a big vision or a big desire. They have every intention of agreeing to something that might require too much too soon. These are situations where coaches may notice clients overpromising and underdelivering, which would be assessed in subsequent coaching sessions. In such cases, clients come back for the next session not having completed the intended actions. Coaches explore what happened that blocked the intended actions, with an eye toward assessing whether the clients have in this case overextended themselves. Overextension might be a onetime situation, or it could be a pattern. Coaches pay attention to which of these might be the case. The clients may need to learn how to check in with themselves to assess appropriate pacing. In this or the next session, the coaches would help the clients begin. A coach might ask a client: "Take a moment now and check in with yourself before you finalize this commitment. Get your calendar and notice what your next week looks like. Where do you see the space, time, and energy to do what you are agreeing to do? Can you write this action in your calendar so you will know that you have a place for it? Finally, check in with your body as you imagine yourself completing this action. Do you notice any places where you are tightening? If so, what's the message for you about this commitment?"

A good rule of thumb is to have clients take action in two ways: (a) Ask them to take the specified action, and (b) ask them to observe themselves during the next period of time, so that they stay attuned to what they think, feel, and sense as they engage in taking action and practicing new habits beyond the status quo.

Several things generally happen within this part of the flow:

- *You identify choices.* When the truth has been told, the story identified, and the gap between current and desired situations cleared, it's time to identify choices the clients can make to close the gap. Some may be obvious; others may tap the coaches' and clients' creativity to generate.
- *You examine commitment.* Since the clients will choose a path, examining their commitment to take action is an important aspect of

the process. A conversation about what it would take to commit to a choice may be in order, as would a conversation about why a choice is or isn't attractive to the clients. Sometimes the choice gets modified in order to increase the clients' level of commitment to it.

- *You identify the action(s).* The clients are about to take an action that they feel some commitment to take. The coaching conversation needs to deal with the specifics of *what* the clients will do, *when* they will do it, and *how* they will do it. To some extent, your work here is to identify the next steps the clients will take to forward the action for themselves. Leaving this step fuzzy leads to frustration on the part of both clients and coaches. As clients take action, they will learn from it, particularly if coaches ask them to self-observe. This in turn will lead to other possibilities and other actions. This might be a place where coaches might consider how the clients could gather some internal feedback to verify that the new action is an appropriate for them at this time.

- *You ensure accountability.* Accountability is the cornerstone of coaching. Clients are accountable to the coaches, but at a deeper level they are accountable to themselves. Coaches serve clients and ask for accountability. Don't leave the session before ensuring that the *what, when,* and *how* of your clients' next steps are clear. (Sometimes it's also helpful to ask clients *why* the action is important.)

THE BOTTOM LINE

In any coaching session, you may repeat this basic 5-step coaching framework several times, or one basic coaching cycle may occupy the entire session. How you use the model within a session depends on the focus, the length of the session, the style and pace of the client, and the alliance you have created together. Sometimes you will linger within a step or recycle back to an earlier step for completion before progressing. Generally, though, a session is not complete without a request for movement of some kind. That is what makes coaching uniquely able to create momentum toward the client's goals.

A TRANSCRIPT OF A COACHING SESSION

The following transcript was taken from a coaching conversation that occurred within the context of an ILCT foundational class. Pat Williams was the coach.

COACH: So last week you said that you wanted to have a conversation about how to rediscover fun in your life. Fun is an area on the Wheel of Life—fun and recreation, and you want to have that be better for you.

CLIENT: Yes.

COACH: So, what do you want to be different regarding fun and recreation in your life right now?

CLIENT: Well, several years ago I had serious knee surgery and had to stop playing tennis. I noticed that ever since, I stopped being able to play tennis and have injuries in my body and don't really feel the athletic person that I was, let's say, 20 years ago, that I'll choose working on my computer. I'll choose staying in the house and organizing because I like that—I'll choose other activities rather than plan something with my partner that would be fun. And because we're both professionals, we'll always say, "Oh, well, if you have work to do" or "Oh, if you have reading to do for your coaching class . . ." Fun is very low on my life design.

COACH: Right. And yet it used to be a big important part . . . because tennis was the way you did it, right?

CLIENT: Yeah, I *loved* it. I had *so* much fun.

COACH: Well, before we talk about other options for a redesign of your life, tell me what was it about the tennis activity?

CLIENT: It was being outdoors in the sun, which I don't do that much anymore. And it was playing with strangers sometimes, or just meeting someone regularly, meeting new people. . . . And it was the physical activity and the contact sport . . . getting better at something. Getting better, taking lessons, practicing my serve, you know, that kind of thing.

COACH: And your physical limitations now prevent tennis?

CLIENT: Yes. They prevent any kind of sport like that, any kind of repetitive sport.

COACH: Where else in your life can you imagine being outdoors, meeting new people, engaging in some meaningful activity . . . it still could be physical to the degree that it's able to be physical. . . . What comes to mind?

CLIENT: Hmmm. . . . That's an interesting question.

COACH: What do you see in other people that you notice, "Oh, that's something to consider?" You could start making a list of things you *think* could be fun that meet those.

CLIENT: I think that's good, only I always come up with that the people who think they have the most fun have a sport—have something like either tennis or golf, which doesn't interest me—they have something that they . . . or sailing, or things that don't interest me. So *that's* my problem. I feel like I almost have to reframe fun, and I don't know how to do that.

COACH: Good, good. What I picked from your conversation were some ingredients that . . . If being outdoors and meeting people were two parts of playing tennis, you can still have those. What you can't have is playing tennis. I don't know if you can't have that, but right now your belief is that you can't have that.

CLIENT: No, I absolutely can't ever play tennis again.

COACH: Okay. . . . I'm closing my eyes a minute as I try to imagine . . . What I'm hearing is it would be very important for you to find a way for fun to be a big factor in your life again, and it wouldn't be just doing busyness to distract you from the time you used to use getting outdoors and doing something . . .

CLIENT: Right.

COACH: . . . and there are physical limitations we know about . . .

CLIENT: Right.

COACH: So who do you know in your life, either that you really know or that you see publicly, like celebrities or anybody that you know of . . . people that have physical limitations and still seem to have fun in their life? Any models that you can think of?

CLIENT: (laughing) No.

COACH: So that would be a great research project, wouldn't it?

CLIENT: Yeah.

COACH: You chuckle. What is the chuckling?

CLIENT: Well, it's funny, because I don't know anyone who would say they have fun. I mean, I heard Ann in class say she has fun with her

29

kindergarten kids doing drawing or scribbling or something like that, and that was fun to her. And I thought that was great. I wish I had something like that, something that I could call fun.

COACH: Yes. And it sounds as if it really is a reframe of . . . shifting . . . "Damn it, my fun used to be tennis, and now I can't do it, and it's a big loss for me and I can't think of anything else to have fun with." That's what I'm hearing.

CLIENT: Yes. That's correct. You know, it might be interesting, when I see people, I could ask them what they do that they call fun.

COACH: Yeah, that's a thought—do some fun interviews with people, what we call informational interviews.

CLIENT: Yeah, what do you do for fun? Ask them that.

COACH: What do you consider fun? Because there's a myriad of activities that aren't physical that some people consider fun. They might be more mental, they might be some community activity—I'm trying to think creatively with you now. . . . But it feels to me, my intuition tells me . . . without getting into great details, I almost need to know the degree of your physical limitations, what the current situation is.

CLIENT: Well, I have problems with my feet, problems with my toes, and so I had to have hammertoe surgery, so every time I kept playing tennis, I had to have another surgery. It was eventually about not being able to walk easily, so I stopped playing tennis. But I still have pain in the bottom of my foot, now that my foot was anatomically changed. Now I have problems in the metatarsal region, so I have pain. So I have orthotics and all that, but I don't enjoy just walking—it's not fun for me.

COACH: So you are ambulatory?

CLIENT: Yes, I can walk, I can hike, but that's not fun. I can't walk fast, I can't run, I can't jump on my toes.

COACH: A little bit of history—when did you take up tennis?

CLIENT: In my teens, when I was about 12.

COACH: And played it from then on, very voraciously?

CLIENT: Yes. And then right before I had the surgeries, I played probably singles four times a week, doubles twice a week. I played almost every day.

COACH: What did you do for fun before age 12?

CLIENT: I rode a bike and played baseball. I ran around.

30

COACH: Is bicycling anything that interests you?

CLIENT: No, not anymore. I fell. (laughing) I live in the mountains now, and it's really hard to bike unless you're really strong. And where I live there's nothing flat, and it's a huge hassle going down to the ocean where everybody is crowded. So there doesn't seem to be a sport. And I think maybe one of the things I'm feeling right now is I'm feeling kind of sad. . . .

COACH: Yeah . . .

CLIENT: . . . the mourning of the fact that there isn't going to be that kind of sport that I've done my whole life.

COACH: Yeah—and if sport equals fun, then that's a big limitation for you.

CLIENT: Right.

COACH: And sport isn't the only kind of fun. It just seems right now that that's the fun you lost.

CLIENT: Right.

COACH: Let's move into the future. Let's just imagine . . . I'm trying to get into your mental space here, by phone, because I really want to believe . . . I mean, I absolutely *do* believe, not just want to, that there is an unknown for you, of having a life of fun, because not only do you deserve it, I think there's also a unique experience that we haven't yet come upon, that would be fun for you at some time in the future. Could be next week, could be next year. So, if you had a future that had fun in it, how would you be different? Who would you become if that were part of your life?

CLIENT: I would feel more rounded. I would feel that my life was more balanced. My life feels out of balance.

COACH: Out of balance, and there's a part missing.

CLIENT: Right. So I would feel more whole. And I would feel happier, I think, because I'd be doing something that doesn't always involve my mind, or busy work that then helps me relax . . . I'd be doing something that wasn't just mind oriented or organization oriented. So that feels better, that there would be something . . .

There is something—I just thought of something.

COACH: Good.

CLIENT: If I could envision a future that had fun, I think I would be involved more in drumming . . .

31

COACH: Ahhh . . .

CLIENT: (laughing and sounding more animated) . . . because I went to this drumming circle two times, and I'm going to go this Friday night. And it's involved because you have to buy a drum, and find people to drum with if you're going to do it in a circle. But it made me have that same sense of connection to strangers, people I wouldn't normally meet.

COACH: Yeah, that's what we were looking for earlier, and that can be done outdoors.

CLIENT: It's actually done indoors, but I suppose . . .

COACH: Oh, there are drum circles that meet down by the beach on a full moon or up in the mountains.

CLIENT: (laughing)

COACH: Trust me, you can find them if you're looking for them.

CLIENT: Right.

COACH: Well, so did you hear the energy shift in your voice and your whole body?

CLIENT: Yeah—it does excite me, that one new thing I only did twice but it did feel like it was fun.

COACH: Yeah, and we don't want to put our eggs all in one basket, but to me, it sounds like—okay, that's something to research and make a big part of your life. It's not going to replace tennis. I know that. But it is going to replace the part of you that's missing—for social connection, for laughter, for fun, for relaxation, for something that's totally away from business and work. This resonates with me as a *very* good alternative.

CLIENT: Yes. The two times I did it, I really couldn't believe it.

COACH: Here's something else I know about fun, just from life experience, that I'd like you to consider. If you just follow your heart, or your intuition, in drumming, my guess is that that's going to be a door opener to other things as well. There's going to be somebody in a drumming group who does something else. Maybe they do . . . what's that new kind of bicycle I'm going to buy?

CLIENT: An elliptical?

COACH: No, where you sit and bicycle . . .

CLIENT: A stationery bike?

ANOTHER CLASSMATE: A recumbent bike?

32

COACH: Yeah, a recumbent bike.

CLIENT: You mean they actually have bikes like that?

COACH: Yeah, I'm buying one next week because I just test-drove six of them. I love it. I mean, I happen to have knee problems, too, and I don't like the seats on most bicycles . . . so that's something to consider. I'm just saying that things will come from being in a drumming group because everybody in that drumming group will do other things in their life for fun.

CLIENT: Right. And the thing about the drumming is that it *would* really help with that other aspect of my life that is very small, which has to do with the spiritual.

COACH: Ahhh . . .

CLIENT: . . . because when people get into drumming, you get into a kind of an altered state.

COACH: Yeah, I love it. It excites me.

Well, I'm going to ask you this big coaching question. That's what you want in the future is for fun to come back in your life, and it sounds as if some of that can be in the immediate future with this drumming.

CLIENT: Right.

COACH: What else do you want?

CLIENT: What else do I want in my life in general?

COACH: For fun.

CLIENT: Umm . . .

COACH: I guess the question is really this: so fun becomes part of your life again. That's great. What's the bigger question? What do you *really* want all that to lead to—really, really, really want?

CLIENT: I want more balance in my life, and more time with my husband.

COACH: Okay. Do you begin to see how all of these are interconnected?

CLIENT: (laughing) Yeah, I see.

COACH: I mean, when you've got a gap in a big area that you've kind of put in a drawer like Peter Pan's shadow, it's like you've hidden that away.

CLIENT: Right.

COACH: And what I know about shadow work, if you will, and this is not coaching right now, it's just some pontificating, from what's coming up in my mind . . . is that our shadow holds what we don't want to look at anymore, but it also holds the part of us that hasn't been expressed yet,

33

that has greatness within what we unclaim. And it sounds to me like your expression is missing that. Fun enlivens your spirit, it increases the partnership you have with your husband, it increases the benefit of that, the happiness of that, the connection.

CLIENT: Yeah, you're touching something—because some tears just formed in my eyes, and I took a big sigh, and leaned back in my chair . . . so I feel like . . . it's interesting.

COACH: Yeah, well good, because those are just feelings. Tears are great.

CLIENT: Yeah, I know.

COACH: So we're touching something that connects heart and spirit, aren't we?

CLIENT: Right. Exactly.

COACH: It's amazing that sometimes we say fun is just fun. It's anything but just fun. It's a demand from your soul that you have some way of getting into this human being part of you instead of just the human busy and human doing part of you. This is a great example of that.

Think of what we call fun. What's the word when people play that we often use?

CLIENT: You mean recreation?

COACH: Exactly. Now look at that word in a new way.

CLIENT: Re-creation. Oh my god! (laughing) That's great.

COACH: So my invitation to you is to try to create a formula in your mind where fun equals re-creation, but put a hyphen between the "re" and the "creation." Because that's really what I sense that you're up to.

CLIENT: (laughing) Yeah, that's totally cool! I never would have thought of that.

COACH: Well, we went from tears to ecstasy there. That's pretty good. (laughing) Do you feel finished enough for this conversation?

CLIENT: Oh yeah. Thank you.

COACH: So I'm just going to end here with a coaching request that you do follow-up with the drumming group and allow yourself to be open to the newness of that. Don't throw it away easily.

CLIENT: Right.

COACH: See what you can do to make it fun, and who you're going to meet, what other social contacts come from that.

CLIENT: Right.

COACH: I don't know if your husband goes with you or not. That's up to you.

CLIENT: Yes, he does.

COACH: Okay, so there's partnership time together, too. And then learn what else comes from that while you're thinking, "What I'm really doing is re-creating who I am in that newfound way."

CLIENT: That's wonderful. Thank you.

Our Comments on This Session

- A coaching conversation is a sacred space, an inspiring space. You need to prepare the space: be focused, be ready to receive the client, be of service. Whether in person or over the phone, limit the distractions. One of the advantages of phone coaching for the coach is that you can stand up. You may want to close your eyes, move around the room, trying to sense the client, the client's world and experience. Do whatever it takes so that your coaching *presence* serves the client and the client's agenda. Be available.

- The transcript illustrates the coach getting the client to do the work instead of handing answers to the client. The skill of *powerful questions* was used frequently. The coach's assumption is that the client has the answers that are right for her, and it's just the coach's role to facilitate their emergence. The questions evoked from the client meaningful qualities and characteristics from the past, which let her map over to what she's experiencing now. The coach encouraged her to draw on the past for clues about what's fulfilling.

- The coach and client didn't hurry through the session, although they did work within the time allotted for this session, which was 20 to 25 minutes. This created space for the client to get to a deep place with the issue. Silence allowed the coach to just stand shoulder to shoulder with the client, without knowing, or needing to know, where the process was leading.

- The coach believed 110 percent that the conversation with the client would lead to a shift in thinking about some possibility, and that the results weren't just magical because she had the answer within—they were magical because both of them (client and coach) were having this conversation.

35

- The client felt supported because the coach was "just there with her"—she felt that there was a space for her to just be, without an answer, and that felt like a very powerful space.
- Later in this chapter we focus on asking powerful questions, the kinds that clients don't normally focus on. In this session, note the power of the question, "What else do you want?"
- Moving into the future shifted things toward greater wholeness— something bigger than "fun" as an activity. This session became a conversation about bigger fulfillment. This is typical of how small issues in a client's life are microcosms of the larger issues. Coaches can use a single issue as a doorway to deeper desires or into habitual patterns of thinking and behaving.
- This session shows the coach and client focused around one area on the coaching tool, the Wheel of Life, which we cover in chapter 8, "Design Your Life." The coach's absolute conviction that people have a right to incorporate fun in their everyday life is a personal assumption he makes, and it illustrates the importance of examining the assumptions coaches bring to their coaching (e.g., Is fun just something for vacations? Does it have to be a big activity? How about 1-minute fun breaks during the day?)
- The coach's implicit assumption is that people know on some level what's true for them and what brings them joy. Creating space for clients to get in touch with it and articulate it opens a door to inner wisdom, and ultimately the surfacing of inner solutions and possibilities.
- The coach's questions lead the client to examining *all* the needs previously met by playing tennis. It was more than just physical activity for her, which led her to thoughtfully consider the issue she brought to coaching in such a way that she would come away with a rich alternative for tennis, one that met needs and desires she had that weren't immediately obvious to her. This is one reason why clients can often maintain the shifts they make, because the obvious answers aren't the ones they come away with from coaching.
- Coaching often draws on models of various possibilities, as this session shows. If the client says, "I don't know anyone like that," the coach and client can create a research project to find people who

might be models. This is a creative way of dealing with a client who has no experience of something.

- The session illustrates the importance of the coach respecting and validating the emotions that arise in the process of exploring an issue. Remember that clients bring to coaching conversations the issues they feel strongly about, and there's likely to be an emotional current to the issues. The coach must allow space for that and convey respect for the information communicated by emotions—from client to coach, and more important, from the client's soul to the client's conscious self.

    When the coach says, "And sport isn't the only kind of fun. It just seems right now that that's the fun you lost," the statement validates the client's emotions while still holding out possibilities. This is very different from a possible therapy intervention such as: "It feels to you like the end of your world," which could allow the client to sink into hopelessness. The coach's reflection acknowledges the importance of sport at the same time as it opens up other sources for fun. It expands the client's possibilities instead of probing the depth of the loss.

- Pointing out to the client the shift in voice, energy, and body helps the client become more aware of what enhances her aliveness, and grounds insights and breakthroughs in the body. This session was a phone coaching session; the coach does not have to be physically present with the client to focus attention on the body.

- The coaching in this case was effective because the coach did not put himself in the role of expert. The illustration of the recumbent bike and having knee problems let the client know that she was not isolated in her need to make decisions based on physical limitations. It normalized the client's experience, which could help the client feel less isolated and more hopeful.

- The coach asked the client, "What do you really, really, really want?" People who are overachievers and overdoers often lose sight of this question and forget to ask themselves this. It breaks through a lot of *shoulds* and helps people reconnect with their center, the place from which great wisdom often emerges.

- The conversation about shadow being in part about the unclaimed parts of ourselves was very powerful and nonpathologizing and a

37

different way to look at the shadow, which contains unrealized creative aspects of ourselves as well as the hidden and sometimes less acceptable aspects.

- The word *re-creation* serves as a kind of touchstone for the whole session. (The client's goal was *recreation,* and the coach realized that this was about *re-creation.*) When the client gets a concise *take-away*—a symbol, thought, or phrase—this helps to ground a session and the learning that took place. The client also gets an action step so she is clear about what's next to support follow-through.

SETTING THE STAGE: THE FIRST COACHING CONVERSATIONS

The first coaching conversation may be the opportunity the coach has to explain what coaching is and how the coach goes about it. In that case, the coach is already modeling what coaching can offer a *prospective client.* That is distinct from the first conversation after the client has hired the coach, when the coach is setting the stage and creating the alliance for the coaching engagement.

We begin here with a discussion of the *coaching alliance* because that alliance is a distinctive feature of the relationship between coach and client that strengthens the power of the relationship between coach and client with a clear understanding of expectations and the cocreation of a partnership.

Many of the participants at ILCT have been trained as helping professionals of some kind: therapists, psychologists, counselors, teachers, human resource professionals, and so on. They know how critical a *system* can be when people are trying to make a change. A system can enhance people's ability to make changes, supporting the direction they want to go, or it can create obstacles that may block change. One of the essential basic systems all professional training considers is the two-person system between the professional and the client. Every training program for helping professionals spends some time focused on the *therapeutic alliance.* The characteristics of that alliance are explicitly designed to further the clients' therapeutic work. While coaching can be therapeutic, it is not therapy. At ILCT, we ensure that students can differ-

entiate kinds of alliances so that they can create, with clients, an appropriate coaching alliance, clearly distinguished in its scope and purpose.

An *alliance,* according to the dictionary, is "an association to further
the members' common interests." Common therapeutic relationship
alliances differ from the coaching alliance in several key ways:

- Many of the expectations for therapeutic alliances have been set by
the codes of ethics and the licensing or governing boards of the
profession, the state, the province, and so on. Other features of the
alliances grow out of the particular beliefs about change that the
helping professionals hold. Consultants often also have beliefs about
the alliances they create with clients. In most cases, consultants have
established themselves as experts, and the resulting alliances that get
created expect that the consultants will often be directive about the
course of the engagement, and assume that the clients lack expertise
that the consultants are bringing. The clients are willing recipients of
the consultants' expertise. This is also generally true of the therapeutic alliance, where the therapist is highly responsible. The
therapist engages in a very specific treatment protocol, generally for a
diagnosed condition. There are protocols for the treatment of severe
depression, posttraumatic stress disorder, anxiety, addiction, and
other therapeutic issues. In each case, the client follows the guidance
and knowledge of the helping professional. The client is generally
leaning on the professional for guidance in getting back to *normal.*
Although many people see therapists for general "problems in living"
where therapists may be working in a more coachlike fashion, we are
referring here to clinically recognized conditions where the client is
suffering and truly needs therapy.

   The figure on the next page (Figure 2.1) illustrates one way a
coach can describe the distinctions between therapy, mentoring,
consulting, and coaching to his clients.
- The coaching alliance is truly designed as a partnership in service of
a particular client's goals and desires, and it is cocreated. In the first
session after a client has committed to coaching, the coach works
with the client to design the facets of this partnership. All facets of it

Figure 2.1

Professional distinctions

Therapy	Mentoring	Consulting	Coaching
Deals mostly with a person's past and trauma, and seeks healing	Deals mostly with succession training and seeks to help someone do what you do	Deals mostly with problems and seeks to provide information (expertise, strategy, structures, methodologies) to solve them	Deals mostly with a person's present and seeks to guide them into a more desirable future
Doctor–patient relationship (therapist has the answers)	Older/wiser–younger/less-experienced relationship (mentor has the answers)	Expert–person with problem relationship (consultant has the answers)	Co-creative, equal partnership (coach helps clients discover their own answers)
Assumes many emotions are a symptom of something wrong	Limited to emotional response of the mentoring parameters (succession, etc.)	Does not normally address or deal with emotions (informational only)	Assumes emotions are natural and normalizes them
The therapist diagnoses, then provides professional expertise and guidelines to give clients a path to healing	The mentor allows you to observe his/her behavior and expertise, will answer questions, and provide guidance and wisdom for the stated purpose of the mentoring	The consultant stands back, evaluates a situation, then tells you the problem and how to fix it	The coach stands with you, and helps you identify the challenges, then works with you to turn challenges into victories and holds you accountable to reach your desired goals

can be designed uniquely, discussed, and redesigned as needed over the course of the coaching engagement.

• The coaching alliance aims to be truly satisfying for both coach and client. Each must be challenged; each must learn. This mutuality is sometimes described as the *interdevelopmental* aspect of coaching. Coaches expect to grow because of the work they do with clients. If they find themselves not growing and learning, they may be saying yes to clients who are not a good fit for them.

The coaches' work truly depends on the quality and kind of alliances that are created. We want to create alliances that empower clients, support their learning and development, clarify the cocreated partnership, and fully embrace partnership between coach and client.

We recommend that you use a client "welcome packet" as a starting point for a formal coaching relationship. The welcome packet is a set of handouts for the client to read and fill out that includes the coaching "contract" or agreement, client goals, policies and procedures, etc. It is a powerful tool for engaging the client in deep and long-term thinking, and it also gives much useful information to the coach.

Other things we do at a first session: If the coach asked the client as pre-work to fill out a welcome packet, the coach reviews that information with the client. The coach describes life coaching, ensuring that the client understands and is prepared for the whole-life perspective the life coach takes. Coaches can also ensure that clients understand how coaching differs from therapy and consulting. This can be particularly important for clients who have been in therapy or who have used consultants, so that they understand that a true partnership is the foundation of coaching. The work of this first session is to specify and create that partnership—the coaching alliance.

After that, the coach begins to design the coaching alliance with the client, starting with questions like: "How do you most want to be coached?" and "What do you most want to gain from our relationship and time together?" The coach reviews any supporting assessments the client has available, such as the Wheel of Life (see Chapter 8), coaching session preparation worksheet, and personality or behavioral self-assessments, such as the Myers-Briggs, the DISC, or the People Map, all personality or behavioral assessments. During this review, coaches demonstrate partnership by asking questions that allow clients to demonstrate their level of understanding and comfort with themselves and their own life.

We find it useful to ask clients to think back to one or two alliances or deep relationships they have had with others that have really forwarded their growth and learning. Clients explore what they did and what the other person did that made these relationships so empowering and supporting for them. Clients may draw upon sports coaches, best friends, mentors, business relationships, or family members. The coaches listen and help clients determine what important facets from these relationships can become essential parts of the coaching alliance.

Other ways a coach works with a client to design the relationship include determining specifics such as the client's long-term goals—what we call "coaching to the large life"—and how the client's short-term desires and intentions fit into the big picture of the client's ideal life.

This alliance is reinforced in every session, sometimes in small ways such as the small talk that can occur at the start of the session. The coach welcomes the client and engages in small talk for a few minutes, as the coach and client are getting to know each other. Small talk helps both coach and client become present to each other in the moment. The coach asks the client what the client most wants out of the session today.

No matter how well the coaching alliance is designed from the outset, the alliance can break down. Sometimes this occurs because the client is making changes and wants from the coaching relationship something different from what was originally desired. Even if the coach frequently checks in with the client, sometimes there can be breakdowns. The signs that the alliance is at risk include:

- The client forgets appointments, is chronically late, or is unprepared for appointments.
- The client has lost interest, or the coach has lost interest.
- The coach or client has personal difficulties that are impacting effectiveness. For example, the coach may be managing the health problems of an aging parent and has become the parent's caretaker. Initially this can create potential distractions. Other situations may include divorce or recalcitrant teenagers. We tell our clients, "Life happens between calls." And as life happens, the coaching alliance needs to be adjusted or renegotiated.

The coach needs to watch for these signs and pay attention to any physical or emotional gut reactions that indicate something has shifted. Behaviors, body symptoms, and language are all potential indicators.

Renegotiating the alliance may be as simple as moving from one coaching session per week to one every 2 weeks, allowing the client more time and focus. A coach could ask the client, at this stage, "Might this be a good time for us to redefine our relationship? What would be most helpful to you right now?"

As in any relationship, clients can be reluctant to end the relationship completely. So if the coach asks, the client may agree that less frequent sessions or *maintenance* calls once per month would be most beneficial. Pat has a client he has been coaching for 6 years. In the last 2 years, that person has simply asked to pay for one 15-minute check-in call per month. The client sends a summary of what has occurred for her during the month. Then she checks in and, during the course of the session, gets a chance to put into words what she is thinking and feeling about that month's life and work. It is as if the client experiences this as a "wake-up call" where she becomes fully present to her life as it is now through the process of putting it into words with her coach. Speaking out loud to another person her successes and her intentions is all she needs to return to self-coaching.

Another sign that the coaching alliance may be vulnerable is if coaches become focused on themselves and their performance, or their agenda, while they are coaching or planning for coaching with the client. Coaches may not be aware of this, falling prey to what the psychological literature calls *self-deception*. Signs of this (Arbinger Institute, 2000), are that coaches are beginning to see clients as standing in less than their full humanity. To the coach, the client begins to be seen as a vehicle, an obstacle, or an instrument. For example, coaches may see clients as a vehicle for gaining similar clients in that particular business. If this happens, the coaches will have some part of their attention focused on that future possibility, and not on the current clients' goals, results, and relationships. Diane Menendez asks most of her business executive clients to read *Leadership and Self-Deception* (Arbinger Institute, 2000), a small book with a powerful message. She has found that executives are particularly prone to putting people "in the box," as this book calls the situation when a person's own self-interests or fears unconsciously affect the relationship and the alliance with another person. Psychological research on self-deception is becoming more common and is perhaps one of the most useful sources for coaches today on pitfalls they can fall into.

43

Designing the coaching alliance begins with the first contact or communication the coach has with the client. Whether the coach's communication is an e-mail, a note on the back of a business card, a voice mail for the client, or an initial phone call, the coach sets the stage for the coaching and creates the alliance from the very beginning of the initial contact with the client. Some clients say they begin to understand the nature of the coaching alliance by reading the coach's Web site, which establishes the coach's SAT (style, approach, and tone).

Coaches generally find that their first contacts with clients come in several different varieties: (a) calls from clients who are committed to coaching and want to determine whether the coach is the right coach for them; (b) contacts with people whom the coach has just met and who have expressed curiosity about what the coach does; and (c) calls from people who don't know much about coaching and want to find out more to figure out whether coaching fits their needs right now. Each of these situations requires a positive initial contact and flexibility from the coach to adjust the conversation to the client's focus for the call.

44

Coaching Conversations: The Initial Contact Call

The phone rings. The coach picks it up and—surprise!—a prospective client is on the phone. She knows that she wants to hire a coach and has some goals in mind. She discovered the coach when a friend of hers mentioned that he had hired the coach in order to improve his work–life balance. The prospective client starts to tell the coach what she's looking for, and then the coach looks at the clock and realizes he has a coaching appointment with another client in 20 minutes. What will the coach do? What will the coach say to the prospective client?

When coaches first begin their business, they often feel a sense of urgency that can manifest in two ways. First, when prospective clients call, coaches feel they must do the initial screening and turn the clients into a paying engagement immediately. It is as if the coaches don't feel they can tolerate any delay, in case the clients change their mind. Second, coaches often agree to coach anyone who comes along in order to gain experience, competence, and confidence. Although this impulse is common and perhaps understandable, we believe that coaches and clients benefit when they are able to be prepared and intentional about initial calls. We recommend designing a structure for this initial interview because clients and coaches ideally should be assessing the fit of the prospective alliance. Setting up a planned initial screening call during which the coach has at least 30 minutes to determine, without feeling rushed, whether the coach and the client fit as partners, is critical. This call has several purposes:

- Coaches discover whether the clients' aspirations and goals are ones that the coaches can get behind and support, whether they fall within the coaches' targeted coaching niche, and whether the fit feels good to the coaches.
- The clients have the opportunity to ask questions about the coaches' style and to assess personal fit from their standpoint.
- The clients hear themselves talk about their goals and desires for coaching, which can be illuminating and valuable, even if they don't end up working together.
- The coaches discover what kind of partnership the clients expect, want, and need from the coaches, and the coaches share their general expectations of clients. (If the two go forward and agree to work together, the coaches will explore this in more depth during the initial call.) This first official session is longer than subsequent calls and covers the client agreement, policies, procedures, and goals for the coaching relationship. We recommend this first session be at least 90 minutes, with the second half being the start of the actual coaching.

Other areas to examine regarding a comfortable fit include the following: payment capability, hours and times available, agreement about the method and frequency of coaching (face-to-face versus phone, weekly versus biweekly), whether the clients fit the coaches' ideal or minimal coaching profile, the coaches' interest in the goals or process, whether there is something the coaches will learn through this coaching experience that will benefit the coaches, and so on.

Through this dialogue, the coaches begin to design the coaching alliance. The coaches' conduct during the calls convey a wealth of information about style and proficiency as coaches: What are the coaches' ratios of questions asked versus information provided? How well do the coaches listen? Do the clients have a sense that the coaches *get* the clients and their situations? These are the coaches' first opportunities to model in the moment what a coaching conversation is like. The coaches need to focus on the elements of the coaching conversation, as described earlier in this chapter, even in these initial interviews.

If the client has caught the coach at a bad time, the coach must not give in to urgency and feel obligated to discuss the possibility of working together at that moment. The coach needs to be confident and to schedule the call at an appropriate time when full attention can be given and the coach can demonstrate the spaciousness that coaching brings into the client's life.

The Living Brochure

The coach's intention is to discover the client's initial coaching goals as well as other long-term possibilities and to enroll the client in working with the coach. Robert Alderman (1996) was one of the first people we know of who used the term *living brochure* to describe a conversation between a coach and a potential client. (The material presented here describes how coach Sherry Lowry of the ILCT faculty uses this conversation.)

The *Living Brochure* is an *enrollment* conversation. It was first labeled "living brochure" because the conversation takes the place of a printed brochure the coach would hand to a prospective client. Coaching is essentially a language-based series of conversations. This is one of the reasons the majority of coaches do not depend on standardized written promotional materials other than what appears on a Web site or is customized for specific clients for business development. Expensive brochures and collateral materials do not demonstrate the power of coaching. Coaching is relationship based, so the power is in the conversation, not in the materials. Clients hire their coach based more on who the coach is and how the client experiences the coach than on marketing materials. New coaches often believe that they can't begin coaching without promotional materials and a Web site, which is a sign of their insecurity. What needs to come first is the conversation. Instead of getting ready to get busy, get busy having coaching conversations.

Essentially, the screening interview conversation takes place through the use of powerful questions that the coach asks the potential client in a conversational manner. When Robert Alderman initially described this conversation to coaching colleagues, he stressed that the coach's intention is to help the client experience firsthand the value of coaches and coaching conversations. Value, of course, is assessed through the eyes of the client. The coach's intention is to be of value. The structure described below is one format for creating potential value to the client through a first conversation.

In the coaching profession, it is common to refer to this as an enrollment conversation. This emphasizes the intention of the coach to enroll the client. We prefer to call this a *conversation for exploration and discovery,* which emphasizes the value of this conversation and the alliance that is beginning to be created even during this one call. There are many different kinds of conversations, identified by their purpose. If the value of the conversation for exploration is apparent to the client, all that is needed at the end of the call is for the coach to ask the client if the client is ready to get started.

Sherry Lowry of the ILCT faculty articulates this well. She recommends that the coach use this conversation to set the stage for creating the most ideal type of client to coach launch or referral. Don't simply see it as an enrollment conversation. It is actually most effective when the potential client has indicated an interest in the coach's work, so there is a reason why the coach and potential client are having the conversation— it is not just idle chatter to pass the time on a plane flight. The conversation may be face-to-face or on the phone. It may have been initiated by e-mail and then taken to the next step. This conversation is intended as a verbal exchange (as opposed to written) because what the coach says and does depends upon the potential client's "real-time" responses. It is an active demonstration of the coach's flexibility and ability to *dance with the client.*

The coach's goal during the conversation for discovery is to create a sense of synergistic partnership. If this type of alliance can be created during the conversation, the match is probably harmonious enough to build a successful coaching alliance.

Below is an example of how Sherry conducts the conversation for discovery. An important note: This isn't a script. Stay focused on outcome, keeping in mind that the coach's goal is to understand more about the potential client's values, desires, intentions, behaviors, attitudes, passions, frustrations, and difficulties.

As the conversation progresses, the coach needs to reassess the outcome. For example, if early in the conversation the coach perceives that he or she is *not* the right coach *for that particular client,* the coach's outcome shifts. The new outcome becomes to determine whether the client is *coachable* at this time in his or her life, and to learn enough about the potential client to make a knowledgeable referral (or at least to make a pertinent suggestion, such as recommending a book or workshop that may be a valuable resource).

If the coach determines that the caller isn't a potential client, the coach abandons the conversation for exploration and instead asks questions that lead to a referral to another coach or to clarity about what the client's next best step might be. For example, the coach may hear the client's desires and intentions, and also realize that the client's life situation—for example, going through a divorce or handling a rebellious child—may need a referral to a therapist prior to coaching. Or the client may be coachable but doesn't fit the profile of the kinds of clients this coach works with. The coach does the most appropriate thing before ending the call, including potentially explaining the coach's thinking behind any recommendation. It is acceptable for a coach to say, "I don't think I'm the best coach for you," even while acknowledge the client's intentions and desires. The coach would then give the caller the name and contact information of two or three other coaches likely to be more be suitable, or refer the caller to the ICF coach referral location at www.coachfederation.org.

The point: The coach focuses on being of service and being a resource to this person. Our experiences show that clients greatly appreciate this and may show up in the coach's life at some future point. They may become a client in the future or refer other clients to this coach. Through the conversation for discovery, the client has learned the kinds of clients and situations this coach best works with.

Here is an example of the *conversation for exploration and discovery* in action.

Step 1. Start with an Ice Breaker
People love to talk about themselves. Encourage this process. Once the coach hears more about the person, the coach will have a sense of how to proceed and will have some language to use. Ask questions like: "Describe yourself in terms of how you see yourself." "Tell me something about how you came to this point in your life to make this contact."

Step 2. Get to the Important Issues
Find out early if potential clients have some important issues and whether they are willing and able to uphold their own interest in a coaching partnership. (This is work as well as pleasure!) Ask questions like: "What are three things you'd like to change in your life within _____ days, starting at this moment?" "If you could add three things of vital importance to your life, beginning this month, what would they be?"

Step 3. Discover Personal Boundary Issues
Get to questions that will uncover issues around boundaries, integrity, needs, wants, and values. Ask questions like, "Do you feel as though you run your job/business, or are there many times when it's running you?"

Step 4. Ask "Ouch" Questions
These are questions that identify sore spots, tender topics, and "pinches" the client is experiencing. Ask questions such as: "Are there any places in your life where you feel incomplete and that need to be addressed?" "Where in your life are you feeling burdened and carrying a heavy weight of responsibility?" "Do any of these places need to be healed or cleaned up?" A corollary question might be: "Is there an area where you would like to become significantly more responsible for something than you are now, and you are disappointed in the lack of responsibility you have?" The goal here is to discover any *unfinished business* or difficult areas that the client would normally not discuss or associate with the context of their goals. A client whose father died the previous month, for

49

example, might need time to grieve before beginning coaching—or not. But if the coach is aware of this, the coach can acknowledge that it could have an impact on the client's energy and attention.

Coaching may assist with these areas, and a proper referral may be suggested. Coaches can work with clients who want to take more responsibility for their children's learning and well-being, or to improve their relationships with their children. Diane Menendez worked with an executive who wanted to be more available to his teenage children. He discovered through the conversation for discovery that it was a source of a deep sense of loss for him that he had been unavailable to attend his children's soccer games and tournaments because of the extent of his travel. Through working with Diane, he turned his loss and disappointment into an intention to realign his time and commitments. Without asking an ouch question, this issue might never have been addressed.

Step 5. Plant the Seed of Self-Care

Part of creating value in the conversation is to plant the seed that doing something for oneself is a beneficial and worthwhile pursuit. For example, ask a question such as, "What kinds of things do you do for yourself when you need time alone?"

Step 6. Discuss Mutual Commitment

It's important to convey the importance of mutual commitment in the coach–client relationship. Say something like, "There is a mutual commitment we both make when we engage in coaching. If this works out for us, are you prepared to _____?" This can be, "Are you prepared to set aside time, energy, and space to fulfill your intentions?" (Make these requests relevant to the coach's practice and the client's process.)

It is useful to ask for a nonbinding commitment to work together for 90 days. The coach may say something like, "After 90 days, we then decide to go forward or determine that we've accomplished what we set out to do. In the meantime, I'll ask you to try on new ways of doing things and looking at your life. Sometimes these may ask you to stretch. For each of these options, I'll ask if you're willing to take on something new for possibly a week, a month, or longer. Would you be comfortable committing to exploring this process with me?"

Some coaches ask for a commitment and discuss the financials from Step 7 at the conclusion to the conversation for discovery. This takes more time, but it allows for fuller discovery of whether there's a match. It's necessary to discuss this as part of making a living as a coach. A major mistake new coaches make is to be reluctant to ask for commitment and to discuss fees and procedures.

Step 7. Get to the Financials

One part of creating perceived value is engaging in a conversation about the professional fee. The coach begins this step by feeding back to the client three changes or intentions the client has stated during this conversation. The coach can ask, "Do you agree that it would be valuable for you to attain these changes? Is it worth it for you to engage a coach to help you?" Then the coach explains fees and options. Most coaches have several different options for working with clients. Fees depend upon the length of sessions, the frequency of sessions, availability of the coach between sessions, and other factors.

Step 8. Focus the Client's Attention on Values

Highlight the choices clients would make if financial constraints didn't exist. Ask questions like: "If you became independently wealthy, what would you do with your life?" "If you knew success was guaranteed or that failure was highly remote, how would you be living differently?" These questions get to inherent values that may be outside the clients' awareness due to a belief that those options are impractical or impossible. These questions allow clients space to reflect on what they really value and what they really want.

For example, a client may say, "If money weren't a problem, I'd live on a Caribbean island and own a coffee shop, like the little one I saw on the island of Saint John last year." Even though that might be a fantasy, what it points to is that the client may want more simplicity and a life of more relaxation. Coaching can help the client surface and realize that intention, even if the fantasy doesn't become a reality. Either way,

51

encouraging the client to take an island vacation couldn't hurt. Or, the client may have articulated exactly what the client wants for the future.

Step 9. Process Check

If the coach has decided the person would be a good fit, this step helps to discover whether the client is ready to go or where the client is in the process of deciding about coaching. A good fit means that the client fits the coach's desired client profile or niche and the coach can fully get behind the client and the intentions. Ask something like, "At this point you seem like the kind of client I love to work with. I want to check in with you. Do you think that your intentions can get realized through working with me? Are you ready to get started?" "When you imagine the life you want, how do you see yourself starting your day?" Follow that up with a "barometer question" such as, "Can you tell me how you are thinking about coaching and its value from our conversation so far?" The coach might then ask whether the potential client has any questions or whether there's anything the coach can clarify or expand on.

Step 10. Testing

This builds on Step 6, where the coach focused on mutual commitment. By Step 10, the coach will have a sense of what the coach can ask of this person in the coaching relationship. Ask questions to check out commitment more fully, such as: "Would you be willing to try new options, even if they are unfamiliar and very different from how you now work and live every day?" "Would be willing to partner with me in discovering your habitual patterns, assessing whether they are beneficial or need realigning, and seeing what new options you might create?"

Step 11. Create Awareness

This step stretches the potential client's thinking about what is possible—the life the client may not be living and the potential that coaching can unleash in a life. "What big opportunities are out there for you personally or in your business that you are not yet taking advantage of?" "What hidden gift or talent might you have that deserves a more prominent place in your life?"

52

This step, along with Step 10, can open up new possibilities and awareness for the client. It also lets the coach discover the client's *mind-set:* how the client habitually attends to possibilities and obstacles to them. This is discussed as part of the Big Five and also in Chapter 1 in this book.

Step 12. Discover What Is Working
With the recent research from the field of positive psychology, we know that coaching conversations are strength based. In this step, the coach takes time to focus on the client's strengths and joys. The coach asks questions like: "What kinds of things make you happy—make your heart dance. " "When do you catch yourself smiling?" "When was the last time you laughed? Is this a regular occurrence or a luxury?" Coaches also ask about how other people view the client: "What would others say you do well?" "What do you bring into their lives?"

Coaches often concern themselves with quality of life and are sensitive to the possibility of an Achilles issue here. If clients say they haven't laughed or smiled in quite a while and that this is an infrequent occurrence, it might be appropriate to ask, "How long has it been since you have experienced joy and fulfillment?" Asking this question might elicit an emotional reaction from the client and help to determine underlying issues. This question also allows the coach to model compassion and a willingness to uncover and normalize emotions in a client's experience.

Step 13. Educate About Coaching
Find out how much clients know about coaching. Many clients will have read articles about coaching and will have some understanding of it. Ask, "Have you read articles about coaching?" Determine whether you need to provide clients with articles or refer them to your Web site or another Web site to learn more about the profession of coaching and how it works.

Step 14. Make a Declaration
Coaches often don't tell potential clients how much they'd like to work with them. It has been reported by many clients that even when they

interview coaches, few ever say, "I'd enjoy working with you. I'd love to be your coach." If this person is someone you want to coach, find a comfortable way to tell the potential client. If the potential client says something like, "I need more time" or "Let me think about it," you can ask, "Are there more questions you'd like to ask now to help you clarify your decision?" or "Would you prefer to contact me when you're ready?"

This is the natural point in the conversation for the potential client to decide if this works. If the potential client is very hesitant or a low risk taker, or if the potential client has financial considerations, you have many ways to work with these situations. Make a nonbinding agreement, for example. Be prepared to address considerations in a 100 percent constructive way. People rarely make good coaching clients if they need to be talked into it.

Step 15. Clarify Issues

You want to be clear that potential clients understand the commitment and concept of coaching. Here's a chance to correct any misconceptions—to clarify that a coach is not a guru or a taskmaster but a partner, a guiding mentor/coach, and so on. Ask: "Can you describe for me what you think my role as coach and your role as client will be?"

You want to listen carefully to clients' expectations. If they seem ready for coaching and you seem to be the right coach for them, move to Step 16. You may need to negotiate with clients their readiness to start and their expectations of you. If you don't seem to be a good fit for them, you may want to refer them to another coach who would be.

Step 16. Make an Offer

Suggest, in specific terms, the next step. "Our next step is to schedule a first session where we review our welcome packet and the agreement, and reaffirm and clarify your intentions and goals for the next 90 days. Can we begin that work on the date of _____ at _____ time?" Or, "My repeat client appointments are on Tuesdays and Wednesdays. Is a morning or evening time better for you? Generally, I reserve a block of time in the afternoon for my personal affairs, but from time to time I can schedule at other times or during weekends or evenings. With 24 hours' notice, there is no charge for rescheduling. After all, we both know *life happens.*"

USING STRUCTURES

There's a truism that safety comes with consistency: what we know we can count on comforts us. Paradoxically, it also provides adequate space for people to make radical changes. The *structures* coaches use support clients in taking responsibility for their life and the coaching work. In coaching, we use consistency in the *relationship* and in *session structure* to create a large space in which the client is given free rein to experiment and explore without needing to worry about whether there will be a safety net.

Two particular tools that give structure—the *welcome packet* and the *coaching session preparation worksheet*—expedite the initial work and set clear expectations for the overall engagement as well as for ongoing sessions.

The Welcome Packet

The coach's intention for a first paying session with the client is to accomplish the following:

- Review the logistics, policies, and procedures
- Create rapport and a beginning framework for the coaching alliance
- Begin to develop the client's long-term intentions and vision, as well as short-term goals
- Model the coaching conversation and the coaching alliance in action

The welcome packet is discussed more fully in *Therapist as Life Coach* (Williams & Davis, 2002) which also offers examples of a welcome packet for new clients, which most coaches have available for e-mail as well as in-person distribution. This packet may include additional forms, articles, and readings the coach finds relevant for a specific

55

client. We suggest that at this time you send only what you will use during the first month: assessments, exploratory questions, policies, procedures, and the client agreement. We sometimes ask the client, "Are you a paper person? How are you at dealing with forms?" This lets us know whether to send the whole packet at one time or send individual pieces just in time for their use.

We believe it's important for the client to have to do some self-reflection as part of completing the welcome packet because reflection will be required during the coaching engagement. Without reflection, the client will simply repeat habitual patterns of thinking, feeling, and acting. Also, requiring the client to prepare will be something the coach will expect for each session. Client preparation is one of the ways that the partnership between coach and client is ensured. An unprepared client tends to foist responsibility for the session onto the coach. The welcome packet is crucial for laying the groundwork for the long-term relationship. Coaches frequently refer back to the client's detailed responses for engaging conversations about original goals and intentions, which may be a resource for identifying new intentions and necessary course corrections.

The welcome packet performs two functions: (a) it introduces clients to the coach's policies and practices and (b) provides them with information about the work you will be doing together.

In order to design a good welcome packet, coaches need to clarify their intentions for using it. Some coaches get their packets to clients via e-mail. Others choose instead to put the welcome packet and other information into a notebook and mail it to clients. The welcome packet can even be sent a few pages at a time in the first month of coaching, so as not to overwhelm the client with paperwork. Ask the client what they would prefer and adapt accordingly.

The Coaching Session Preparation Worksheet

Most coaches also ask clients to prepare in some way for their calls in advance of phone sessions. Many use *coaching session preparation worksheets,* which are faxed or e-mailed to the coach before the phone sessions. These are commonly one-page forms that help keep the coach and client focused on what the client wants from each session. Coaches keep completed forms as a resource for documenting the clients' progress and accomplishments. We like to ask clients, as part of the coaching session preparation worksheets, to record successes and highlights of the time between sessions, as well as opportunities and challenges they see now. We also ask them to identify priorities for the sessions that will become the session agenda.

Great Questions for the Discovery Conversation,
Welcome Packet, and First Sessions
We discuss "powerful questions" as a coaching skill in more depth later in this chapter. However, questions that are evocative and stimulating to the client are essential to a client beginning to experience coaching as a unique and powerful conversation. Without powerful questions, the coaching conversation can fail to inspire. What follows is a list of a few powerful questions that can be used in a variety of contexts but that are particularly useful in engaging the client in the beginning. The coach may want to use them for a living brochure, include them in the welcome packet for the client to think about in preparation for the first session, or ask them during the early sessions. Many of these questions are "edgy"—they'll stretch both the coach and the client.

57

- What gives you energy?
- Where do you get most discouraged?
- What strength, skill, or gift do you wish to use more fully?
- What do you most want from coaching?
- What are three changes you could make right now that would move you closer to your desired outcome?
- How do you get in your own way?
- Where do you find yourself feeling cautious or careful about making changes in your life?
- How will you assess the value of our work together?
- How can I best coach you? (What might I do that wouldn't be helpful?)
- When do you find you waste time and energy?
- How do you like to learn?
- What three things do you really want to accomplish in the next 60 to 90 days?

- How do you handle conflict in your work or at home?
- How might I recognize when you have something difficult to express to me?

The First Coaching Session

Set aside a minimum of an hour for the first session. The coach has several major goals for this first session:

- *Clarify expectations.* Clarify with the client the nature of the partnership and discover what will make the coaching valuable from the client's perspective. True value lies in how the client attributes value to the coaching, not in how the coach perceives value. Discuss requests and expectations you and the client have of each other and the processes you will use for the coaching (face-to-face, prep sheets, e-mail in between, and so on). Review how to use the coaching session preparation worksheet.
- *Discover intentions and desires.* You will already have asked questions that provide insight into the client. Ask more about things that interest you about the client, listen well, and draw forth the client's aspirations, desires, and wishes through powerful questions (see pp. 62–70).
- *Begin work on the client's goals.* The welcome packet should contain worksheets where the client lists goals. Use these to clarify and expand the understanding of goals and their importance in the client's life. Then begin to set a timeline. Most coaches review and clarify information on goals by time frame: 30-day goals, 90-day goals, and longer-term goals.
- *Coach the client's being and life.* The client will discover rapidly that he or she needs ample energy to accomplish goals. Taking time to focus on energy drainers can be useful. If the welcome packet includes a form asking the client to list things that drain his or her energy, you can review this during the first session. This information provides insights into the client's current life and obstacles. You can directly help *clear some of the deck* by identifying ways in which the client can eliminate or reduce energy drainers.

58

- *Model how it is to be an authentic human being.* Listen fully from the heart. (A first session should be about 80 percent listening.) Walk the talk. Allow for periods of silence—"the fertile void." Pave the way for the basic coaching conversation. The coach's authenticity is paramount to the coaching relationship because, like it or not, your authenticity is a model for clients' movement toward increasing authenticity in their lives. Many of their workplaces—like much of their lives—support inauthenticity rather than authenticity because the workplace is under the illusion that authenticity brings about conflict and gets in the way of achieving results. In coaching, authenticity encourages people to show up as who they really are—*warts and all*—and to create results that flow from their authentic desires, strengths, and uniqueness.

Preparing for Coaching Sessions

Coaches need to have practices they use for becoming present, focused, and centered in order to bring their best self to each coaching session and maintain the spaciousness needed for great coaching. Coaching by telephone requires discipline in order to avoid getting distracted by things in the environment. Even though the client can't see the distraction, the session will be negatively impacted by it.

A good practice is to build in at least 10 minutes between coaching sessions and do the following before each session:

- Clear the desk of materials not specifically relevant to the session and eliminate any distractions.
- Get centered: quiet your mind, meditate for a few minutes, and breathe.
- Hold the client in your consciousness and review materials and notes from the last session.

At the end of the session, allow enough time to provide good closure. Set the next appointment, summarize commitments (yours and the client's), and close comfortably without feeling rushed to the next appointment. The tone on which the coach wraps up the session will stay with the client, so be sure to end in a manner that reflects your commitment to the client.

Personal Ecology: Working with Energy Drainers

Energy drainers are those things one is tolerating, ignoring, or putting up with that are draining. They can be mental clutter or physical clutter, but when handled they allow the client to reclaim the energy that is being used up. Giving an early coaching focus to energy drainers is a wise strategy. You can even begin to address this issue during a complimentary session. Ask clients to prepare a list of energy drainers and send them to you in advance. This will prepare clients for the session and will give them some immediate success in areas of life that could block them from attaining the success they seek.

The advantages of dealing with energy drainers is illustrated in the following excerpt from a holiday newsletter by Phil Humbert (2001), a longtime coach and author of a personal success newsletter.

> *Mary and I spent most of today cleaning out closets. It wasn't supposed to be that way, but we were giving a table and chairs to Goodwill, and started thinking about what else we ought to give.*
>
> *We ended up taking six blankets and assorted towels and linens to a local shelter, a large box of books to the public library, and several boxes of housewares, clothes, and assorted odds and ends (along with the table) to Goodwill.*
>
> *My point? Well, along with feeling virtuous and bragging about how "generous" we are, there is something much larger going on here.*
>
> *If success is about efficiency (and it partly is), then anything that clutters up the coach's life, or adds friction, or distracts the coach, or gets in the coach's way, undermines the success. That's what the concept of "tolerations" is all about. When we tolerate a few frustrations—a few nuisances and annoyances that sap our energy and reduce our concentration—pretty soon the impact on our effectiveness becomes significant. Don't do that to the yourself!*
>
> *As I look at closets that are the neatest they have been in years, my life is richer tonight. As I look at a dining room that will be more useful and more inviting, I know our meals will be more pleasant, which may reduce stress and improve digestion, communication, diet, nutrition . . . and the list goes on. All from giving away things that have cluttered our home and our lives.*

Your Personal Eco-System™ consists of the immediate environment—your home and the people and things around you—and that environment either supports you in achieving your most important priorities, or it slows you down. Your home, office, car, friends, and loved ones function as a system to either support you or slow you down.

I think of a highly efficient environment as being a Personal Support System,™ while highly inefficient environments not only create friction and hold us back, but at some point they can actually become toxic and can kill our dreams—even kill our sense of ambition and hope.

This holiday season, along with the parties and year-end celebrations, take time to clean out your personal ecosystem. Clean up the nest. Clean up any misunderstandings or personal hurts. Clean out the closets, both literally and figuratively. It will enrich you with an immediate sense of well-being and will allow you to perform at a higher level with greater focus and clarity in the months to come. And, isn't that what success is about?

If the first coaching session and the welcome packet are well designed, coaches and clients both will have learned a great deal about who the clients really are, as well as the clients' intentions and any ways in which clients block themselves. These pieces of information alone can provide major value to the client. We recommend to ILCT students that they keep each client's welcome packet easily available. Coaches can use it to do a 3- or 6-month review, looking back at the client's original intentions in detail. Unless the coach prefers a paperless office, a useful practice is to create a file folder for each client. Staple the welcome packet to the inside left panel of the folder. Keep coaching session preparation worksheets and coaching notes to the right, with the newest one on top. This gives coaches the opportunity to rapidly review critical information and bring back issues the clients may have taken off their radar screen, perhaps because they were superseded by crises or by current pressing issues. In essence, the coach can return the client to focus on enduring intentions and desires by referring to the welcome packet information.

Transparent Language, Powerful Questions, and Purposeful Inquiry
As we have said, coaching takes place during conversations we have with clients. A coaching conversation differs from an everyday conversation because the coach uses language intentionally and powerfully. Our

61

language—words, rhythms, timing, nuances, metaphors, stories, and tones—becomes the most potent resource the coach has in working with the client.

If you listen to a coaching conversation, the language of coaching sounds simple. Simple, yes—easy, no. It is deceptively simple. The coach's language encourages depth of thinking and self-reflection. Its intention is to be *direct* and *transparent* so that the client's thinking, language, and processes are highlighted. The coach's language is free of unspoken judgments and assumptions. (See David Grove's work on transparent questions on page 67.)

New coaches sometimes go astray by believing that questionnaires, forms, articles, and models are essential to great coaching. In fact, the language you use with the client—the questions you ask—will be the most powerful resource you can bring to your coaching practice. It is through your *language* that much of your *presence* is communicated.

POWERFUL QUESTIONS

Stuart Wells (1998) wrote that strategic thinking is critical to the future. He offered three key questions that every leader must ask repeatedly:

- What seems to be happening?
- What possibilities do we face?
- What are we going to do about it?

These three questions mirror the questions asked throughout the coaching process. The coach's primary tool is the use of powerful questions that reach deep inside the client and allow the client access to new possibilities.

How skillfully and successfully you navigate the basic coaching conversation depends on your ability to ask questions that form the foundation of coaching because they guide and focus the client's thinking. A coach's questions need to go well beyond the pedestrian; they need to be powerful in their ability to catalyze the client's thinking and behavior.

Powerful questions have the uncanny power to focus attention, change the way a client feels, and prompt the client to make choices and to take actions not previously considered because they were outside of current awareness. Jerry Hirshberg (1998) noted that powerful questions "are often disarmingly simple and are particularly effective in jarring 'The Known' loose from its all-too-familiar moorings, the thick, dead underbrush of old associations and assumptions, allowing for fresh light on a subject, and the potential for the growth of new ideas." We know from studies in neurobiology that the human mind cannot resist answering a question. The common experiment of asking someone not to think of a white elephant illustrates how the mind responds to suggestions. Questions work the same way. Ask the client a question, and the client will begin to search for an answer.

Helping professionals are familiar with the power of a great question. Steve de Shazer, one of the founders of solution focused brief therapy, is known all over the world for one single question he invented. His simple—but profoundly provocative—"Miracle Question" (de Shazer & Lipchik, 1984) is used by thousands of therapists every day:

What if, overnight, a miracle occurred, and you woke up tomorrow morning and the problem was solved? What would be the first thing you would notice?

Like the Miracle Question, powerful questions serve the client in three ways:

- They draw out the client's hidden or untapped potential.
- They focus the client on high-leverage points for change.
- They speak to the client's creative powers and resources to generate new options.

Questions serve many purposes in coaching. Questions can open up an area and expand, or they can probe and intensify a focus. As guides for the client's attention, they can be used to:

63

- Encourage, support, or validate
- Initiate, uncover, or surface issues
- Draw out and discover what is not apparent, or clarify what has been surfaced
- Generate new possibilities
- Respectfully challenge thinking, behavior, and limitations
- Identify assumptions.

We sometimes ask new coaches to watch a few of Peter Falk's *Columbo* movies, where Falk's ability to ask an apparently stupid question is actually a wise and skillful way of focusing attention on what's missing or what's occurring that hasn't yet become transparent to Columbo or others. Therapists reading this book might be familiar with the questions Milton Erickson asked, which were designed to cause creative confusion for the client and to create an opening beyond the client's present awareness and habitual ways of thinking. For example: "Do you think you will begin to change this Tuesday or will you wait to begin next week?" This kind of question implies that change will happen, focusing the client's attention on when it will take place.

Erickson also used questions to interrupt the client's habitual patterns. We have used questions this way, requesting that clients ask themselves during every hour of their workday, "Right now, how am I being the leader I want to be?" A question like this forces the client's attention onto reflecting on the previous hour, something the client otherwise may not have done.

A good practice for coaches is to tape their end of a coaching conversation and record the questions they ask. This practice lets coaches assess whether they are limiting their questions in any way and whether their questions actually land powerfully on the clients' ears. When a client says, "That's a good question," the coach knows the question has had a powerful effect on the client.

Inquiry: A Special Kind of Powerful Question
A particular type of powerful question is the *inquiry*. Many spiritual traditions use *inquiry* practices as ways of developing self-awareness and self-understanding. An inquiry is a question that a person holds in mind

continuously and contemplates over a specific period of time. When a coach requests that the client do an *inquiry,* the client will be living with the inquiry question daily until the next session. This is a great example of the famous quote by Rainer Maria Rilke (1992):

Live your questions now. And perhaps even without knowing it, you will live along some distant day into your answers.

Other examples of inquiry practices include Zen koans and contemplative meditation. At ILCT one of our senior instructors, Lynn Meinke, suggested that we call these *coaching koans.* Inquiries are questions that encourage clients to reflect deeply. Because they live with the question over a period of time, they find many ways of answering it. The principle of inquiry is that the human mind can't *not* answer a question. When we put the right question in front of us, we open up avenues for exploration and answers that would not have appeared to us before.

Readers may be familiar with how journaling and silent retreats may help someone outrun habitual ways of judging and certainty, and create an opening for internal dialogue. This is the principle of inquiry at work. It's powerful and life-changing. These are questions that don't have easy answers. Socrates made these famous through the *Socratic inquiry* process he used with his students. He would walk with them out to the town gate, asking difficult and penetrating questions about virtue, peace, ethics, etc. History shows us that Socrates was murdered because he asked too many questions that challenged the status quo. In life coaching, that is exactly what we want to do. We want to ask questions that challenge clients to think beyond, aspire beyond, and act beyond their current status quo.

In the field of coaching, inquiry can radically deepen and expand clients' personal experiences of their capabilities and assets, as well as their ability to notice *how and what they notice.* Two main purposes of inquiry are to generate self-awareness and to encourage clients to increase their awareness of their beliefs, behaviors, and life, so as to create more choices and responsibility.

Coaches model for clients the ability and willingness to be "in the inquiry," that is, being comfortable with open questions, and empha-

65

sizing curiosity and discovery. Like our clients, sometimes we just want to *know*, or we wish we knew. Yet because coaching is a learning model, we serve our clients in significant ways when we stay willing to not know—even when we'd prefer to know.

Coach Marilee Goldberg (1998) made a useful distinction. She said there are two mind-sets from which questions develop, the *judger* mind-set and the *learner* mind-set. Judgers focus on problems, noting what is wrong, assessing issues of control, making assumptions, and attempting to be right. If coaches come from the judger mind-set, they will not be effective. *Learners*, in contrast, focus on what is right (about me, about the other person, and about the situation), what the choices are, what can be learned in a situation, and what they are responsible for. The learner mind-set is the mind-set of the coach. The coach's stance is to be willing to be "in the inquiry" instead of "in the answer."

Many business leaders commonly come from the judger mind-set, constantly looking for closure and drawing conclusions. Malcolm Gladwell (2005) illuminated how this works in the human mind and body. *Blink* focuses on the value of the judgment mind-set and its risks. As Caldwell showed, judgments about people and situations are often made within a fraction of a second. In much of human life over centuries, this has served humans well. It has allowed us to make snap decisions about safety issues and to take appropriate action.

Habitual quick judgments can be helpful or can hinder clients. Inquiry is a method coaches use to ask clients to examine their mostly unconscious patterns of judging, in the service of creating a new way of being that will allow them access to their intentions.

Accountability Questions

Coaching brings movement in clients' lives in part because it creates accountability on the part of the clients to coaches, but even more important is accountability of the clients to themselves. At the end of each coaching session, coach and client want to have the answers to these questions:

"What will you do?"
"By when?"

"How will you know you have been successful?"
"How will I know?"

Some clients, particularly those in the business world, have become victims of their accountability drives—their habitual tendencies toward accountability. They overuse accountability, driving themselves to accomplish tasks at the expense of self-reflection on the worth of the tasks and assessment of whether the tasks lead to desired outcomes.

Staying Close to the Client's Language

The chapter has focused extensively on the ways that coaches use questions, an essential part of the coaching conversation. When coaches hear the term *powerful questioning,* they frequently put pressure on themselves to make every question they ask a *powerful* question. In fact, the simplest questions can have a powerful impact on clients. Coaches often don't know whether their questions will be powerful until they ask them and the clients respond. Powerful questions, as we think of them, are not *guru questions,* coming from a place of demonstrating the coach's expertise or superiority.

As an antidote to the tendency of new coaches to overfocus on having every question be powerful, coaches can explore the brilliance of very simple questions that stay very close to the clients' language. Many ILCT students come from a helping profession background, so they are familiar with trends in this profession such as work with narratives and with language and its assumptions. We ask ILCT students to explore therapist David Grove's (1997) work on transparent questions, through reading the Web article, "Less Is More: The Art of Clean Language."

The authors, students of Grove, summarized how Grove's focus on clean language creates the opportunity for clients to fully self-observe. Grove's questions enable clients to experience their own patterns of thinking, feeling, and responding in "real time." As a result, transformations occur. The clean language Web site contains a number of examples showing how closely the clients' words are reflected in the active listening responses. Grove teaches therapists, but his lessons apply equally to coaches and others who are providing mirrors, reflecting back to the clients so that the clients can learn. In Grove's view, ideally the coach's words reflect what the clients say, adding little, but tracking so closely that the clients truly hear themselves.

We're calling this use of language "transparent" because it doesn't clutter up the lens of clients as they work with their own goals and current situations. The coach uses as few words as possible so that the clients have more time and space to think, work, and express themselves.

Transparent language doesn't add to what the clients say; rather, it closely tracks and reflects the clients' language, allowing the clients to see more clearly who they are, what they want, and where they will go.

A client might say, for example, "I've felt very stuck about my job for a long time. I'm trapped in this job, and I have no way out of these golden handcuffs." A coach could ask a question such as, "What resources of courage and determination would you need to leave?" This could be a useful and powerful question for the client. However, Grove's work suggests that the coach is adding a new lens and filter, adding to the client's current construct of their situation. The coach is not working transparently because the coach is focusing the clients' attention on the option of leaving the situation or mustering up the resources to do so.

This might be a useful approach. On the other hand, it shifts the clients' focus to what could or should be done. Another alternative for the coach is to track very closely the clients' own language and stay with them—within the current frame of their thinking. The coach might ask any of the following and be working fairly transparently with the client:

CLIENT: "I've felt very stuck about my job for a long time. I'm trapped in this job, and I have no way out of these golden handcuffs."
COACH: "What kind of stuck is this for you?"
or
COACH: "What is your experience of being stuck in your job for a long time?"
or
COACH: "What is your experience of being stuck and feeling trapped with no way out of the handcuffs?"

Each of these questions asks the clients to elaborate for themselves and for the coach on their current experience of the situation. To use a phrase from gestalt psychology, these questions ask the clients to work with the figure-ground of their situation. Their figure is what they are most attending to—it has arisen out of the ground of all that they could be attending to in this situation. In the excerpt above, the coach's question asks the clients to focus more and more attention on their own experience of being stuck. The coach's questions ask the clients to gather more information about their current situation—their *what is*—before moving to a course of action that will shift things. The coach's questions invite clients to examine their thoughts, then their experiences—their sensations, awareness, emotions, etc. This richer view of what is happening now—a richer figure in the language of gestalt—facilitates an understanding on the part of both the coaches and clients of what will facilitate a shift to a more satisfactory situation for the clients. With more richness and texture in the clients' awareness, several new directions may emerge. The clients may discover that being stuck somehow has a payoff for them. Or the deep exploration of feeling stuck may invigorate and energize them toward doing something different.

The second choice for the coach, still working transparently, could be to explore the clients' *desired* situation. Once the current situation has been explored, the coach might ask, "What would happen if you could find a way out of the handcuffs?"

In essence, *transparency* means staying within the language used by the clients—not adding different metaphors, a new framework, or a different context to what the clients are saying. Many coaches surprise themselves when they tape their part of a coaching session and discover just how much they are adding: information, assumptions, directions. Coaches need to ask, "Have I stayed close to the clients' language and given it enough time through so that the clients have a full, rich sense of their current situation?" Coaches need to restrain themselves from adding too soon, even if their intention is to add consciously, intentionally, usefully, and respectfully. Coaches need to maintain good and appropriate boundaries, and working transparently and cleanly communicates respect for the clients' boundaries and the clients' ability to understand and create.

Questions form a major vehicle for moving the coaching conversation along. But when a question contains an assumption, the clients can

69

absorb that assumption without realizing its impact. Every assumption establishes a framework that creates some choices and obscures other choices that are outside the framework.

A better vehicle may be for coaches to *directly state* what they are thinking—to share the assumption directly. A coach might say something like, "I'm aware of how powerful the term *handcuffs* is as you speak it. I'm aware that handcuffs call up the term jailed to me in a very visceral way." We believe that coaches need to experience the power of *not* adding anything and develop confidence in the power of simply tracking and reflecting before starting to voice assumptions, however overtly. We believe we owe it to clients to be responsible about what we add and how we shape thinking—theirs and ours—through our questions, assumptions, and framework.

Chapter 3

Coaching as a Developmental Change Process

In our training, we often begin a discussion of the developmental change process by quoting the poem "Wild Geese," by Mary Oliver. The poem is a meditation on a flock of wild geese who are heading home, and the poet's elaboration on the deep connection human beings have to each other and to the world, their home. The poem's perspective is one that appeals to many people in midlife and after. Oliver is a deeply spiritual poet whose writing has gained broad appeal during the past decade as more and more people find themselves searching for meaning and purpose beyond their current boundaries. A Pulitzer Prize winner and winner of the National Book Award for Poetry, Oliver writes poetry and essays that emphasize the great connectedness of human beings with the universe. The longing for such deep connectedness—to other human beings and to something universal—draws clients to the powerful process of coaching, particularly in midlife. When such people work with life coaches, their journey often takes them in new directions.

Life coaches support clients in the search and in walking the new path toward desired change. They do so by being able to bring *multiple perspectives* to the client work. They remain fully appreciative of the unique gifts and strengths of each individual client. At the same time, they can see how the client's work fits within the context of how human beings generally develop over the course of a life span.

Before we go further, let's examine the case of a client whose profile and situation are best viewed from the lens of developmental issues.

change is the law of life, and those who look only to the past or the present are certain to miss the future.

—John F. Kennedy

CASE STUDY: GEORGE

George is a 52-year-old professional, a successful chiropractor who built his business from the ground up and whose reputation for sensitive and caring work keeps him very, very busy. He lives in the same city in the northeastern United States where he grew up. George comes to you because he feels tremendously disenchanted with his work. As a young man, he had hoped to become a veterinarian, and his first love has always been animals. He has ridden horses all of his life and currently owns one, which he doesn't get to ride frequently enough. He has also had a longtime dream of owning land where he could raise llamas. He is tremendously gifted with his hands, can sculpt and create, and plays several stringed instruments well. However, he has little time for practice, sculpting, or playing. George became a chiropractor because he was urged to do so by his parents. His father was a chiropractor, and his older brother is also a chiropractor. To George, both of them seem to be contented in the field. He wonders sometimes why he is not and tells himself that he should be contented. Yet that doesn't bring him contentment.

George has been feeling frustrated with his chiropractic practice for some time. He gets easily irritated with some of the people who come to see him these days, which never used to happen. He is upset with himself because of these feelings. He knows that any irritated or angry energy he gives off can interfere with the patient's healing processes. He acknowledges to you that he is aware that he has always liked animals better than people—he has a great sense of connection with and compassion for them. He gets impatient when people complain all the way through a chiropractic session. He tells you the story of one current patient who greatly annoys him. She is 75, tremendously anxious, and a victim of a traffic accident. She comes in twice weekly, talks incessantly through the sessions, and chronically complains about everyone as she talks. Uncharacteristically, last week, he told her, "Just shut up and let me work!"

For the past several years, George has had a lack of energy and motivation, which disturbs him. He wonders whether this has anything to do with getting older. George has been happily married for 20 years, is active in his church, and has twin sons who are seniors in college. George's wife, who is 45, is in the last stages of completing her doctorate in social psychology. After teaching elementary school when they were first married, Joanne quit to take care of the children. When the boys were in junior high, she returned to school. She is excited that she will be completing her degree and can turn to university teaching.

Discussion

At the Institute, students examine these questions before they discuss the case of George.

What stands out to you about George's situation?

What are the first questions you want to ask George?

What emotions arise in you as you read about George?

What do you empathize with most about George and his situation?

What do you feel most distant from or impatient with about George's situation?

If George were 35 or 65, how might you approach coaching him differently?

We use these questions to prompt students to think about their planned approach as well as their internal reactions. Keep in mind as a coach that you won't read a synopsis; you gain this information through conversations with the client. And as those conversations occur, any of these questions and many others may prompt you to respond in a coach-like manner. However, coaching questions can only grow out of the ways that coaches understand human beings, including whether they understand stages of development and archetypal patterns that are fairly representative of human beings all across the world.

When coaches are ignorant of human developmental issues, they miss great opportunities for zeroing in on what may be a source of the client's drive toward change. They may unfortunately join the clients in avoiding the clients' real work. We use the following theories to help coaches understand some widely accepted theories of human development. When coupled with Prochaska's theory of readiness for change, coaches can understand where most effectively to enter the client's landscape of living.

James Prochaska's work initially emerged from the field of addictions counseling and was research-based in applying a theory and strategy of the counselor's behavior and style that would be best matched to the stage of the client's readiness for change. We believe Prochaska's theory applies as well to coaching clients, even though it is not a treatment application. A common coaching example is given below, using Prochaska's stages. As part of clients' goals for coaching, clients want to improve their health and begin an exercise routine. Prochaska (Prochaska, Norcross, & DiClemente, 1994) identified six well-defined change stages that clients move through, although not necessarily in a linear way. The important thing for coaching is that coaches may be working with clients who are not yet ready for action, and so the coaches' role is to assist the clients in helping them to get ready for action.

1. *Precontemplation.* In this stage, clients actually are not yet considering making a change. Clients are unaware of the need for a change or unaware of their current patterns or behaviors. If coaches see that the clients seem to be at the precontemplation stage, the clients are not ready to make big changes. That may be in line where they are at developmentally as human beings. When coaching clients at this stage, the initial exploration and assessment phases of coaching can be critical.

   Clients who want to improve their health are already beyond this stage. It is not as if precontemplaters can't think of a solution; it is that they don't identify a problem. The clients above have already identified a problem and have reframed it as a goal: to improve their health and begin an exercise routine. Coaches are unlikely to find clients at the precontemplation stage, unless perhaps they have been sent by their employer for a problem they have not identified themselves. Sometimes, however, clients come to a coach for one reason and something else emerges. In this case, the clients may be at the precontemplation stage around a particular issue.

   It's important for coaches using Prochaska to recognize that the stage is related to the specific area: a client may be at several different stages for several different goals, which requires flexibility from the coach. You may be working with a client on work issues or on improving his fulfillment in relationships when the client goes to the doctor and discovers his cholesterol is high, blood pressure is high, and the doctor recommends he focus on his health. Here, the client has received *assessment data* from his doctor. Sometimes assessment data is received from the coach, as in 360-degree feedback assessments in corporations. Three-hundred-sixty-degree assessments, or full-circle feedback, are surveys that colleagues, bosses, and sometimes others (like clients or customers) are asked to fill out on a person's strengths and weaknesses. In either case, one of the coaching strategies for moving a client from pre-contemplation to the second stage, contemplation, is the use of assessment data. A coach would be looking here to see if the client is accepting the information or denying that there is a problem that he can choose to address.

2. *Contemplation.* Clients in this stage are considering making a change and also may find themselves quite ambivalent about it, or they may not know what to do to make the change. They can endlessly weigh the pros and cons but not actually decide to get into action.

The coach can assist clients in this stage to examine how the current situation and their habits, behaviors, and patterns work for and against them. For the client who wants to improve health and initiate exercise, the coach might ask" "What have you thought of to start doing?" "What kind of exercise do you most enjoy?" "What will you have if you keep things as is and don't make any changes?" "What are the pros and cons of initiating a regular exercise program for you?" The clients may be busy executives who travel quite often and feel time-pressed. If so, the coach's role might be to help the clients examine the consequences of allowing work to overtake their time and schedule, to the detriment of their health. In addition, the coach helps the clients explore their motivation to change versus their motivation to keep things as is.

Diane Menendez uses Barry Johnson's (1992) *polarity management* model to help clients who get stuck weighing the pros and cons of two sides of an issue for themselves. While we won't discuss this here, the model asks clients to map out the pros and cons of two poles of an issue—in this case exercise program or no exercise program—and to identify the positive and negative aspects of each side. Then the coach works with the client to create ways of avoiding the downsides and securing as much of the upsides of each pole as

75

possible. The coach is an ally who helps clients find the pathway for moving forward.

3. *Preparation.* In this stage, the client is preparing to change: gathering information, assembling resources, checking out possibilities, etc. This is where the accountability coaching brings with it can be paramount. The coach also can help the client discover resources, identify what's needed, etc.

    Helping the client move from the contemplation stage to the preparation stage can be a significant accomplishment in itself. The client begins to overcome the inertia that characterized the contemplation stage where the action was all simply thinking about action. Coaches sometimes feel that they have failed when their client doesn't jump into action. Instead, the preparation stage is critical. The coach's work is bringing about change if the client seeking health, for example, is researching on the Internet some local resources for health clubs, trainers, classes, etc. This is movement—though sometimes the coach who is unfamiliar with Prochaska's stages doesn't see it that way. Coaching with Prochaska's model in mind, the coach maintains the patience to allow the client to move through each stage, knowing that the client's ultimate success will be better ensured if each stage is addressed fully according to the client's needs.

4. *Action.* This is the classic stage where the clients actually take action, practice new behavior, and try new things. The coach's role is to ensure that the clients' action is congruent with who they are. The clients have been empowered through the work at the initial three stages to identify their own ways of taking action. The ideas for action haven't come from the coach's preconceptions nor the coach's advice. The actions have resulted from the cocreative process of coaching.

    A client's action may be hiring a personal trainer, buying a piece of exercise equipment and using it, or setting up a regular workout schedule.

5. *Maintenance.* In this stage, the clients have maintained the chosen actions for a long enough time to have created new habits and integrated them into the rest of their life. This usually indicates that new habits are being installed. Coaching at this time continues to

acknowledge and endorse the change. Often the clients may have not been successful at maintaining change in the past. The coach's alliance with the clients increases the likelihood of success: the clients finally have an ally. If the clients slip back to old habits or circumstances change, the coach helps them to reset their goals or recalibrate their actions.

Just as in car maintenance, occasional tune-ups and adjustments are needed so that the current situation can be addressed. Clients sometimes believe that they can consistently maintain actions over time, no matter what. Yet life brings changes. A client may develop a health issue that requires that he change his preferred way of exercise. This can be more difficult than he expected. Or a new child in the family requires realignment of the parents' use of their time.

6. *Termination.* Prochaska used this term because it reflected the fact that the client no longer needed a programmatic approach to the behavior that needed changing. The new behavior has become a natural part of the person's life, and it happens without much thought on the part of the person. For the clients above, the exercise program has simply become a part of what the clients do each week—a new habit, perhaps even a new joyful habit.

In coaching, Stage 6 may not mean an ending of the coaching per se. It may simply mean that the coaching will no longer focus on a particular goal—the need to focus has *terminated,* so to speak. Some clients may feel that they have gotten where they wanted to go. The coach helps the clients distinguish between terminating coaching for life and recognizing when ongoing maintenance coaching or coaching for new issues will be beneficial to the clients.

These steps are not linear, they are spiral. It is important to keep in mind that change is a process, not an event. On any desired change the client may cycle through these stages in a nonlinear fashion. Coaches commonly see this: Clients may say, for example, that they commit to taking action by the next session. Yet when they appear for the session, they have moved back from the action stage to contemplation. The coach's role is to support the clients' movement through the cycle and to accept the clients where they are now.

VIEWS ON HUMAN LIFE AND CHANGE: PSYCHOLOGY, PHILOSOPHY, AND HUMAN DEVELOPMENT

Our introductory chapter includes a broad overview of the history and evolution of life coaching from its psychological origins. The roots of coaching run deep into the ground of psychological change theories and practices. Like all other psychological practices, coaching is a process concerned fundamentally with change: change in the clients' external life, changes in observable results, and changes in the clients' subjective experience of themselves, others, and their world. All too often, media articles about coaching focus *only* on coaching's *action orientation,* to the detriment of the profession. They miss a critical aspect of great coaching: *the coach's intention is to build the long-term capacity and capability of the client.*

Having the client take *action* is only one aspect of the client's change process—often the most observable and quantifiable aspect, but not necessarily the richest, most enduring, and most satisfying outcome of coaching. Coaching is not simply quick-fix, results-oriented work. Yes, coaching does produce performance changes and short-term results. However, the benefits of coaching accrue because clients build their capacity and create greater capabilities for the long term—for life. Coaching's great gift remains that coaches focus on clients' *learning and development* as well as on *achieving desires.* James Flaherty (1998) stressed the need for the coach to focus on long-term client capability building.

What Coaches Look For Is What They Find

We all know that once we decide to buy a car and determine what kind, suddenly we notice that the world is full of that particular kind of car. If we've decided to consider a sports car, for example, we begin to notice how many of them are riding alongside of us. That's the consequence of expanded awareness. Something we were formerly unconscious of becomes very prominent to us, or becomes a *figure,* as gestalt psychology calls it, that emerges from the ground.

When we were in training to become mental health professionals, we learned a set of assumptions, theories, techniques, and behaviors that became part of our repertoire as helping professionals. Like other helping professionals, we studied more than one school of therapy and have adopted what works from a number of different approaches. As *The Family Therapy Networker* (1998) reported, the most common way that therapists describe themselves, when asked what "school of therapy" they practice, was "eclectic." We think the same eclectic approach needs to be true for coaches. Coaching should never begin to appear overly reliant on techniques or be limited by a single theoretical approach. That's an important lesson that new coaches need to learn. Masterful coaching takes all the lessons, techniques, and theories, integrating them into a personal flow so that the coaching becomes transparent. This process is analogous to what happens when learning to drive a car. When teenagers learn to drive, they are overly observant of the pressure on the gas pedal, the turn signals, the nuances of driving a car for the first time, including all the rules and regulations of the road. By the time they become proficient drivers, driving becomes a set of automatic habits. They no longer think of all the techniques and details—they simply drive.

As Albert Einstein is believed to have said, "Theory is extremely useful, because your theory determines what you can see." For coaches who come from a therapy background, much of what they have learned as therapists can be useful to their coaching practice. Whatever field coaches may come from, they need to consciously examine the mind-sets and assumptions they have learned as part of their professional development to date—about the client, about what is necessary to bring about change, about the value of digging around in the past, and so on. Lawyers who become coaches may have internalized a set of assumptions about the need to offer advice, ask probing questions, and never ask a question they don't know the answer to. To become successful as coaches, lawyers will need to consciously examine and adapt their style of relating to clients, maintaining what is consistent with the coaching alliance and relationship, and discarding what doesn't fit in coaching. The challenge for each coach is to sort out what is useful from what is likely to be detrimental—or at the very least what will slow down the change process for the client.

In the past 20 years, some schools of therapy have begun to look more and more like coaching. Solution focused therapy (SFT), for

79

example, uses a set of questions to focus the client's attention and awareness on *what works.* If therapists have received training in SFT, they have learned a valuable set of tools that they can use as coaches. Life coaches also know that there are limitations to transferring tools that were designed for therapeutic applications.

For example, the *Miracle Question* used in SFT transfers very effectively to many coaching situations. Asking the question, "If a miracle occurred overnight and you had the change you wanted, what would be the first thing you would notice?" directs the clients' attention specifically to what they desire. Asking this question of George the chiropractor might move him out of his lethargy and disenchantment to consider the possibilities available to him.

However, there are limits. For example, in many trainings, including SFT, helping professionals encourage the clients to create actions based upon what worked in the past. The assumption is that what worked in the past will also work effectively now. Perhaps it will. However, that assumption discounts a *developmental perspective.* In fact, taking an action that worked before may discourage the clients' development, although it may allow the clients to achieve a short-term goal.

KEN WILBER'S FOUR QUADRANTS OF CHANGE

ILCT encourages a more integral and developmental perspective (Wilber, 2000; Figure 3.1). We believe that partial and piecemeal approaches to complex situations are likely to be ineffective in the long term. Whether coaches are addressing individual and personal issues of meaning and transformation—as in the case of George—complex business problems, or large-scale global issues like war, hunger, disease, and education, clients are likely to benefit from seeking approaches that grow from more comprehensive, holistic, systemic, and integrated perspectives. As you review the development models, keep a current client's desires and situation in mind. Or use your own current situation and your transition to becoming a coach and developing your coaching business as the situation to analyze. Coaches can source comprehensive perspectives by using models and approaches such as those described on page 81.

Figure 3.1

The client and the context (Adapted from Wilber, 2000)

	Interior	Exterior
Individual	**I** **INTENTIONAL** emotional, mental, spiritual: impulses, perceptions, sensations, levels of trust for self, other, world, values, belief, moods, etc.	**IT** **BEHAVIORAL** physical, neurological, body, brain, behavior, things encountered, neural patterns, physiology, etc.
Collective	**WE** **CULTURAL** relationships, community, service, morals and ethics, myths, social expectations and rules, world view country of origin	**ITS** **SOCIAL** systems and institutions: rules, patterns, machinery

Quadrant 1 is the interior/individual aspect of change—the "I" domain, as Wilber describes it. This is the interior reality of clients, including their thoughts, feelings, beliefs, and yearnings. In this quadrant, people focus on what only they can know, from the inside. This is the realm of subjective experience that is only fully known by the clients, living their unique life. A client may come to a coach for Quadrant 1 work out of a desire for inner development. The client and the coach can gain access to this domain when the client engages in self-observation. Over time, self-observation reveals patterns of feeling, thinking, and response. This quadrant is a key determinant of change; people make changes only when they believe and feel that change is possible and that they have the resources necessary to accomplish the changes.

Most coaches find themselves naturally asking questions and working with the client using a Quadrant 1 approach. They spend most of their time here. Sometimes that approach is sufficient, but it is also limited.

As a coach works with George, she will naturally pay attention to Quadrant 1 issues: George's lethargy, his sense of boredom and irritation, his shame at how discontented he is, and his anger at his own frustration.

81

when you boil rice, know that the water is your own life.

—Zen saying

Quadrant 2 has to do with the exterior-individual aspects of change—
the "it" domain. This quadrant includes what can be observed about the
individual from the outside. Quadrant 2 gets a great deal of attention
from coaches and world-class athletes. Executive coaches work with this
domain when they observe their clients leading meetings and notice
patterns of language the clients use. This quadrant is where life coaches
pay attention to developing individual behaviors and supporting the
physical ingredients that spark motivation and congruent action. Nutrition, exercise, and posture are all components of this quadrant.

A coach working with George in this quadrant might notice that
when George describes his work as a chiropractor, his body hunches
over and his chest seems to collapse. It appears to the coach that
George's voice becomes shriller, and the coach notices how frequently
George sighs and then falls silent. The coach observes these factors and
can choose to feed them back to George. If the coach asks something
like, "How do you feel when you sigh?" George will report from Quadrant 1, the quadrant where only he can be aware of how he feels
because the evidence relates to his interior thoughts and feelings. The
coach can instead observe from Quadrant 2, which can lead into a
Quadrant 1 inquiry. George may not be aware of his physical responses.
As the coach shares his or her observations, George can become more
fully aware of his physical responses and how they link to his moods and
emotions.

Quadrant 3 deals with the interior-collective aspects of change— the
"we" domain. This is the domain of culture, family history, and so on. It
is the interior, often hidden, territory of shared assumptions, collective
projections, and images and associations that direct what happens when
people come together. This is the domain of myth, story, unwritten rules,
and cultural beliefs. This domain includes the practices, roles, rituals,
stories, and meanings that determine perceptions of possibilities within
specific groups. This is the domain of shared history and shared visions.
They create themselves through conversation and dialogue, through what
is said and what is left unsaid and subject to interpretation. Coaches and
therapists know how strongly this quadrant can impact the client's Quadrants 1 and 2, as when a client's family background has a defined set of

expectations for gender roles—for what it means to be a man, a woman, and a parent.

One of the difficult things for many clients is that the interior-collective domain is one of *internalized* values and morées. This quadrant represents the clients' internalization of values as reflected in their social systems (work, church, family, culture, neighborhood, country of origin, national identity) and the deeper meanings of symbols, purposes, vision, and values. These values are not necessarily reflected in overt messages inherent in their social web, but are more the subtle messages encoded in their day-to-day interactions. How a clients' "I" domains mesh with their "we" domain is a rich area of exploration in coaching.

George's coach could work with him in Quadrant 3 by asking him to identify what he learned from his family and upbringing about work, about changing jobs and roles, and about a man's role in his family. George's family heritage is German. His coach could ask him what that has meant to him and to his family—what that heritage assumes and perhaps does not discuss about work, family, roles, and so on.

Getting this cultural conditioning out into the open would help George notice what in his background and current relationships supports him in making changes and what blocks him. Coaches are able to expand their impact by asking questions from this quadrant. This is particularly important when doing cross-cultural coaching. An Hispanic woman working in a U.S.-based corporate environment may have different perspectives and conversational practices than many of her colleagues. A company that has offices around the globe needs to teach its managers to inquire about Quadrant 3 issues and to be aware of its impact on human change, not limiting themselves to a superficial understanding of employee behavior and values.

Quadrant 4 is the exterior-collective aspects of change—the "its" domain. It is the quadrant of systems and institutions, including social systems, family systems, and work relationships observed from a systemic perspective, in other words, observed from the outside of the client. (The cultural impact on the client is the province of Quadrant 3.) This domain, like Quadrant 2, is concerned with observable, tangible, and measurable aspects of reality. Quadrant 4 reminds coaches that system design deter-

83

mines performance, and that if we want to get the system to perform at a substantially higher level, we must design for it.

To avoid confusing Quadrant 3 (the "we"), and Quadrant 4 (the "its"), we teach our students to think of *cultural* as the internal, introjected, and historical impact of the clients' cultural heritage, views, and ethics on them as individuals. Quadrant 3 is concerned with the unspoken aspects of the culture, whereas Quadrant 4 is concerned with the observable interactions, structures, and rules of relationships. Often this quadrant is exemplified by the policies explained in print, as in an organization's orientation training or policies manual.

A key point for coaches is that each of these quadrants is related to all the others. Change or development of one quadrant is inextricably bound up with all the others. Each quadrant affects all of the others, and each one is powerful. Clients may find themselves more powerful in one or the other of the domains. Sometimes becoming aware or more powerful in a neglected domain forms the focus of the coaching. Ignoring any domain can lead to haphazard or incomplete results.

George's coach might work with Quadrant 4 through asking George to examine the social groups he is a part of. The coach might ask, "Where in your life do you have social groups you are a part of—a church, Rotary Club, professional group, or family system?" George would list and identify these for the coach. Then the coach could turn to Quadrant 1, asking George, "How fulfilling are each of these groups for you right now?" The coach might also work in this quadrant by asking George to examine his environments, noting the arrangements of spaces, furniture, and so on, and then identifying how he interacts with his environment because of the way it is organized. He could also look at the records George keeps on his calendar. How does he systematically use his available time? Each of these is a potential avenue for changes that has the potential to yield greater satisfaction.

LEVELS OF CONSCIOUSNESS DEVELOPMENT

Dr. Clare Graves, the founder of what is now known as Spiral Dynamics, described human development on his Web site as a never-ending quest:

At each stage of human existence the adult man is off on his quest of his holy grail, the way of life he seeks by which to live. At his first level he is on a quest for automatic psychological satisfaction. At the second level he seeks a safe mode of living, and this is followed in turn by a search for heroic status, for power and glory, by a search for ultimate peace; a search for material pleasure, a search for affectionate relations, a search for respect of self, and a search for peace in an incomprehensible world. And, when he finds he will not find that peace, he will be off on his ninth level quest. As he sets off on each quest, he believes he will find the answer to his existence. Yet, much to his surprise and much to his dismay, he finds at every stage that the solution to existence is not the solution he has come to find. Every stage he reaches leaves him disconcerted and perplexed. It is simply that as he solves one set of human problems he finds a new set in their place. The quest he finds is never ending.

Robert Kegan is one of the foremost researchers to have developed a theory of human development. The material in this chapter is drawn from his books and sources about his work on the Web, such as www.theleadershipcircle.com, which focuses on applications of his work to leaders in organizations. An essential principle of Kegan's work is that movement from stage to stage of development is really about a transformation. It does not happen all at once. Transformation may take years to unfold. Without practice in new ways of thinking and behaving, shifts from stage to stage do not happen (Kegan, 1983).

When shifts do occur, they are always associated with the emergence of significant new capability. Research also shows that people seldom regress permanently to a previous level, although they can regress temporarily under stress or trauma. Their new order of consciousness transcends the limits of the old order and is better matched to the demands of the world the client now inhabits. It simply works better. When stress or crisis occurs, the client may temporarily seem to move backward, but normally the recovery will be rapid. If clients revisit issues, they consider them through new levels of complexity. The trajectory forward definitely has been set into the human being.

Kegan's theories focus on changes in the way people differentiate between their sense of self and their environment. Sometimes these are referred to as boundary issues. As Kegan says, development is a lifelong process of differentiation and integration. We, as human beings, are pulled toward autonomy and inclusion, and the various ways we work with these issues over the course of a lifetime is somewhat predictable—not by age (for adults) but by developmental level. Since our interest is in adults, we will focus primarily on the latter stages of development.

The Egocentric Self (Stages 0–2, Birth Up to Age 12–16)

Between the time a child is born and the end of adolescence, with full biological growth, an egocentric self has evolved. During these early developmental stages, the self consists of needs, interests, wishes, impulses, and perceptions, but does not truly have a shared reality with others. During the time of adolescence, a self concept emerges, which produces a consistent notion of "me." During this stage, young people lack true empathy because they can't imagine the feelings of others. Others are *instrumental:* people who meet their wishes, desires, and needs.

At this stage, young people relate to the "other" to get their needs met because they don't yet know how to make another person's needs important to them.

Adolescence is a stage when adolescents learn how to pursue their wants and needs within a larger system of competing needs. It is a difficult time because they are accepting that the world does not revolve around them and that they need to give up their egocentric agenda in order to take up membership in society. Adolescents do not know that this shift will actually aid them in achieving what they want within a larger system.

Research suggests that 15% of adults do not fully make the transition beyond the egocentric self. These people can be self-centered and controlling, or they can have a tendency to play out the victim or rebel roles.

The Interpersonal of Socialized Self (Stage 3)

Most of us successfully make it through adolescence and become effective, well-functioning adults. Research suggests that the majority of adults in our society function in the interpersonal self stage. In this stage, people take up a role in the larger society and identify themselves with their role. The new structure of the self can be articulated as "I am my role." At this stage, the self is made secure and valuable by belonging to and succeeding within prescribed socially accepted roles. As coaches, we find that this stage is limited by the discrepancy between people's own awareness of themselves and their actions, and what they actually do, what they are good at, and to what extent and how others accept them. At this stage, people are unaware of how their goals and behaviors are actually predetermined by others or by the culture; they are essentially defined from the outside in, but if asked they would say that they define their own life. They have an illusion of autonomy, as if they have truly authored their own life. Yet that is not so.

Clients at this stage do not yet see the extent to which they are directed by their cultural conditioning—the expectations and rules voiced by significant others and institutions in their life. In this stage of development, clients are not yet free to follow the song of their heart. They may hear the heart song and ignore it, dismiss it as impossible, or struggle with how to respond to it. Most often, fear gets in the way of actually moving toward it when clients are at this stage of development.

When clients at this stage serve as leaders, they often function as benevolent parents, maintaining the social conditioning yet caring deeply about the people around them.

In relationships, Kegan describes this person as interpersonal but not intimate. "There is no self to share with another—you are the other needed to complete me." At this stage, the client has difficulty managing anger because it jeopardizes relationships. Instead, sadness, roundedness, or a sense of incompleteness occurs when anger surfaces.

If we think of this existence of the individual as a larger or smaller room, it appears evident that most people learn to know only a corner of their room, a place by the window, a strip of floor on which they walk up and down.

—Rainer Maria Rilke

The Independent Self (Stage 4)

Transitioning to an Independent Self is the major transition of adult life. Only 25% of adults in our culture complete this transformational process. To make this transition, clients can no longer ignore or distort the call of the soul. They face the fact that following their own path often means disappointing others, risking failure, and/or contradicting the norms that link them to society and that make the socialized self worthwhile and valuable.

This transition is particularly difficult because to make this journey, clients must let go of the deeply held beliefs that worth and value are tied to action. The self, for the first time, *becomes (or is)* an identity; the self still *has* relationships with other people but is not defined by them, nor completely defined by cultural expectations.

The challenge of this stage is to first create an internal self. This is the first developmental level where clients can be truly *self-reflective* about their roles, norms, and self concept. Although this process opens up many possibilities, clients may also experience pain as they look back on who and what they were at earlier stages.

Clients at this stage may begin to focus diligently on self-development as well as the development of others. They are keenly aware of what is authentic and what is inauthentic in their lives. Action becomes an authentic expression of an emerging sense of inner purpose. As clients begin to see and experience the power, creativity, freedom, and satisfaction of living from a true, authentic center, they also value those traits in others. They may become impatient with what they regard as deception, and they become defensive when chaos threatens the order and structure of the self they have created. Self-expression and cooperation become new organizing principles.

The Integral or Interindividual Self (Stage 5)

At this stage, the self is a vast tapestry of personal systems. There is a sense of expansiveness and vastness, but it is not of the self but rather of the context in which the self operates. At this stage, clients understand the systems and groups that have shaped them and of which they are a part. They are capable of seeking out information that causes them to make changes in behavior and they are capable of constructive negative judgments about themselves. Now they truly have a self to share with others. This is the first time they are capable of true intimacy.

According to Kegan, only about 1% of adults reach this stage. However, another 14% are in transition to achieving it. Here, the inner self-definition shifts from "I am a whole and complete self that coordinates with other whole and complete selves" to an internal realization that, in fact, "I am not whole and complete." Rather, "I am many selves."

Jungian psychology may be attractive to people in transition to this stage because they recognize that there are parts of themselves that they have ignored and not developed.

Clients at this stage no longer need to pretend to be whole and complete, and can bring compassion and curiosity to their own development and interaction with unacknowledged aspects of themselves. Clients are now able to hold the whole complexity of personality—the good and the bad, the light and the dark, the hard and the soft. They can see this inner complexity without flinching or needing to engage in some strenuous self-improvement regime. Better still, they can see others this way—as complex multidimensional beings. They also can see the world in this way—as a dynamic interplay of forces. Seeing the self as a rich ecology of discord and harmony opens them to the richness and complexity of the workplace and the world.

The Sacred Self (Stage 6)

Research suggests that spiritual practices such as meditation and contemplative prayer accelerate the development through Stages 2–5. Level 6, the sacred self, seldom, if ever, develops without a long-term spiritual practice. Up to this point, the self has been largely seen as located within the body-mind.

At the stage of the sacred self, an incredible shift takes place: the client realizes that "I am not the body, nor the mind." A client at this stage identifies with the soul—a soul in communion with the divine. The client realizes that the integral self, with all its rich nuances, is useful for acting in the world. It is functional—a useful tool of the spirit. At this stage, the client experiences the world as unity, as one. This oneness is a literal experience of oneness with life itself. This is the birthplace of universal compassion.

George, the chiropractor, is likely to be on the brink of Stage 4 in his development. His coach sees him struggling with authenticity and hears him speak that word frequently during sessions. His coach sees him beginning to want a more comprehensive spiritual life than his traditional German Catholic religious focus has given him. He wrestles with the distinction between spiritual understanding and interconnection and the

89

"religious dogma," which is how he describes his experience of his religious upbringing and tradition. (Notice that, using the Quadrant model, the dogma occurs in Quadrants 3 and 4, while his personal experience of its impact is a Quadrant 1 issue; an understanding of this may guide the coach's questions.)

Otto Laske, a researcher who studied with Kegan, has developed methods for coaches to use with their clients that are based on Kegan's work. Laske has written articles that are referenced on the ICF Web site, at www.coachfederation.org, and included in the ICF Research Symposium proceedings (Laske, 2003). He believes that a coach cannot work effectively with someone unless the coach is at least at the same developmental level as the client. Preferably the coach should be at a higher developmental level than the client.

For coaches who work with executives, a powerful developmental model, the Leadership Development Framework and Profile, has been created by Suzanne Cook-Greuter and William Torbert (see www.cook-grueter.com for more information). It builds on work by Robert Kegan and offers a nuanced method for describing leaders at several developmental stages.

Torbert et al. (2004) identify each stage of their model as an action logic, a way of making meaning of one's role, function in the workplace, relationships, interactions, and problem-solving preferences, all of which results in a pattern of action the person is likely to take. Their model is based on the early developmental work of Jane Loevinger (1998), who created a measurement instrument to assess adults' meaning-making level, the Washington University Sentence Completion Test (WUSCT), which has been highly validated through thousands of research tests. Where Kegan's methods for identifying developmental level are based upon an interview (and therefore dependent on the interviewer's skills), the WUSCT asks clients to write their responses on a series of sentence stems, which are then coded by an expert coder based on an extensive manual. Torbert et al. extended Loevinger's work by developing methods of coding the higher levels of action logics, which is why their work is so useful to executive coaches.

Their stages focus on the action logics seen in business settings

Stage 1.   *The Opportunist* (4.3%) (correlates with Kegan's Stages 2 and 2–3). Opportunists focus on their own needs and desires, and want to protect themselves. This results in a short-term focus on concrete things and what is good for themselves. Opportunists may use sarcasm and show hostility toward others. They can be manipulative and resist feedback.

Stage 2.   *The Diplomat* (11.3%) (correlates with Kegan's Stage 3).Diplomats focuses on doing what is socially expected and what will gain approval from others. They avoid conflict and focus on preserving their status and membership within a particular group. They want to save face and can get involved in "us versus them" discussions.

Stage 3.   *The Expert-Technician* (36.5%) (correlates with Kegan's Stages 3–4). People at this level have strong beliefs and can be dogmatic, as they work from the logic of their professional craft, focusing on using their expertise, creating procedures, and being efficient. They can get rigidly stuck in the details and be perfectionistic, although their constant desire to improve things makes them the darlings of the quality movement.

Stage 4.   *The Achiever* (29.7%) (correlates with Kegan's Stage 4). Many leaders in larger companies seem to be at this stage, which focuses on achieving results and effectiveness. Achievers are proactive, use scientific problem solving, and set high standards or goals for themselves. We believe that many coaching clients come to coaching at the achiever level.

Stage 5.   *The Individualist* (11.3%) (correlates with Kegan's Stage 4–5). At this stage, the focus is on systemic connections, relationships, and the interactions of the self and the system. Individualists understand issues of unintended consequences and are able to question their own assumptions. Individualists are able to adjust what they do to the context they are in, but without being manipulative in doing so.

Stage 6.   *The Strategist* (4.9%) (correlates with Kegan's Stage 5). At this stage, leaders recognize that reality is a social construction, which accounts for its complexity and the many interrelationships between factors. Strategists are highly tolerant of individual and system differences, can create win-win results, and value feedback as a way of making sense of their world.

Stage 7.   *The Magician/Ironist* (2.0%) (correlates with Kegan's Stage 6). Leaders at this stage are aware. We think of people such as Gandhi, whose ability to focus on transforming self and others grew from his highly developed awareness of systemic issues and dynamic interactions, and an ability to make meaning by combining a vast array of practical as well as spiritual principles.

Stage 1 is considered a preconventional stage; few opportunists succeed in leadership roles in larger organizations. Stages 2 through 4 are considered conventional stages.

In *Action Inquiry,* Torbert et al. (2004) described cases of leaders at various developmental levels and the results of their attempts at organizational change efforts. They believed that a leader must be at least at the Strategist level to successfully undertake a complex change effort. His work makes fascinating reading for coaches who practice within corporations undertaking systemic changes.

In this developmental model, George might be considered to be moving from the Achiever level to the Individualist level. He has placed a high value on achieving results and building his business well. At an earlier stage, his excellence as a chiropractor may have been indicative of the Expert stage. Now he seems to be in transition to an Individualist focus, where he sees himself as part of a system and feels dissatisfaction when he looks at the entirety of his life.

A coach who wanted to use the action logics might ask George to take the WUSCT and have it scored by Cook-Greuter's firm, at www.TopTier-Mentoring.net. The feedback generated from this test is also highly valuable for coaches themselves, as it points to the natural frameworks and focus they will bring to their work with clients.

Midlife and Its Changes

No matter what stage of development a client is at, midlife seems to be a time of transition and change.

Frederic Hudson (Hudson, 1999; Hudson & McLean, 2000) proposed a cycle of change (referred to in figure-form as the cycle of renewal; Figure 3.2) that recurs throughout the course of an adult's life. (See www.hudsoninstitute.com for a fuller explanation.)

Figure 3.2

The cycle of renewal (© The Hudson Institute of Santa Barbara)

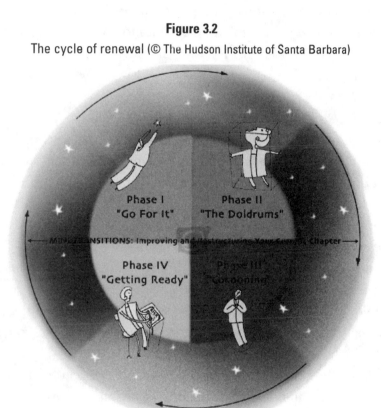

Hudson proposed four phases to this cycle, which recur throughout an adult's life. He called the cycles "life chapters."

Phase 1. Go For It

This is the beginning, essentially the positive part of a life chapter, when client seeks to live their dream and take actions toward fully living it and maintaining the success and well-being they experience. In Phase 1, clients feel as if they are "on purpose." Life just seems to be working.

George probably felt like this when he first started his practice, and perhaps also when he first got married, as these phases can apply to any aspect of life. Many professionals rejuvenate themselves and return to Phase 1 through learning. They go to seminars and learn new ways to work with clients. Examining George's history, his coach realizes that George took seminars frequently, upgrading his skills and chiropractic office tools, which he reported brought him a burst of energy. At this point, he has begun to study acupuncture. Before he came to coaching, he thought that new pursuit might return him to an energetic and satisfied place. He is surprised that it hasn't, although he is still interested in acupuncture.

Phase 2. The Doldrums

This phase is a "downtime" when there is a sense of general malaise and decline. In this phase clients are unhappy with the situation but not certain about what to do. Generally clients hang on to what was good in Phase 1, hoping it will return if they just work harder at it. The doldrums are meant to serve as a wake-up call, an invitation to restructure or reinvent life so that it works again.

George has clearly been *in the doldrums.* Sometimes the doldrums can be purposeful for clients. Clients may not get stuck in their reactions to the doldrums if they realize that they signal them to do a little "cocooning," the next phase, and to engage in reflection and consideration of their choices.

However, the doldrums may also be a manifestation of burnout—*or rust out,* as some career coaches describe it. People are tired and are ready for something new. They continue to do what they know and to experience dissatisfaction with the known.

The Mini-Transition

One way out of the doldrums is to make a mini-transition. This includes correcting and improving the chapters the clients are in by taking a shortcut across the Cycle of Renewal, by sorting out what works from what doesn't and creating a personal plan. According to Hudson (Hudson & McLean, 1999), clients keep the main themes, roles, and

94

characters of their chapters, but make some significant changes as well— perhaps geographical location, job, career, or relationship. The mini-transition renews the clients' chapter, bringing resilience, hope, and challenge. The clients return to Phase I with renewed energy to continue their life chapter. For George, a mini-transition might involve bringing in a business partner so that he wouldn't be working alone.

This category includes what is commonly called a midlife crisis, with people often attempting to create a mini-transition by changing spouses. Others add something to their life: a vacation home, a boat, or an adventure vacation that takes them out of the known and adds stimulation to their life. Done with full consciousness and thought, the mini-transition is very healthy. Choosing a mini-transition unconsciously and impulsively leads to unhealthy choices, such as quitting a job with no forethought, having an affair at the office, or making an expensive purchase that is outside of the client's budget. These radical behavior shifts are done without consideration or reflection, which is different from what George might do: donating a month or two of his time to do chiropractic work as a volunteer in a poor African country. Doctors Without Borders is an example of an opportunity for a medical practitioner to experience a mini-transition.

95

Phase 3. Cocooning

Cocooning is the phase where human beings imitate butterflies and enter a chrysalis in order to engage in transformation. This is a detachment from a chapter that wasn't working and the beginning of a major life transition. In cocooning, the client takes an emotional "time-out" to heal, reflect, and discover new directions for life, eventually leading to renewal and revitalization. Cocooning nurtures and nourishes the soul, giving birth to a new script and the beginning of a new story for the next chapter of life.

Clients can cocoon in several ways. Some might take an extended period of time off, such as a sabbatical, to reflect and discover. Others might build cocooning time into their regular schedule over a period of time. Clients may cocoon, for example, by going on a month-long silent retreat or by building in half-day retreats to their weekdays. Either approach works. A person could even have a special room for cocooning more briefly: a place for meditating, reflecting, journaling, exploring in the silence, and coming out rejuvenated.

George might choose to cocoon by taking off one day each week, going into nature and reflecting on his needs and desires at this stage of life. The coach can help George by partnering with him to build inquiry questions and disciplines that will enable George to explore deeply, making the best use of his cocooning time each week.

Phase 4. Getting Ready

This phase is a time for experimenting, training, and networking, resulting in a launching of the clients' next chapter. The clients test the possible paths ahead that will allow them to live their purpose and values. At that point, they write the script for the next chapter of life and plunge into it. They have arrived at Phase I again.

Coaching can be crucial for clients in Phase 4 as a means to help them develop their ideas beyond the abstract notion and into fruition— making the changes they want to make. George may determine, through his cocooning reflections, that he wants to bring in several junior chiropractors, fresh out of school, to mentor them and then to manage his business with them serving more clients. Ultimately, he will be able to sell the business. In the interim, he may choose to take a monthlong acupuncture training session in China and also a course in nutrition. He will be able to add these to the business offerings and will be the provider of these services within the business.

MAKING THE SHIFT

Taking a developmental, cyclical, and integral perspective on the client's life and goals marks the holistic activity of life coaching. How coaches have been trained, as well as the style and focus of their current profession, will be partial determinants of how they make the transition from their current profession to coaching.

Transition always requires both a *holding on* and a *letting go*. Generally, this needs to occur before something new can be embraced. Like a child receiving presents on a holiday, new things can't be added when the arms are already full.

All people who successfully make transitions clarify and engage in both holding on and letting go. Clients like George must consider what to hold on to and what to let go of, as do professionals moving into coaching.

An in-depth awareness is required for coaches who plan to continue practicing their current profession as well as beginning to coach. ILCT asks participants to focus on which skills are readily transferable from their current work to coaching, which skills are not transferable, and which shifts they will need to make—for example, shifting "therapist habits and mind-sets" to "coach habits and mind-sets."

Many therapists become very aware at this time of how deeply ingrained their habits of thinking and behaving as a therapist have become. They may habitually move to ask clients about their feelings first. They may avoid challenging clients because their habit is to see clients as fragile and in need of extensive support to make changes. They may not hold clients accountable. These are all habits the therapist will need to change in their coaching.

How long does it take to change a habit? Various estimates, ranging from 90 days to 60 repetitions, have been given, depending on the frequency with which the person engages in the thinking or behavior that is the target habit for change. Regardless of the exact time span, the question remains: How can *this coach* develop the habits needed to become a great coach? What shifts will this coach need to make? We describe these new habits as shifts because if therapists, for example, continue to do therapy, they will need to shift back and forth between these two sets of assumptions, behaviors, attitudes, and skills. Coaches will need to be flexible to ensure that they are using the right habits in the right settings. This can be enabled through some changes in the environment. If therapists will be doing face-to-face coaching in the same office where they do therapy, they may want to change chairs when they coach so that they coach from the chair that their therapy patients usually sit in. This will provide them with a new perspective, which can help them to use other habits and practices than they habitually do when they sit in their

97

therapist chair. Because body and mind are so intimately connected, this shift of body can assist in the shift of mind.

The exercise below (Exercise 3.1) is useful in examining the shift from therapist to coach. You can use it to brainstorm some things you may want and need to release, discontinue, continue, start, or enhance. To begin this process, we have written some examples from earlier coach training classes:

EXERCISE 3.1
Shifting from therapist (or other helping professional) to coach

Read the samples below, which are suggestions we've gleaned from other helping professionals who were transitioning to coaching. Then add your own.

CONTINUE DOING

1. Great listening from the heart

   _____

2. Use my intuition

   _____

3. Look at the client's life within systems

   _____

4. Use reframing

   _____

5. _____
6. _____
7. _____
8. _____

START DOING

1. Do more self-disclosure

   _____

2. Ask for payment in advance

   _____

3. Set fees according to what I'm worth

   _____

4. Call myself a coach, and believe it!

   _____

5. _____
6. _____
7. _____
8. _____

An exercise for anyone making a transition, client or coach, can be to complete Exercise 3.2 below, one commonly used in organizational development work. Completing each frame, the person asks, "What do I need to do more of or start, do less of or stop, and what can I continue?" Exercise 3.2 was completed by a therapist in transition, who for the short term would be keeping her therapy practice while beginning to coach.

EXERCISE 3.2
In transition

CONTINUE

1. Maintain my office as is

2. Keep the schedule I have created, with Mondays off

3. Maintain my administrative support

4. My optimistic attitude about the coaching opportunities I have

5. My reading of the literature and research on coaching

6. Attend local ICF chapter meetings

DO MORE OF/START

1. Feel free to disclose

2. Share more of who I am

3. Use humor

4. Challenge

5. Be very active

6. Tell people that I am adding coaching opportunities to my business

7. Attend networking events

8. Become a member of the International Coach Federation

EXERCISE 3.2 (continued)

LET GO, DO LESS OF/STOP

1. Go for feelings as the main route to change

_____

2. Feel as though I must be the expert

_____

3. Believe I'm dependent on insurance

_____

4. Always put the client's needs first

_____

5. Think of clients as "patients"

_____

6. _____

7. _____

8. _____

If you as a reader are in transition, we suggest you complete this fieldwork to help you apply the work from this chapter.

- Identify the two major actions you need to take to help you make the shift from your current profession to coaching. Work with a coach or a partner to identify an action plan. You will need to identify supports and resources for each of the shifts you want to make. Take at least one action this week to develop a new habit for you as coach.
- Self-observe this week how you are within your relationships with others, your relationship with yourself, and your relationship with what is larger than you. Maintain your attention and focus each day. What does this suggest about your level or stage of development?

PART II

Beyond the Basics

This section builds upon the fundamentals of coaching introduced in the first three chapters. Primarily it emphasizes specific skills and ways of using oneself that the coach uses with clients within sessions.

In Chapter 4, "Empowering the Client," we introduce six types of conversation that can occur within the context of coaching, as well as seven specific micro-skills that create an empowering conversation.

Chapter 5, "Stretching the Client," introduces the 10 steps of the Coaching Continuum in addition to five specific skills for challenging clients to stretch.

Chapter 6, "Creating Momentum With the Client," includes six strategies and common practices for creating and maintaining coaching momentum.

Together, Parts I and II provide the platform for a coach to work with the client on the "Coaching From the Inside Out" processes described in Part III.

Chapter 4

Empowering the client

When Jackie Robinson was signed by the Brooklyn Dodgers general manager, Branch Rickey, he became the first African American to play major league baseball. But "Number 42" became the target of considerable racist hatred and death threats. Rickey had warned Robinson that things would be tough and that he should learn to turn the other cheek. Prior to one game, however, Jackie received a telephone call that brought him to his tipping point. He was so devastated that he couldn't concentrate on the game and struck out with the bases loaded. During another inning he made a fielding error. The crowd's obscenities escalated.

Pee Wee Reese, the white shortstop from Kentucky and Jackie's teammate, called a time-out. Pee Wee put his arm around Robinson and is reported to have said, Jackie, let me tell you something. I believe in you. You are the greatest ballplayer I have ever seen. You can do it. I know that. And I know something else: one of these days you are going into the Hall of Fame. So, hold your head up high and play ball like only you can do it. Robinson was uplifted by these sentiments and went on to deliver the game-winning hit for his team.

Many years later when he was inducted into the Hall of Fame, Robinson recalled that day on the field with Pee Wee as being a turning point and a moment when Pee Wee gave him hope when all hope was gone.

Pee Wee Reese, a great natural coach, intuitively knew that a few well-timed words of encouragement can change the course of an event or a life—or even the course of history.

Empowerment is a word that has been overused—and it is often used incorrectly. Some people talk about empowering as though it is something coaches do for clients. In fact, no one empowers anyone else. Clients must be the ones who discover, claim, and boldly stand by their own power. What coaches can do is to create a climate that encourages the clients to be powerful. The coaches can ask questions that point the clients' attention toward sources of potency. The coaches can help the clients identify any blocks to their recognition of internal power and wisdom, and then can assist them to explore ways to overcome the obstacles. We often use the analogy of boulders and a whitewater rafting trip: You will definitely meet boulders on the rafting trip. You will either go around them in a controlled manner or sometimes might hit them head on, followed by bouncing off, turning around, and moving on down the river. Obstacles are like boulders in the river. You can't always avoid them, but the key is not to get stuck on them.

We believe that this way of thinking is behind Robert Hargrove's definition of masterful coaching. In his book by the same name, he says masterful coaching is about "empowering people to create a future they truly desire, based on unearthing what they passionately care about . . . to create their lives based on what is deeply purposeful to them" (1995, p. 20).

As coaches, we hold the intention that clients feel empowered to take action in every sphere of their lives. Clients sometimes don't like to see themselves as "powerful," possibly because they have had bad associations with power. A common distinction coaches may make is between *power* and *force*. Power comes from the inside and does not have to be forceful. It just is. Claiming personal power does not mean that the clients become an aggressive, forceful energy. It simply means that clients recognize and claim the unique power they already have to shape their life. Coaches assist clients in having full access to resources that may be lying dormant or the manifestations of which may be currently invisible. This invisible resource is the positive aspect of what Carl Jung calls the *shadow* archetype of our personality. People often assume that the shadow holds only the darker and more destructive aspect of the self. But it also hides unrealized strengths, gifts, and abilities. The coaches help the clients to claim these. Remember Wendy in Peter Pan? Wendy helped Peter reclaim his shadow as a part of himself and sewed it back on for him.

We judge the effectiveness of our coaching sessions by gauging the level of the clients' motivations by the end of the session. Generally, clients end sessions feeling more capable, competent, empowered, clear, and passionate, as well as better able to take action. The result of a coaching session is usually positive because we work with skill, wisdom, and humor, while holding in our focus the clients' highest good. That is, our entire focus and intention are on their empowerment. We know as coaches that coaching is essentially about *insight, learning,* and *choosing to act.* These three empower the clients to feel naturally generative and naturally empowered.

WHEN DO COACHES USE EMPOWERING SKILLS?

Clients tap into their creativity—the ability to see other possibilities for action and life—to make changes. The major obstacles that prevent clients from achieving all their potential come from within: the inner critics, the gremlins, the internal voices that challenge the clients' belief in themselves. Shakti Gawain (1997) puts this elegantly in *Meditations:*

> *As adults, the major block to our creativity is our inner critic, that part of us that internally criticizes what we do. We have standards of perfection incorporated from the world around us, ways that we think things should be done. We have a critic within who criticizes us when we are not doing things the way the critic feels they should be done. For most of us, this inner critic is what stops us from taking the kinds of risks that need to be taken.* (p. 62)

Julia Cameron (2003) makes an eloquent statement about how, when courage and creativity are released, that energy builds and creates its own momentum.

> *It is when we fire the arrow of desire, when we actually start a project, that we trigger the support for our dream. We are what sets things in motion; people and events resonate toward our fiery resolve. Energy attracts energy. Our arrow is the speeding pickup truck that attracts summer dogs to chase it down the road. We generate the energy and excitement. Then others will give chase. Build it and they will come. Creative energy is energy. When we are worrying about creating instead of actually creating, we are wasting our creative energy. When we are vacillating, we are letting air out of our tires. Our pickup is not speeding*

105

down the road and may never even get out of the driveway. Our project goes flat. Does this mean we should race off wildly? No, but it does mean that once we have a heart's desire we should act on it. It is that action, that moving out on faith, that moves mountains and careers. (p. 20)

When coaches focus on heightening clients' awareness of their potency and their choices, the clients' motivation rises, creating energy and momentum to sustain their work.

In general, coaching enhances the clients' ability to recognize, embrace, and use their key strengths. Knowing and using *signature strengths* is one of the ways that clients create lives of authentic happiness and true fulfillment. We refer here to strengths as they are described by Martin Seligman (2002). Calling specific attention to strengths, gifts, and choices assists clients at all phases of their work. While coaching isn't therapy, it boosts clients' self-esteem and confidence (as well as their toolbox of strategies) to identify and acknowledge specific strengths.

Coaches focus on empowering the clients when:

- An obstacle has been encountered and the clients are discouraged.
- The clients discount a resource or skill that has the potential to enhance current effectiveness or aid in achieving a goal or desire.
- The clients label as a weakness something the coach sees as a strength.
- The goal seems temporarily unattainable or the clients are blocked in seeing a pathway toward it.
- The clients have forgotten their vision and need to be reminded of possibilities.
- No one in the clients' lives believes they can attain what is desired.
- The clients need an advocate, in which case the coaches model how to become effective advocates.
- The clients' inner voice is predominantly discouraging or negative. Empowerment counters the inner voice with a strong compassionate message—the voice of the coaches.

SELECTING THE RIGHT TYPE OF CONVERSATION AND THE RIGHT SKILLS

The coach's intentions fulfill themselves through the use of skillful conversation and through seven empowering skills. The conversation type and the skill must work together to create a platform for empowerment.

The Case of the Dentist

As you read the material below about the types of conversations and skills, consider the applicability of each one to this case, a dentist in search of a career change.

You have a new client, a dentist who has been in practice for 10 years. His goal is to build his business and make it more profitable in order to possibly sell it and retire in 10 or 15 years. You discover in the course of coaching him that he is living for a future time when he no longer will be working. When you ask him about his work, he begins to tell the truth more deeply. He is bored with dentistry and would love to do something else. But his wife is scared to death of the prospect of this type of change, especially if it jeopardizes their current comfortable lifestyle. Their two sons, ages 7 and 8, both go to private schools, and his wife does not currently work outside the home, although she volunteers for a number of charitable causes. Both are active in their church.

You learn that the dentist has always had an interest in music and the arts, and that during his early college years he wanted to be a sculptor. However, he pursued dentistry because he is talented with his hands, and his father had a dental practice. While his father was alive, your client enjoyed the practice, as well as the relationship and comradeship with his father. When his father died 5 years ago and he began a solo practice, dentistry lost its savor for him. He is discouraged about reigniting his interest in dentistry, although he has a passing interest in dental surgery. He likes to mentor others and has considered adding several dentists to his practice who are fresh out of dental school.

107

Your client has had a lot of fun creating a Web site for his practice and wonders whether he would enjoy being a Web designer or the owner of a design shop. He loves to mentor people and is lonely and dissatisfied in a solo practice. He is clear that his wife and his sons come first, though, and he does not want to jeopardize their family harmony or their security.

Six Types of Conversations

Ellis (2006, pp. 52–55) describes six types of conversations we use every day. As you read these descriptions, consider the value of each one to the case of the dentist, as well as to your coaching practice.

Sharing

When you share, you communicate the essence of who you are, what you think, and how you currently feel. This is a quick but heartfelt snapshot of yourself that you provide in a few minutes. Sharing might sound like this:

> *Life's tough these days. I've been having problems with my boss, and my teenage daughter is rebellious. I wish I had more time to deal with these problems.*
>
> *I'm worried about my health. My doctor said that I need to come in for three difficult tests, and I'm scared. I love being active, and I don't want anything to get in the way of that.*
>
> *I really enjoyed the trip that I recently took to San Francisco. We had a great time visiting with people and exploring the city. In general, life has been such a celebration.*
>
> *I just received a $3,000 raise, and I am really surprised. I feel so pleased that my hard work has been recognized. Now I'm starting to think about what to do with the extra money.*

One way to be a powerful life coach is to demonstrate and ask for sharing—speaking deeply, authentically, and comprehensively about where you are in the present moment. You and your client can learn to converse soulfully from the depths of your beings about who you both are in this moment. This is a sacred way to be with each other, and it is a rare and precious experience.

Many people find sharing difficult to do at first. When someone asks, "How are you?" many people give a brief, superficial reply, "Just fine, thanks." Other people habitually go into a long weather report full of unrelated details. Both kinds of responses can conceal who we really are in the moment.

When we share, we do not always have to reveal deep, dark secrets, nor is the release of emotion always necessary. The main idea is to reveal an authentic and personal experience to the listener. This kind of conversation is deeply felt, soulful, sincere, candid, and direct. When a person speaks truthfully, candidly, deeply, and briefly with another person, the two individuals are able to create a symbiotic cosmos. Powerful sharing moves us deeply and alters subsequent conversations. Sharing gets thing off the clients' chest so that they can become present and mindful to what they want to create now.

As a life coach, you can model this kind of speaking and request it from each of your clients. You can start sessions by asking your clients to share. If they respond instead with their agenda for the session, you can describe sharing in more detail, demonstrate it, and again ask them to share.

The most powerful thing you can bring to someone's sharing is full, committed, and heartfelt listening. This might be as challenging for you as authentic sharing is for the client. When people share, coaches are often tempted to give advice, launch a discussion, or piggyback on their comments by relating an experience of their own. Instead, your job is to postpone a personal response and simply receive what the client shares.

We can even do others a favor when we ask them to receive in this way: "Please don't give me any advice about this. You don't have to make any suggestions or do any problem solving. I just want you to listen. Just witness. I just want to share."

Here is a powerful role the coach can play by just being a witness: someone who observes and creates a safe container for the client to share. Witnessing in this sense is a neutral and supportive role. Human beings on many important occasions ask people to witness their experience as a way to honor it: we ask people to come to weddings and funerals as a way of witnessing experiences and honoring their place in the human life cycle.

Debriefing

Debriefing is different from sharing. While sharing is about who someone is in the moment, debriefing is a list of what someone has been doing since the last session. When clients debrief, they give a detailed report. Like a newspaper article, debriefing relates the breaking events and answers the who, what, where, when, and how questions.

Sharing offers a taste of how someone is in the moment; debriefing serves up the "whole enchilada"—a long list of what they have done and felt since you last saw them. In the process of sharing this information, clients begin to feel refreshed and focused.

People benefit from debriefing. Clients can:

- Learn from their recent history by talking about what worked and what didn't work. With that insight, they are more likely to repeat what *does* work.
- Forgive their mistakes, celebrate their successes, and then release the past. Debriefing can include all of these elements.
- Set goals. As clients review the last few days, they might realize what they want to change.

Encourage clients to debrief regularly with a variety of people in a variety of ways. Clients can debrief with other significant people in their life. They can debrief in private by writing in a journal, speaking into a tape recorder, or simply talking out loud to themselves. You can suggest that your clients commit to this new behavior, and you can also monitor how often they debrief on their own.

Bring debriefing into your coaching and into your life. It is a habit well worth acquiring.

Clearing

Another form of conversation with a unique purpose is clearing. When clients clear, they vent feelings. Clearing is pure, emotional release where your client's aim is to speak about a topic until they "get it off their chest."

Where sharing tends to be brief, clearing may be either brief or lengthy, depending upon the clients' personal style, as well as the intensity of their response. Unlike debriefing, clearing does not result in a detailed review of recent events in the clients' life. When clearing, your clients can focus on a single event and their emotional response to it.

Clearing is a powerful form of conversation that you can facilitate in a variety of ways. Coaching isn't a therapy session, so the purpose of clearing is not catharsis. You may simply ask, "Is there anything you need to clear in order to move into today's session? Is there anything left over from the meeting you just left?" Clearing can occur in just a minute or two. The client speaks it, you hear it, and the two of you are ready to move on. Clearing could be simply a sentence or two where clients put into words their frustration with a meeting they just left. You create space for the clients to express and release whatever needs clearing. This, too, is a form of witnessing.

Ask yourself:
Would you use this kind of conversation with the dentist?
How would it be empowering (or disempowering) to him?

Discussion and Debate

Discussion and debate are probably the dominant forms of conversation in our society—in large groups, in small groups, and even in pairs. These two ways of communicating occur when people express their views and opinions. Both ways can promote learning, which takes place when we approach a subject from a variety of angles. We come away with a different point of view that is larger than what any one person originally brought to the conversation.

Discussion and debate work when people share the conversation and when space is created for everyone's brilliance in the arena. To recognize this shared space, it is necessary to give everyone equal time to speak.

111

Discussion and debate generally do not form a substantial part of the coaching process. Instead, coaching relies more on what David Bohm (1996) described in his extensive work on dialogue. Bohm contrasted discussion with dialogue through the root meanings of each word. *Discussion,* which is similar to the root of *percussion,* contains a sense of beating against something. *Dialogue,* on the other hand, comes from the root word for "flowing through." And that's how it often works in coaching. Allowing for silences, listening, intuition, something flows through the conversation that is larger or deeper than either individual alone brings. Even Socrates' method of inquiry was to create discussion and debate, but for the purpose of deeper thinking about common human striving. Socrates was recognized as the teacher, however, so his relationship with those he taught was not a coaching alliance. We recommend that coaches focus on dialogue, as we have said above, because dialogue is consistent with the coaching alliance.

In a coaching frame, the purpose of discussion and debate is never to focus on right or wrong, only to create deeper thinking through dialogue. Sometimes clients like to debate, and you can participate in this form of communication in a playful way. There may be occasions when a client wants your opinion or wants to debate a particular topic. This kind of communication should not focus on forcing your opinion on the client. Stay light and playful. By not expressing a point of view or not taking a stand on a particular issue, you convey your open-mindedness and can bring a fresh perspective to the conversation. You also demonstrate that it is okay not to have a point of view and that there is no need to adopt one immediately.

Teaching

Another way we can be in conversation with each other is through teaching. Teaching occurs when somebody says, "I know something that you may not know, and I would like to share it with you." When others want to learn from this person, they often listen intently, take notes, search to understand, and ask questions about the information until they are clear. Sometimes in a teaching environment, debate and discussion occur; in an unusual teaching environment, even sharing may occur.

We recommend coaches be cautious with teaching. It is tempting to become the source of wisdom for a client, but it can undermine partnership. On the other hand, some clients may need to learn exactly what the coach can teach rapidly. In small doses, teaching can be very effective.

In the case of the dentist above, you might want to teach the client how to do a simple breath-counting meditation as a way of centering and focusing between patients. Before you begin teaching, you might say, "It could be beneficial for you to be able to do a brief centering exercise between patients. Would you like to learn that now?" If the client accepts your invitation to learn, at that moment you have shifted into teaching. It is important to explicitly say to the client that your role has shifted. "I'm shifting into a teaching mode for a moment."

Ask yourself:
Would you use this kind of conversation with your client, the dentist?
How would it be empowering (or not empowering) to him?

The Coaching Conversation
There is one more unique and distinct way that we can be in conversation with each other, and that is through coaching. This type of conversation takes place when people explore what they want in the future and choose ways to attain it—without getting advice.

In the context of a coaching relationship, you do many different things with clients—exploring, problem solving, creative thinking, generating multiple options (including contradictory ones), and experimenting with new strategies and techniques. Sometimes coaching simply means listening fully and occasionally feeding back what you hear, which is a huge gift we can bring to people. Throughout this activity, the clients' purpose is to generate their next new action—something that does not happen in sharing, debriefing, discussion and debate, or teaching.

Seven Skills for Empowering
These skills evoke the clients' best resources, allowing them to realize what they already know but may doubt, undervalue, or treat as insignificant. Keep the case of the dentist in mind as you review these skills.

113

1. Focusing on Strengths

Remember the Big Five model we introduced back in Chapter 1? Focus, the first of the five, asks this question: Of all the possible places to direct their attention, which do the clients choose? You also make choices as to where to direct the clients' attention. Shining the light on their strengths serves them well and counters the habitually critical climate the clients may inhabit.

How often in our lives do we hear what we are doing right? Many clients are only minimally aware of their strengths. They may have been told that a strength is a weakness or a liability by others who do not want them to apply that strength. We all have strengths; however, most of us are more aware of our weaknesses. We hear more about our weaknesses, beginning early in our childhood, from parents, teachers, and others. Some of us even find it impossible to talk about our strengths, either because we are not aware of them or because we feel it is inappropriate or even arrogant.

As a coach, you want your clients to recognize, articulate, and fully embrace their strengths, whether they be attitudes, skills, or behaviors. You may find it helpful to begin coaching certain clients with an assessment of strengths, such as the one found on www.authentichappiness.org.

Clients come to coaching with a unique combination of strengths and weaknesses. It is important to examine these characteristics in the context of the goals the clients have set. Some of their weaknesses can be improved on, but others may be impossible to change. For example, clients may have been diagnosed with attention deficit disorder (ADD). We have found several high-level executives who learned that they have this condition when their children were diagnosed with it. These executives are often highly creative, synthesizing and building new ideas from disparate sources. On the other hand, their ADD may bring with it a short attention span, a fidgetiness that others notice, and certain other qualities that may not be subject to change. Some executives choose to use medication but others do not, except when they must sit through long meetings. Most other factors that clients might consider weaknesses may be amenable to change, but it just may not be worth the effort for the clients to do so.

114

As a coach, you can best facilitate your clients' success through a combination of:

- exploring with them where and how they can use their strengths;
- exploring with them new behaviors and skills they can learn;
- supporting them in making peace with weaknesses that cannot be changed or strengthened, since acceptance itself can be a powerful strength when wisely applied.

When clients are aware of their strengths and know how to best apply them, they can follow the path of least resistance in addressing a challenge or goal.

2. Acknowledging and Endorsing

No matter how strong clients may seem, all clients benefit from being acknowledged and endorsed for something they do well or a quality or a *way of being* they display. Great coaches pay a good deal of attention to endorsing and acknowledging their clients.

Often, clients may find it difficult to hear positive acknowledgments or validating statements. And as a coach, you may find it difficult to deliver acknowledgment and validation. This may be particularly true if you did not receive much recognition from important people in your own life.

Endorsing and acknowledging are not the same as complimenting. When we compliment someone, we comment favorably on something the person has or does. A compliment expresses your opinion, and by extension your approval of something that is part of the clients' life. Generally, we tend to compliment people on their belongings or external features—a material possession or a new hairstyle—much more often than internal qualities.

In contrast, when we acknowledge clients, we sincerely voice our recognition of an accomplishment or a quality the clients have demonstrated in a particular situation. A good acknowledgment needs to be specific. It names the quality and elaborates on how it was effectively used or demonstrated.

In the world of politics, an endorsement is given when the endorser fully stands behind the other person. Essentially, the endorser says, "I stake my reputation on your integrity, your ability, and your intentions. I have unshakable faith in you, and I'm willing to go public with that in order to lend my name to your campaign." When you endorse clients, you verbalize your appreciation and recognition for who they consistently are—the essential qualities they show again and again in their life and in their work. You look beyond their actions and possessions, and focus on their deeper self—the essential people they are now or are *becoming.*

Endorsing language can actually recharge clients' energy levels, in the same was as recharging a battery gives it new power. When the clients' energy level increases, they are more likely to be motivated to move into action.

3. Standing For

Are you familiar with the experience of having someone be an advocate for your desires and for your ability to create the future you want? We play this role as coaches when we hold on to the clients' dreams and desires even when the clients temporarily forget who they are or what they want. We *stand for* the possibilities that the clients have said they want for themselves.

We empower our clients when we acknowledge or endorse a part of their behavior or being. We also empower when we *stand for* the clients—their goals, their desire for a more fulfilling life, and their potential to create the life they wan.

When you stand for clients, you remind them of their goals and their power to achieve them. You advocate for them. *Standing for* has the power to sustain the clients' energy and focus when they have temporarily lost one or both. It calls forth latent creativity from the clients.

Standing for is an important coaching skill. As a coach, you give great power to clients' dreams and desires when you remember them, hold on to them, and believe in them. You stand for your clients when you remind them of what they want, remind them that they can achieve their desires, and hold their vision and agenda for change.

4. Reframing

Human beings are essentially story-making and meaning-making beings. We have an inborn desire to connect events and draw relationships between them, creating explanations for phenomena. *Reframing* and *perspective-taking* are two skills that assist the clients by offering other possibilities for their current story. Reframing is essentially putting something in a new frame, which offers a different perspective on it. We know how important a frame is to a piece of art. Some frames diminish the work, and others enhance it, drawing our attention to features that were not originally highlighted. (Anyone who has reframed a favorite picture knows the power of putting something into a different context; it's amazing how a new frame can give life to something.)

Reframing as a coaching skill is simply shifting the clients' attention to consider a new perspective or view. When you reframe, you find new language for something. You place a behavior or motivation in a new context, or frame, which causes the clients to consider it differently. Reframing takes place when you draw the clients' attention to the upside of something that the clients may consider a liability, such as the creativity that comes with clients who are easily distracted. Rather than a weakness, it is now viewed as a strength. When you reframe as a coach, you find an authentic way to put a positive spin on an issue. The issue now appears as opportunity rather than failure, or as a strength rather than a weakness.

When a specific reframe works extraordinarily well, it runs the risk of becoming a cliché. This is what happened with the "reframe problem into opportunity" cliché in many business settings. When a manager shows up at a staff member's desk saying, "I have an opportunity for you," the staff member is likely to hear it as, "I have a problem for you!" That is because the word *opportunity* as a reframe for a problem has been highly overused in business settings, with people wanting to avoid negative connotations around work assignments involving difficult problems.

A reframe can be powerful and compelling, and when used masterfully it will retain its power. Often it doesn't because it simply calls attention to the person's attempt to hide a fact. As a coach, it is obligatory to find unique ways to reframe when you work with clients. Do not allow a reframe to become a cliché.

117

Great teachers have always used reframing. In the movie *Dead Poets Society,* a prep-school poetry teacher, played by Robin Williams, uses reframing masterfully. He asks each student to come up to his desk and stand on it in order to give them a different view of things. That is often all that is needed to shift a client's apparent block or obstacle into a positive and hopeful frame—and hence to create forward movement and effective action.

5. Meta-View or Perspective Taking
Whitworth, Kinsey-House, & Sandahl (1998) introduced the notion of *meta-view* as an extension of the coach's listening. Using meta-view, the coach takes a big-picture view of the situation, sharing with the clients a statement of the big picture and providing a new perspective on the situation or issue. In essence, perspective-taking and meta-view accomplish reframing for the clients. They are specific tools for reframing. We think they are deserving of a place of their own, too. For example,

CLIENT: I've been discouraged for a long time about my work. I used to enjoy it so much. Now, after twenty years, I've lost interest in it. I just can't figure it out.
COACH: It could be that you're entering a new cycle of change and are finding yourself in what we call "the doldrums." That's a natural part of the cycles of change we all go through, particularly when we've stayed in one career for a long time, as you have.

In this example, the coach uses a teaching concept to offer a perspective that provides the clients with a broader perspective of their experience. The coach's understanding of natural cycles of development serves as a resource for finding a useful meta-view. The clients now see the issue as common to many people at their point in life.

Coaches help clients examine situations and shift perspectives through asking them to generate multiple frames as possible answers to questions. For example, you may ask the dentist to draw a wheel diagram, with the question or issue to consider in the center. The dentist's question might be, "How can I become more fulfilled?" His task is to fill in each of the spokes of the wheel with a different way to create fulfillment. Each of the spokes may represent a specific area of his life, as in the Wheel of Life (see Chapter 8).

We all use perspective-taking to shift our sense of what we can choose to do, or to call up other options than those that first occur to us. When coaching executives, Diane Menendez asks her clients to raise and answer the question, "What is life calling for here?" when they find themselves frustrated or irritable. Asking this perspective-shifting question can help a leader get beyond their initial reaction in order to access other truths and other ways of identifying options than they might think of initially. Another question we use to help clients shift perspective is "What don't I know about this that could change my options here?" If clients have a role model, they might say, "What would John do in this situation?" All of these add possibilities for the client to choose from.

Shifting a client's perspective can be accomplished in many ways.

CLIENT: I intended to give myself permission to slow down today and play. Instead, I spent the day handling crises or putting out fires, one after another. Finally at the end of the day, I'd had it. Just when I thought it couldn't get worse, my computer hard drive crashed.

After you as the coach have listened and mirrored, a shift in perspective might be called for. Here are a few options. Take a moment to reflect on the changes and opportunities that each perspective offers. Then ask the client

- "How would someone you really admire respond to this situation?" (For example, "What would the Dalai Lama do?")
- "How would the teacher Robin Williams portrays in *Dead Poets Society* respond to this kind of day?"
- "If this were a movie, who would you ask to play you?"
- "What will be important about this situation 10 years from now?"
- "I wonder what principles are at work here." Remember Murphy's Law: If there are two or more ways to do something, and one of those ways can result in a catastrophe, then someone will do it.

119

6. Never Make the Client Wrong

As a partner in designing the life your clients want, it is important for you to hold on to the clients' agenda—not your agenda for the clients. Sometimes we can clearly see what is possible for the clients or where an action is headed, but the clients cannot or do not see it that way. We would love to be able to give the clients the boost of our perspective. But our job with the clients is to support their agenda. By understanding this, you will never make the clients wrong.

Remember Carl Rogers's discovery of the power of unconditional positive regard? When clients know they can expect this attitude from their coach, they are free to experiment, knowing they are not risking your judgment. This is one way they learn to tame the power of their self-judgments—by experiencing your freely offered regard for them.

You can lead your clients by asking powerful questions, by having them engage in inquiry, and by using future pacing, but be sure to stay joined with them. Don't lead them where they cannot or do not want to go at this time. For example, if clients does not complete their assignments between calls, you can listen. You can also explore with them other assignments and other methods, or you can simply ask if they want to refocus on the original goal. All of this can be done in a direct and caring way, without adding the element of blame.

7. Possibility Thinking

We discussed earlier the concept of "coaching to the gap." When clients live with a gap between where they are now and where they want to be, they often are unable to see how to close the gap and how to create fulfillment for themselves. They may have become immobile, limited by their habitual patterns of thinking and acting.

Part of a coach's job is to be a possibility thinker—to partner with the clients in exploring alternatives and in seeking possible solutions, new methods, strategies, or directions the clients can take.

Possibility thinking offers the clients an opportunity to suspend their usual reality and to explore a world of potential. When they do, clients often can return to the current situation and see clearly, perhaps for the first time, the blocks they have been living with and ways to eliminate them. For example, clients who have been paralyzed by fear may not realize it is possible to act despite the fear and to break through the fear by not surrendering to it.

If you find yourself having difficulty staying with possibility thinking for clients, it is time to do an inquiry yourself. The clients' dilemma may be similar to one you currently face, or the clients' issues or styles may be triggering something in you. Take time for reflection and inquiry. Ask for some *shadow coaching* from a mentor or a buddy coach. A shadow is a reflection of yourself that mirrors your own stance and actions. Shadow coaching is where you review with someone you trust what happened on a coaching call. Shadow coaching can help you discover blocks that hinder your ability to see the possibilities in your clients.

The skills covered in this chapter are tools for the coaching toolbox. They are there to choose from, to mix and match in ways that are appropriate for the situation. As you learn the techniques, don't allow these tools to own you. If you find yourself enamored of a skill, you are likely to overuse it or use it in situations where it isn't the most appropriate tool. Using a wide range of tools supports you in being a masterful coach.

121

Chapter 5

Stretching the client

In Chapter 4 we looked at a skill called *standing for* clients, where the coach recalls for the clients the truth of what they want for themselves and the real possibility of attaining it. *Standing for* is an example of a coaching skill that, in the moment, provides a clear *challenge* to the clients' current way of thinking.

A great dictionary definition for *challenge* comes from the *American Heritage Dictionary:* "To summon to action, effort or use; to stimulate." At our best as coaches, we challenge the clients by using our language and ourselves to stimulate the clients to achieve their best and to summon them to act in new ways.

Let's consider challenging and stretching and their location in the coaching continuum (Ellis, 1998).

Over time, coaches develop distinctively different styles, like all helping professionals. Some coaches may frequently direct the clients' attention and focus; others primarily forward the coaching through questions. Some coaches follow Carl Rogers's view that people solve their own problems when they are fully listened to and affirmed. Consider the coaching continuum below, which ranges from the least directive responses at one end, beginning with "Listen Fully and Affirm," to the most directive practices at the other, ending with "Give the Answer."

THE COACHING CONTINUUM

1. Listen Fully and Affirm

This is full, heartfelt, and soulful listening with great empathy and heart. Soulful listening invites the clients to bring to awareness what they know, think, sense, and feel. After a time, clients reveals their most intimate thoughts. In some spiritual practices, this is called the *inquiry.* You stay fully present and silent while the clients speak for an extended period of time, 5 to 15 minutes. Then you share what you are noticing, thinking, and feeling.

2. Listen Fully and Feed Back the Problem

At this level of listening, you listen fully and soulfully for a time, affirm the clients, and then feed back the issues to them. You summarize *briefly* the essence of what you hear as the focus for the clients—the key issues to coach.

3. Ask the Clients to Generate a Few New Possibilities

You begin to be directive. You listen, feed back what you hear, ask questions, and specifically ask the clients to identify several new possibilities for attention and action. At this level on the coaching continuum, you might ask, "What are two possible new ways to overcome these obstacles?" Some people might wonder why you'd ask the clients since if they knew, they wouldn't be asking for input from a coach. But it doesn't work that way. Often the clients do have an idea or two but haven't been challenged to identify any alternatives themselves. Your question affirms to clients that they are likely to have some ideas to offer.

4. Ask the Clients to Generate Many Possibilities

You listen, affirm, mirror, and feed back, but this time you focus on stretching the clients to generate many, many possibilities. Ask for several, maybe even as many as 10 or 12, possibilities that will address the clients' issues or concerns. If a dozen options seem too easy to generate, ask for more. The point is to act as a guide for your clients and to stretch them to move outside their comfort zone. For example, let's look at a client who is working on ways to feel more fulfilled and satisfied during the workday. The coach might ask him to generate 25 or more small things that he can do during the workday to create a sense of satisfaction. It would be important to have many options available in a case like this so that the client doesn't become habituated to just one or two. This client, for example, might put a screen saver of his children on his computer. He might incorporate some stress busters at certain inter-

123

vals of the day, like breathing, stretching, and walking outside. He could use a program like *Desk Top Yoga* periodically. This sets the tone for out-of-the-box thinking. The important thing is to get the client to stretch beyond the obvious—beyond the thoughts that he generates readily.

5. Add Your Input to the Clients' List of Possibilities

At this place in the coaching continuum, you join the clients in brainstorming, adding suggestions to their list of possibilities. You and the clients brainstorm back and forth, with you adding some of your best thinking in the moment without an intention to take over for the clients. This adding, which is more directive, runs the risk of moving the clients' focus to where you want it to be. The risk is that the clients mistake your possibilities for suggestions or advice. You need to work hard at letting the clients know that these are just additions to the list—they are not necessarily better ideas than those the clients have generated. Your perspective as an outsider does mean that you are likely to see possibilities outside of the clients' blind spots or current perspective. In a sense, your possibilities may *reframe* or expand the clients' view of the situation. You may be of service to the clients at this level if their creativity seems low or if they feel stuck. Sometimes a coach needs to jump-start clients' thinking, although we believe it is usually best for the client to offer the first several ideas.

6. Present at Least 10 Possibilities (Some Contradictory)

You are more directive at this point in the continuum, placing yourself in charge of identifying and creating possibilities for the clients. You may stretch the clients by including possibilities that are far outside the realm of their comfort zone. You may think that presenting 10 possibilities seems like a lot. It's important to offer contradictory possibilities so that the clients must choose between very different arenas of action. Be sure to make some of them practical and doable. Clients may seize upon your ideas to springboard their own creativity when you use this strategy.

For example, a client is frustrated with a female employee. At Stage 6 of the continuum, you might offer ideas like these:

124

- Just fire her!
- Or, you could decide to focus on her strengths and do everything possible to turn her into a better employee.
- Pay for her to go to a training program in the area in which she needs improvement.
- Hire her a coach.
- Assign her a new role that enables her to develop in her weak area.
- Get her a mentor who is excellent in the area she needs to grow in.
- Ask her to shadow someone who is great in the area she needs to grow in.
- Ask her to take a vacation.
- Tell her that she has 2 weeks to up-level her skills or she may have to postpone her vacation.

The purpose of these seemingly contradictory suggestions is to stretch the clients' thinking into the realm of all possibilities, even into the realm of the absurd. When you and the clients start laughing about the possibilities, you know you are on the right track. You've moved the conversation into a mood of lightness from which the clients will have a new perspective and from which creativity can emerge.

7. Present at Least Three Possibilities

At this level you offer three possibilities of equal value. We call this level a directive action because you are essentially limiting the clients' choices. Be sure that when they hear the possibilities, the clients do not hear them as advice. Take time to work through the benefits and consequences of each one so that the clients can fully consider them.

You might wonder why Stage 6 generates 10 possibilities and this stage generates only three. Stage 6 aims to stretch the clients into the realm of many possibilities. Stage 7 focuses the clients' attention on choosing not between absurd options, but between doable, realistic, practical possibilities, each of which the clients could really choose and implement, although they may be quite different from one another. When you offer these possibilities, you must make sure that these are not offered as definitive solutions.

In the case of the client frustrated with an employee, you may say, "Of all the options we've discussed, I'm aware of three possibilities that seem doable right now for you."

- Discuss with the employee the possibility of specific training in communication skills.
- Discuss with the employee how being assigned a mentor in communication skills would be beneficial to her, preferably someone in a different department of the company.
- Hire a coach for the employee with defined goals and outcomes mutually agreed upon between the coach, the employee, and the client/supervisor.

At this stage you offer the three possibilities and then invite the client's feedback. "What do you think about these? What ideas do you have that might build off of these? Remember, these are just possibilities. As you hear them, what do you think?"

8. Teach a New Technique

You are directing when you are teaching. However, there are times when clients need to learn something new or request that you teach something new so that they can move beyond where they are now. You might find yourself teaching a relaxation strategy, for example, or a method of preparing to resolve conflict, or time management skills.

Teaching is more effective later in a coaching relationship, after rapport and trust have been built and after the clients have become used to the alliance as a partnership of equals. Be cautious when you find yourself teaching early on in a coaching relationship, as the clients may find this easy and useful, and come to depend on it. Your alliance will be considerably different with the clients if that happens. If it is done too early in the coaching relationship, the clients will be less apt to see themselves as active agents and might begin to look more often to the coach for answers. If that occurs, it takes more effort to undo or remedy that pattern. We suggest you avoid setting it up in the first place.

9. Offer an Option

This situation is even more directive because you are offering only one option for the clients to consider. If the option is on target or if it acts as a reframing strategy, it can be effective in getting the clients out of their current situation. Offering an outrageous option can help the clients focus. It may also bring lightness into the conversation, which helps the clients reframe the situation and bring more creativity to it.

For example, if a client complains about his boss, you might offer the one outrageous option: Move to another country and get away from him. The one outrageous option will likely elicit an immediate reaction from the client and will probably produce a long list of ways to act in order not to have to consider the option of moving!

10. Give Advice or Give the Answer

At this level, the most direction oriented in the coaching continuum, you are probably not coaching. Giving advice or giving the answer is more the province of consulting. If you do find yourself giving advice, be sure to label it as such.

On the other hand, a very direct *telling the truth* as you see it may be needed. Remember the 5-step coaching model (pages 22–25), where you *say what is so*. This provocative intervention can be useful when the client is trapped in confusion, when resistance or fear is entrenched, when the game is destructive and repetitive, or when it is time to end what seems like self-destructive sabotage. These client interventions can involve phrases such as "I can't support you selling out in that way. I believe you are strong enough. You know you are strong enough. Just do it."

CLIENTS STRETCH TO MEET CHALLENGES

Masterful coaching involves times when you must challenge your clients in supportive and encouraging ways rather than simply listening. Your goal is to offer a challenge that helps your clients stretch and grow.

Challenging is stronger than just "wanting for" or making a small request. It is straightforward, but it is never disrespectful. A strong request for a big change might appear to clients as a challenge.

127

There is a useful analogy from the sports arena about the style of delivery for challenging others. Bobby Knight, former coach of the Indiana University basketball team, often challenged his players. He is an in-your-face guy, often belligerent and loud. He has even been known to throw chairs and other items. After 25 years as Indiana University's coach, Knight lost his job because he challenged *disrespectfully* after being warned to stop.

On the other hand, Roy Williams, another highly respected college basketball coach, demands the same amount of excellence from his players that Knight did, but he wisely challenges them by teaching them and building on their strengths. During a game, he rarely loses his temper or shows disrespect. When he takes a player out of the game, he doesn't do it as punishment. Instead, he sits down next to the player and teaches him what he could do differently. The game will be going on, and Roy Williams will be down on his knees in front of the player, seizing a teachable moment with him. Williams tells the player why he yanked him out of the game and tells him what the player needs to do differently. Sometimes after a minute, the player will go back into the game, having been challenged to upgrade his skills.

Obviously, Roy Williams is the better model for coaches. You must challenge your clients when appropriate and always do it respectfully. Experienced coaches let their clients know when they begin challenging—when they "up the stakes" because the situation calls for it.

Making a huge request or a challenging call for evidence of progress may activate the clients to make a huge shift or a leap forward. This kind of challenge communicates to the clients that you are confident they are capable of taking on such a big challenge. They may succeed because they begin to share your belief in their possibility and promise. Challenging clients, which takes courage, it is another way of *standing for* them.

As we begin to examine ways that coaches challenge their clients, consider the case of Rob:

Several nights ago you gave a speech on creating a fulfilling life. One of the attendees called you to inquire about coaching. He is a 33-year-old single male who works as a computer programmer. When you ask him about his coaching goals, he says he wants to lose weight and to create a financial reserve for himself. You start to work with him. During the first two calls he says the following: "I love listening to CDs, reading books, and collecting comic books." "I eat out all of the time and love food." "I'm sort of down lately; sometimes I feel anxious. Even though I have a decent job, I feel stuck." "I'm fat and pudgy, and I don't like it. I want to be trim."

Ask yourself:
What do you hear from Rob that calls for using challenging skills?
How might you challenge him on this first call?

MANY WAYS TO CHALLENGE

Coaches productively challenge clients in many ways. Common ways to challenge include:

- Make huge requests.
- Double the goal.
- Reduce the time to accomplish something.
- Ask the clients to document and provide evidence of progress.
- Measure the clients' results and establish benchmarks.
- Ask the clients to raise their standards and expectations for themselves or for others.
- Ask the clients to do just the opposite of what they would normally do.
- Ask straight questions that no one else in the clients' world has the courage to ask.
- Expect a great deal from the clients—perhaps more than they expect of themselves.
- Ask for fieldwork and practices to keep the clients focused.
- Maintain high standards and be rigorous about examining the clients' accomplishments and actions.
- Be patient and press the clients to consider the truth, not just the first answer that may come to mind.
- Be diligent about asking the clients to commit to their promises.

129

- Consistently help clients draw distinctions (introduced below). Encourage clients to make big shifts and to grow in perspective, approach, attitude, mind-set, patience, and so on.
- Ask the clients to only live their life purpose (see Chapter 7) for the next period of time.
- Ask the clients to begin a new discipline or practice that requires reflection, such as keeping a journal or beginning a meditation practice.

SKILLS FOR CHALLENGING AND STRETCHING THE CLIENT

Use Distinctions

We began this chapter by consider the coaching continuum. Most of the time, we remain nondirective and we use our listening, mirroring, and questioning skills to forward the action. At times, however, the clients' situation will not move forward on its own because clients are thinking in a habitual way that isn't helpful and empowering. In Chapter 14, we explore more extensively this issue of how clients' mind-sets affect them and the coaching relationship. At these times, the best approach is for you to first offer a concise, clear statement of how you see the clients' situation. This statement uses clean language, is direct, and is an empowering and potent way of looking at the situation. Then you offer a *distinction* that holds the key to a new way of thinking or action. If the clients can incorporate this distinction, they might be able to shift the situation to a more desired outcome. Offering a distinction is a *part* of the coaching process, not a magic bullet.

Remember that our ability to grow and develop depends on our language. It's no accident that the Bible contains a very early chapter where names are given for all of the creatures of the world. The ability to name something, to put it into words, gives human beings the ability to choose, create, modify, and grow. We can only enact what we can name.

When you use distinctions, you intervene directly in the clients' learning and awareness. Your intention in using distinctions is to offer the clients a chance to see something about the situation that has not been visible to them. The value of a distinction comes from the new avenues for acting and becoming that it makes possible.

A distinction allows the clients to consider making a *shift* in thinking and noticing. A shift is a cognitive, emotional, or behavioral movement from one state to another. The following examples of distinctions have the potential to support clients in making a shift:

- Unconscious incompetence versus conscious incompetence
- A goal versus a pipe dream
- Just being competent versus achieving mastery
- Having to be right all the time versus allowing others to be right as well

When you use distinctions, you offer the clients the words to notice something that may be subtle. You may also help the clients articulate the distinctions. Here's an example:

CLIENT: I want my work life to go much more smoothly than it has been going recently. Everything that comes my way at work seems to be getting more and more difficult. It's an ongoing battle with my boss and my staff.

COACH: You're seeing work as if it were a battlefield. In order to experience something else, you need to let go of your armor. (ASSESSMENT of the situation)

CLIENT: Right. I am so tired of struggling"

COACH: "What would it take for you to move from being in a struggle at work to making work seem easy and natural? Giving up the going-into-battle way you enter work means putting down your arms and armor, and making peace—with your boss, with your situation, with those you work with, and with yourself.

Notice that the distinction the coach is offering here is "work as a battle" versus "work as peacemaking."

CLIENT: I don't know how to do that.

131

The coach might follow up with statements such as those below to reinforce the new distinction about how the clients carry themselves into work. The next step would be to find a *practice* and an action the clients could take that would begin to explore the new distinction and put it into practice. The coach might ask:

> "What would be the first sign that you were going into work unarmed, unarmored, and ready not for battle but for peace?"
> "How would you start your day?"
> "What would you be telling yourself as you entered the building?"
> "How would you prepare yourself for work as a place of peacemaking?"

To use distinctions effectively, make sure that your voice tone and words remain nonjudgmental. Stay unattached to whether the clients seize and use the distinction. You may find initially that the clients don't grasp the distinction or its power, but then return a week or so later to explore it.

132

Ask yourself:
What distinction does Roy, the client mentioned earlier, need to learn in order to achieve a shift or move forward?

Use Metaphors and Analogies

Andrew Ortony, a Stanford University researcher in learning and cognition, made a radical statement some years ago: "Metaphors are *necessary,* not just *nice*" (1975/2001, p. 29). He went on to show that using metaphor creates powerful, rapid learning by linking what is unfamiliar or novel with what the clients already know.

Many coaches treat metaphors and analogies as if they were adornments, enhancements in language—like a delicious frosting on an already tasty cake. Metaphors and analogies are powerful tools for two reasons. First, a metaphor offers the clients a new perspective on an issue. Second, the perspective rapidly becomes potent because it links with preexisting thoughts, emotions, and beliefs that the clients have already internalized. Consequently, metaphors and analogies work quickly and naturally to change thinking because they work holistically, bypassing linear, analytic explanations and client resistance.

Poets and writers know about the potency of metaphors—how they can shake emotions as well as the mind. Consider this poem, by Antonio Machado, translated by Robert Bly (Bly, 2004):

The wind, one brilliant day, called
to my soul with an aroma of jasmine.

"In return for the odor of my jasmine,
I'd like all the odor of your roses."

"I have no roses; all the flowers
in my garden are dead."

"Well then, I'll take the waters of the fountains,
and the withered petals and the yellow leaves."

The wind left. And I wept. And I said to myself:
"What have you done with the garden that was entrusted to you?"

133

Here the soul and spirit of the speaker are compared with a garden, entrusted for safekeeping but left to die by someone who did not take care of them. Machado's poem calls upon a classic metaphor for our lives and our spirit, that of the garden.

The use of metaphors has proved extremely powerful in many professions—mediation, therapy, consulting, and now coaching. Coaches use common metaphors to direct clients' attention to aspects of their situation and possibilities not yet considered. Below we illustrate how a coach might use the garden metaphor as well as several others in a way that draws the client's attention to other possibilities.

Here's the situation: A working wife is discussing how difficult it is to create time for herself and for any sense of balance. She says, "I'm struggling to stay focused on my work and on my relationship with my husband because the kids seem to need me so much at home. Just keeping groceries stocked and driving them back and forth to games is hard. Yet there's so much pressure on us about money now, with college coming up in just a year for the oldest."

Using the metaphor of a garden for her family situation, the coach might use the following statement:

"Imagine your family life is a garden where you are all growing. A garden is something that requires soil preparation, thought about what to plant, and then conscious, purposeful nurturing. A garden doesn't just grow by throwing seeds out there and forgetting them. All gardens have diversity—a variety of plants that contribute to the beauty of the whole design. All gardens have weeds, but you want to pull out any before they choke the plants you are nurturing. Sometimes you need to prune. So, gardening requires frequent watering, weeding, and tending. What needs tending here in your family? Where do you need to cut back or prune things to really let you and your family grow? And further, what needs fertilizing or nourishing?"

Using the metaphor of a journey, the coach might use a statement like this:

"A trip is different from a journey. In a trip, you have an exact route and a specific place to get. In a journey, you may have a destination, but you don't have a specific route planned. And furthermore, you are aware that things may occur that are unplanned. You may take side trips—due to weather, car trouble, road conditions, etc.—that are unexpected or unplanned. Often these side trips lead to some of the best experiences of the journey. If you begin to view your family situation as a journey for all of you, what's the vehicle you are in, and what would you like to be in? What experiences do you anticipate? How are you handling unexpected challenges, route changes, and things that take you off course? You are one of the drivers here: What changes do you need to make to get on a course that brings you satisfaction?"

Using the metaphor of a game, a coach might say:

"I know your kids play soccer and you like to play a lot of games together like *Monopoly*. Think about your situation as a game. In order to make the game work, you need to understand how to choose the right game and understand the rules. You can also take a time out. Are you and your husband on the same team with the same game plan? How about you and the kids? Does anybody need to take a time out from the play? Can the game as a family be seen as a time together that brings pleasure, not a competitive race where there's a defined way of winning?"

Games are a ubiquitous experience for many family trips. If you are working with someone old enough to remember road trips before cars had built-in DVD players, he or she may remember passing the time looking for license plates from all locations, or playing the alphabet game, where you look for road signs or advertisements that start with the letters A through Z. These are games to pass time and build relationships, and experience connectedness by having fun. In today's world we know that in many families, especially in North America, trips are taken in which everyone but the driver has a personal iPod, and the family connection seems to be lost. The goal of the coach is to draw on positive experiences that have a universal quality and increase the client's connection to him- or herself and to others. Use a metaphor that will work positively and be matched to the client's situation.

Notice how each of the three above metaphors—a garden, a journey, and a game—illuminate different aspects of the choices available to the client. One might work better than the others, depending on the client and his or her intentions. Just like a picture is worth a thousand words, a metaphor seems to shift the way a person sees the situation.

Metaphoric language is also common in the business world. Using metaphors in corporate coaching is an excellent means for highlighting aspects of the situation that can help the client think differently. Listen to the client's language for the buried metaphors the client is using, such as the following common ones:

- We're missing a piece of the puzzle
- We need to level the playing field
- We need to think out of the box
- We need to push the envelope

- We need to get on the bus
- We need to get in the zone
- We need to draw a line in the sand
- We need to stand up for ourselves

Raise your antenna and listen to your client's metaphors, then use that as you work with them. For example, your client might say, "I wish our group could think out of the box better." Ask yourself how you as a coach can work with this "box" metaphor to create a more useful way of thinking about the situation. As coaches, we are looking for metaphors that expand opportunities and widen the horizon for whatever the client's situation is. Sometimes a metaphor is off-target for a person. In business, for example, the metaphor of football can be considered exclusionary to women. Coaches may need to ensure that their clients are using metaphors that work for them as well as others in their work or personal lives.

An effective metaphor in coaching needs to meet two requirements. First, the clients must be familiar enough with the metaphor that they don't need to ask questions about how it applies to the situation at hand. Second, the metaphor should create the intended emotional effect on the clients and be carefully chosen for the situation the clients face.

Some metaphors work so well that we use them again and again with clients. Clients know instinctively that when they work with coaches, they are going somewhere. Consequently, metaphors about journeys and gardens work effectively with almost all clients who consider the path they are on and the patient growth required.

These questions can help you generate metaphors:

- What is the client's journey most like? Possibilities might include a plane trip, slow walk, trek around the globe, a walk at night in dark woods, a horse-and-buggy ride, and so on. One of our journey metaphors, given to us by Kira Freed, involves imagining a road trip from California to Maine. If you're always saying, "Are we there yet?" you'll miss the Grand Canyon and all the other amazing sights, as well as all the turns along the way. The best way to get there is to be present at each leg of the journey.

- Then there is the difference between a trip and a journey. Say you want to go from Denver to Portland, Oregon. You can call AAA and get a Triptik, which provides a route map, hotels to stay in, driving times, road conditions, and so on. All of the details regarding the best or quickest route to the destination are identified. Or, you can take a more leisurely route, taking county roads, veering off on side roads, and seeing sights that are unexpected. This would be more of a journey where we anticipate that unexpected pleasures will be part of the experience. This can be more time consuming, but it may be more fulfilling as a journey than a faster-paced trip. Pat Williams learned the distinction between trip and journey when he went from Denver to Vancouver, Canada, choosing to avoid the interstates and take county roads through smaller towns. The journey became as much fun as the final destination.

- What kind of vehicle is the client journeying in—and is it appropriate for the trip? A client who wants to travel by spacecraft may really need to slow down and take a car ride, stopping to admire the scenery along the way.

- What kind of growth occurs in the garden where the client is working? How is the client preparing the ground, planting seeds, caring, weeding, fertilizing, watering, pruning, thinning, and sprouting back? Marge Piercy (2003) wrote a wonderful poem called "The Influence Coming into Play: The Seven of Pentacles," related to this point, which reminds us to honor the pace of things. Clients often forget this key point—that human experience and human lives often have their own pace. We can urge a baby to be born quickly, but that will not change the 9 months needed for gestation.

Metaphors and analogies deepen the clients' intuitive understanding of issues and encourage deep exploration. Select metaphors that match the clients; create metaphors out of stories you tell, drawn from your own life. You can find several articles on using metaphors at www.devco. demon.co.uk/Magic-of-Metaphor. html and www.devco.demon.co.uk/ learningmetaphors.html. Below are metaphors from students that express how they learn:

137

Planting flowers—A seed is planted in my mind, which I nurture with water and sun in the faith that it will sprout and grow.

Playing cards—I divide things into four categories and look for patterns across the suits until the logic and meaning emerge and I know which card to play.

Savings account—I invest the time to accumulate data and information until there is enough interest that I can roll it over into the next idea.

Switching on a lightbulb—It's not until the light switches on that I have an insight or an "aha!"

Eating—You need to take in the basic meat and potatoes before you get to the mouth-watering dessert.

Being a detective—It's all about uncovering the facts, looking for clues, and asking the right questions until the whole mystery makes sense.

Peeling an onion—I peel off a layer, which reveals the next layer to be peeled off. Each time, something informs me that I am getting closer to the center of the issue.

A quest—I'm searching for that elusive something, and every step I take brings me closer to what I need to know, but I never get there . . . it's a continuous journey.

Sculpting—You start with the raw material and shape it into a form that's pleasing to the eye.

Wrestling—I struggle with the ideas until they're pinned down and I've captured them.

Other suggestions: Listen to your clients' language and create metaphors based on the words they use. If work is like a battlefield for them, use that image as a jumping-off point for generating a series of metaphors to expand the conversation and explore the issue. Remember that you can also ask your clients to generate a metaphor for the coaching work they are doing.

Ask yourself:
What metaphors would you use to describe the coaching
process for clients who are stuck?

138

Ask yourself:
What metaphor could you use with the client who is frustrated with the employee?

Make Big Requests

As we stated in Chapter 1, Fernando Flores developed one of the most useful coaching tools—making requests—through his exploration of how language really brings action into being (Budd & Rothstein, 2000). Imagine an aspect of people's lives that isn't working. They may expect, or at least fantasize, that they'll be told what to do differently. However, a coach's job is not simply to hand clients the solution, for two reasons. First, we don't know it ourselves; even if we are aware of a possible solution that has worked for others, it's not necessarily relevant to these particular clients' lives. And second, even if we knew the solution, handing it to the clients robs the alliance of the process of exploring the issue together. It robs the clients of the learning experience of working through the steps to the solution, and it robs coaches of the opportunity for joint discovery that is an integral part of the coaching relationship.

An empowering way to engage clients in the exploration to discover a new approach to a problem is to make a request. Coaches request a very specific action or choice from the clients—and most often uses the word *request* in the statement. The request is not complete until the specific behavior or action is identified, until both clients and coaches understand the time expectations for when the request will be completed, and until both clearly agree on what constitutes a successful accomplishment of the request.

A request is *not* an invitation, although it may seem like one because the clients are free to respond to it. It is also not a suggestion or a piece of advice. It does convey a sense of urgency because the clients *must* respond to a request *right away.* The clients can accept it, turn it down, change it, or suggest an alternative. No matter what the clients do, a request leads to some action—even if it gets changed in the process.

Requests sound like this:

- "I request that you stop suffering this week. Talk to the people you need to talk to right away."

- "I request that every morning this next week, you use your planner to prepare a to-do list, with each action labeled as either an A, B, or C priority, before you begin your day. Will you agree to do this?"
- "I'm requesting that you demonstrate how serious you are about increasing your sales by making twice as many calls to prospective clients this week as you have during the past 2 weeks."
- "I request that you open up to your boss and tell him how you really feel when he criticizes you publicly at work."
- "What is the one big request I should make of you to get this moving? Whatever it is, that's what I'm requesting."

The clients must respond to the coaches' request. Silence is not an adequate response. The clients have three response choices: "yes," "no," or "no, but here's what I'll do instead." When clients reject your request, explore the idea further. Requesting is a commonly used tool to elicit action steps for the clients to consider. When coaches make requests, it's to further the clients' agenda. Furthermore, do not become attached to the specific request you make. The clients may not agree with it, or they may create a variation. Be willing to *dance* with your clients when you make requests. Let the clients lead the dance. You join into the rhythm.

Why use requests? They clearly identify the commitments the clients are willing to make. They rapidly move the clients into action without undue thinking or lag time, which is particularly useful when the clients tend to ruminate before taking any steps. Requests encourage clients to experiment with actions they would not normally consider. They offer something else, too: the opportunity for the clients to be faced with the choice of saying yes or no. Clients may discover that they have difficulty declining or reshaping a request. This creates the opportunity to explore what it means when the clients feel compelled to say yes.

Requesting is more open and fluid than suggesting. A suggestion can be interpreted as a recommendation from an expert. A request is a consideration for the clients to accept or reject. The power of a request is not found in the specific action requested; it is found in the way coaches communicate confidence in the clients' ability by requesting something *bigger* than they might have been willing to request of themselves.

140

A key to skillful requesting is to make the request specific. Be clear and very targeted. Make your language as focused, accurate, and direct as a laser beam. Pause after the request to let the silence hit.

An experienced coach intuitively senses what to request of a client. The joy lies in creating the request in the moment, based on what the client presents to the coach. Beginning coaches sometimes think there is a "perfect" request that they are unable to discover. The perfect request does not exist, but the coach can be precise about the action the client should take, when and how it should be taken, and how the client will determine whether the request has been met.

✎　*Write two requests that you could make to the client who is frustrated with his employee.*

Identify and Name Contradictions and Inconsistencies

Sometimes clients contradict themselves from session to session. For example, one week the client says that a balanced life, with time to attend his children's soccer games, is the top priority. He loves to see his kids in action. The following week, the client takes on a new volunteer role on a local board of directors, which will require afternoon and evening meetings every week. He speaks excitedly of his interest in the assignment and the challenge of turning around a troubled agency.

You can't help but notice that the client's new choice will get in the way of honoring his commitment to his children. Your obligation is to point it out to the client so that he clearly sees the inconsistency. With new clarity, he can explore the attraction of each path and what might block him from effectively accomplishing both. (Even the best coaches can't help clients be in two places at once.)

Putting the contradiction into words might sound like this: "In our last session you were excited about your commitment to attend your daughters' soccer games this season; you told me what a high priority this was for you this year. Today, you are about to commit to a board assignment that will prevent you from consistently attending the games. What's going on?"

Inconsistencies abound in all of our lives. Look for opportunities to point them out to clients when they really add value to the coaching. Over time the clients can learn to detect them themselves and can

141

become self-correcting. When inconsistencies surface, coaches spend the time to explore how they came about. Are they due to competing values? Competing desires? Lack of time and attention to calendar issues and a realistic appraisal of the requirements of fulfilling a promise?

Common inconsistencies include:

- what the clients are saying they want versus what they are doing to make it happen
- what the clients say they feel versus their nonverbal behavior, energy, and so on
- what the clients are saying are their priorities versus their actions, which are more accurate indicators of their priorities
- what the clients say are their strengths and/or weaknesses versus what they are truly capable of.

Ask yourself:
Identify an inconsistency or contradiction in the client (for example, the case of the father who wanted to demonstrate more commitment to his children). How would you identify this for the client?

142

Use the Compassionate Edge
Master coaches get faster and more powerful results because of their willingness to use the *compassionate edge*—to send a message to the clients with laserlike truth and brevity that gets right to the heart of the matter. The compassionate edge provides a very *direct* challenge to the clients because it is put into words and is part of the conversation.

This challenge comes from the desire to help the clients avoid mediocrity, while simultaneously maintaining a compassionate and empathic stand toward the clients. This combination of qualities can move clients to a deeper acknowledgment of truths and an accelerated ability to take action on their own behalf.

Mastery of the compassionate edge has benefits for coaches, too. Once you become skilled at it, you may find that you will attract high-powered clients who expect the edge. They are not just learning the skills; they are high achievers who want to do what it takes to "go for the gold."

Here are some examples of the compassionate edge:

"That's good work but not nearly what you are capable of. What else can you do here?"

"Tell the truth—do you really want to do this? I don't think you do."

"When are you going to be really, really honest about what you want here?"

"You are complaining. Turn your complaint into a request. Who do you need to say what to?"

✎   *Using the compassionate edge, write a statement that you might say to the client who is frustrated with his employee.*

The focus of this chapter has been about maintaining a fierce commitment to the clients' goals as well as compassion for their journey. We believe there is power in taking it to the mat with clients in order to overcome obstacles. The next step will be to create momentum toward new behaviors, which we discuss in the next chapter.

143

Chapter 6

Creating Momentum with the Client

Coaching is all about *learning* and *action*—not learning and action for its own sake but in the service of a longer-term aspiration, goal, or performance that drives the choice of action. As coaches, we want to ensure that our clients don't just reach a goal or achieve a performance, but that they maintain it. We want them to master the ability to become generative and self-correcting around their goals.

Stated another way, coaches work with clients' goals—performance, coaching focus, skills, and outcomes. This aspect of coaching focuses on what the clients want—the *what* of coaching as opposed to the *who* of coaching, which is focused on who the clients are, their *way of being* in the world. We also work with clients to build long-term capability and capacity so that they can sustain their goals. We want them to leave the coaching experience fully able to observe their behaviors and with the ability to correct themselves when they realize they have diverged from their goals.

THE KNOW IN ORDER TO GROW PRINCIPLE

Sometimes insight needs to precede learning, and powerful questions enable learning by helping the clients unlock new insights. Once learning occurs, the clients can choose options for action. Without insight and learning, action may just be compulsive doing. But without action, insight and learning will not help the clients achieve their goals. That is why *forwarding the action* is at the heart of the coaching relationship—and it is the biggest difference between coaching and traditional psychotherapy. When a coach "forwards the action," the coach helps clients move from insights into specific steps, propelling them toward their goals. Forwarding the action means that the coach's work leads to progress toward what the clients want from coaching.

Action for the sake of action, however, doesn't suffice. Clients hire coaches to attain goals that will offer long-term fulfillment and satisfaction. Consequently, the coaches need to focus on how clients can *sustain* and *maintain* what they most want. It's not enough that the clients are taking action. The coaching process focuses on assisting the clients in being able to sustain the results—to sustain the excellence—over time. We're looking for ways to support clients to incorporate new ways of thinking and behaving into their habits and daily repertoire.

In order to do that, coaches keep several questions in mind:

- What new perspective(s) do the clients need to be able to hold to ensure long-term success?
- What new behaviors do the clients need to consistently perform in order to ensure long-term success? How can they practice these until they become second nature?
- What emotions or states of being do the clients need to be able to access in order to ensure long-term success? How can they practice accessing these until they become second nature?
- What do the clients need to do to incorporate the thinking and behaviors into what they do naturally and habitually?

145

FOCUSING ON "RIGHT ACTION" THROUGH FIELDWORK

The media has focused extensively on the ways clients take action when they are being coached. As you can see from the previous list, several kinds of actions are necessary to ensure long-term excellence and fulfillment.

Experienced coaches end each session with a summary of clearly stated actions that will forward the clients' learning and growth, often described as *fieldwork*. Coaching conversations are not complete until the clients have identified actions that lead to accountability for change. Fieldwork may include actions the clients agree to take that have been discussed during the session, and it can also include requests made by the coaches that hold the clients on course. It is important to state here that any fieldwork is generated through collaborative discussion with the clients; it is an assignment by the coaches. Coaches may make requests that, if the clients agree to them, become part of fieldwork. The coaches may say, "I have an idea for some fieldwork that might be helpful to you this week." A good question to ask clients is: "What has emerged in our session today that generates some fieldwork for you between now and our next meeting?" In some sessions, fieldwork is generated throughout the entire session, particularly when the clients and coaches have been working together for some time. A client should always have several agreed-upon actions to take or complete between each call. Regular fieldwork helps clients make progress by emphasizing their accountability for results and providing them the satisfaction of taking steps toward their goal.

As with requests, good fieldwork is specific. Clients know exactly what to do, what completed actions will look like, and how to assess whether the actions were taken successfully. Do *not* overload your clients with fieldwork—two or three assignments between calls are sufficient to create and sustain momentum. Initially, make the assignments small until you have a sense of your clients' capacity for completing fieldwork successfully between sessions. Fieldwork should stretch the clients, but appropriate assignments are those that the clients have a great likelihood of successfully completing.

The best fieldwork is likely to take into consideration all three factors that create momentum for the clients: *results-oriented action, awareness observation* (of self and other), and *practices* to create new habits.

To clarify how these three can be used with clients, imagine you are coaching this client:

The Stressed Attorney. Sharon is a 35-year-old unmarried attorney who wants to become a partner in her law firm. Her work environment has become more and more stressful—she works long hours, comes home very fatigued, and finds she has little energy. She seldom goes out in the evening and doesn't see friends. She has a church community she belongs to but has become much less active than she was previously due to her great fatigue every day. She tends to overeat, especially chocolate and sweets, when she comes home. She's eating more snacks, not exercising, and finding that her situation is growing worse. She wants to work with you, her coach, on getting her eating and exercise habits in order so that she can better manage her stress. You discover that this is an old habit of hers— she's managed stress in the same way ever since her college years.

Results-oriented actions are the most obvious, readily available assignments. These are steps that directly and transparently further the clients' movement, step by step, toward the goal. For the attorney, *results-oriented actions* might include throwing away all chocolate and sugared snacks (making her home a "snack-free zone"), buying a supply of fruit and vegetables, and taking a 15-minute walk at lunch 3 days a week. These actions would get the client moving in the right direction. However, they might not be sufficient to allow her to create and maintain a healthy lifestyle over the long term. To do this, she also would need to be able to be self-aware and to self-correct—to generate solutions as new issues come up.

Self-awareness observations improve the clients' ability to notice their individual habits and patterns of sensing, feeling, thinking, and behaving. In order to *grow* themselves, the clients need to *know* themselves and their world—their thoughts and desires. Self-awareness exercises ask the clients to observe self and others, and often to record what is observed. A self-awareness assignment asks clients to *inquire* into their way of being in the world—but *not* to take action on the awareness.

Self-observations for the attorney might include the following:

- Setting her watch to sound at 8 a.m., 10 a.m., noon, 2 p.m., and 4 p.m., and each time recording what she is doing and the level of stress she is experiencing (using a scale from 1 low to 5 high). She can notice when she feels the most stressed, what is happening at those times, where she is, who else is there, and what time of day it is. This exercise might also include sensing in her body whether she feels hungry before she eats.
- Identifying five specific qualities that represent her at her best; making a chart to track each of the qualities every day for a week;

147

indicating when and where she experiences herself using each quality.

- Identifying the emotions she feels regularly each day and the surrounding context in which they occur.
- Asking herself these questions: "In what situations and with which people do I feel most stressed in my body?" "When do I feel over-whelmed?" "When do I feel impatient?" "What gets in the way of my ability to eat healthily?" "What are my standards for healthy eating?"

Observations of others also might promote reflection during the week:

- Who do I know who eats healthily?
- What does it look like when others around me manage stress well? What are they doing differently?

In Chapter 2, *inquiry* was discussed as a coaching tool. Inquiries can serve as self-awareness tools. In this case, the fieldwork inquiry is designed to stimulate reflection, deep thinking, and learning for the clients around an issue that may be related to their goals, life, or current issues and experiences.

Ask yourself:
What are two self-awareness observations, or observations of others, from which the stressed attorney might benefit?

Practices are specific actions in which the clients engage with the intent of building specific cognitive and behavioral habits. Similar to daily practice sessions to which musicians, dancers, and sports profes-sionals commit, coaching clients also need disciplined practice times to develop the ways of being and acting that will enable them to achieve their goals.

To help clients build practices, coaches need to understand a clients' visions of *excellence*. If the attorney said that excellent eating habits included eating five servings of fruits and vegetables daily and no more than three pieces of chocolate per week, this information could contribute to the clarity needed to design practices for the client. What other supporting ways of thinking, behaving, and acting would assist the client in attaining this level of ability to eat healthily?

One example might be to avoid purchasing candy and junk food at the supermarket—which might involve saying no and bypassing that aisle. Other examples might include learning to relax and giving hourly attention to specific goals. Following are possible practices the client can take until she develops natural habits toward her goal:

Practice 1. Schedule the maximum number of hours she will work during each of the next 4 weeks. When breakdowns occur in the schedule, she will cancel activities instead of adding hours. At the end of each week, she will analyze the time and keep correcting the schedule until she has achieved the maximum hours without stress.

Practice 2. Ask her to do one of the following each day: carry her lunch to work and eat it outside when the weather permits. Include only vegetables, fruits, and cottage cheese for 4 weeks. Notice and record how she feels at the end of each day.

Practice 3. Ask her to learn and practice a daily 20-minute breath meditation and/or prayer time for a minimum of 5 days each week for the next month. At the end of the week, note what she has learned about herself from this practice.

An excellent resource with examples of observational and practice-oriented fieldwork is Flaherty (1998). While his focus is primarily on coaching within corporations, he includes examples of working with the client's personal life as well.

149

Ask yourself:
What are two additional practices you might offer
the stressed attorney as fieldwork?

SKILLS FOR FORWARDING THE ACTION
WITHIN THE COACHING SESSIONS

Five frequently used skills support coaches to forward their clients' action within and during coaching sessions: Using accountability, contracting with the clients, acting *as if,* stepping into the future, and creating alternative actions and choices.

Accountability

The people we coach are intelligent, hardworking, and usually very successful, but they cannot do it all alone—or at least not as efficiently and effectively as they can when they partner with us.

Coaching sets a context of accountability, which includes regular contact in the form of weekly or biweekly sessions. These sessions provide the clients with someone outside of work and family who cares about their success and who will share in and celebrate their progress. Most of us do not have this accountability regularly in our personal and professional lives.

Accountability is a gift we give our clients. Remember, if they could do it by themselves, they would have already done it. Accountability leads to sustainable results. It is the difference between paying for "training" in weekend workshops and actually translating those lessons into action. Countless people have taken time management seminars and then never made the time to implement what they learned. Coaching can make that happen.

Successful coaching sessions end with clearly defined commitments by the clients—actions the clients commit to take before the next coaching session. One of the powers of coaching lies in accountability. The clients are fully accountable for the actions they take and for the results they get. At every session, the coach asks to hear about actions taken and the outcomes that resulted. Through accountability, the clients creates sustainable results over time.

Ask yourself:
How would you use accountability with the stressed attorney?

Contracting with Clients

When you contract with clients, you create a verbal agreement. You and clients establish an understanding about the clients' plan to do something differently or in a new way that will move them forward in the direction of their desired outcome.

Often, this can be strengthened for some clients by contracting with them for agreed-upon behaviors or actions for the coming week or weeks. Contracts can be verbal or in writing; both lend power to the relationship, which holds the clients accountable for what they promised to do.

Experienced coaches often ask clients to e-mail, fax, or phone a message to report their progress on the actions agreed on in the contract. You can request feedback on a daily basis or at some agreed-upon time interval between coaching calls. Checking in like this works better with some clients than others. The best way to assess the appropriateness of regular check-ins is to ask the clients what will work best for them.

Ask yourself:
How would you use contracting with the stressed attorney?

151

Acting *As If*

Earlier we described powerful questions that elicit ways something *could* be different in the clients' present or future life.

Clients sometimes want to achieve something but feels frozen or stuck. They may be unable to move forward and reach a goal. A helpful exit from this stagnation is provided by coaching conversations that ask the clients to act *as if* their desired change had already taken place. It helps them see *whom* they need to become in order for their desired future to manifest. Twelve-step programs ask participants to "fake it until you make it," which is similar to acting as if.

An example of an "as if" strategy would be asking the clients to imagine that it is now 6 months into the future. Their life is more satisfactory; goals they came to coaching for are now realized. You ask the clients to comment on how things are now, as if everything had occurred as they imagined. They will speak from that time 6 months in the future as if it is the present. You ask them to speak personally, from the "I." You follow this by asking your clients to now look back and identify what actions they took to get her there.

Ask yourself:
How would you use acting "as if" with the stressed attorney?

Stepping into the Future

The previous skill of *acting as if* asks the clients to speak from the future and then to look back at the steps and actions that got them there. *Stepping into the future* is a slight variation of that, where you ask the clients to step into the desired future and describe it in detail: what they see, how they feel, how their environment appears, and so on. Then they begin to notice what is possible from that future view.

Remember Martin Luther King Jr.'s "I have a dream" speech? Most of us marvel at the compelling effect this speech had on millions of people from all different walks of life. King's speech propelled many people into a desired future. King had a skill that great leaders have: the ability to paint a compelling, detailed view of the future by stepping into it and then noticing what is possible from that place.

When clients have difficulties determining forward actions, stepping into the future can be a powerful tool. It can help them "try on the future for size" by feeling what it is like to be there and by looking back to see what it took to get there. Stepping into the future is a way to preview the steps, see possible snags, and develop alternatives. It also can be compelling for the clients, motivating them to begin making meaningful strides toward the future that is now so vivid for them.

Ask yourself:
How would you use stepping into the future with the stressed attorney?

Creating Alternative Actions and Choices

The power of a strong collaborative relationship cannot be underestimated. The level of mastery a coach brings to the coaching relationship provides a foundation for this collaboration in the following ways:

152

- Skillful coaches have professional mastery of core coaching competencies integrated well into their style.
- Skillful coaches have a large enough body of relevant experience—both coaching experience and life experience—on which to draw so that instead of being a rote recapitulation of techniques, the coaching is fluid and is a unique response to the individual clients. This includes being able to zero in on relevant issues to address and tuning out the rest, knowing intuitively where space needs to be created in the clients' lives in order for shifts to happen.
- The coaches move between thinking and nondirected awareness, and between analyzing and reflecting.
- The coaches are able to accurately assess the clients' readiness to change and to choose appropriate strategies so that the strategies are enough of a challenge but not so challenging that the clients are overwhelmed.
- The coaches foster the flow state in clients, finding "an optimal balance between one's perceived abilities and the perceived challenge at a high enough level to avoid both boredom (too much skill for the challenge) and anxiety (too much challenge for the skill). . . . In flow . . . an individual is engaged in a challenging situation that requires fully engaging and stretching one's skills at a high level in response."
- The coaches can create an intuitive flow in which coaches and clients are in sync with each other and are engaged in a generative dialogue.
- The coaches create a trusting relationship where the clients know the coaches are completely aligned with their goals, are "on their side," and are dedicated to looking through the clients' eyes and life.

In addition, coaches and clients both have a high level of emotional intelligence and competence in creating and sustaining relationships. The experience of coaching can accentuate both of these skills for the clients, building additional emotional and relational competency. The coaching relationship itself fosters and strengthens these attributes in clients.

153

Adept coaches use the skills in this chapter to cocreate a variety of action plans with the clients. As the clients work to achieve their desired result, the coaches can also point out previously undisclosed choices or alternatives for the clients to consider as additional options. Together, coaches and clients discover alternative methods, choices, and strategies that neither one may have been aware of individually.

In every moment, life is about choices, but in everyday life it is often difficult to recognize a full range of options. Hence, clients benefit greatly from having coaches who will see, hear, point out what is being missed, and work collaboratively with them to explore alternative methods, choices, and strategies that neither of them had previously considered.

Ask yourself:
What would you do to create alternative actions and choices with the stressed attorney?

Coaching From the Inside Out

Being a life coach is about helping clients create satisfying and fulfilling lives. Up to this point we have provided you with skills and strategies to support clients to discover what authentic and happy lives would be, set and achieve their goals, remove obstacles, and create visions and plans.

Part III, "Coaching from the Inside Out," describes a unique set of tools and methods for coaching your clients to design their lives for fulfillment.

Part III illustrates in detail how coaches can work with clients to gain clarity about what a fulfilling life is to them. It focuses on the clients' need to reflect on and create a vision of personal fulfillment, separate from the agenda of their parents, teachers, culture, spouse, children, or anyone else, and provides coaches with tools to assist clients in identifying blocks to living a fulfilled life and transforming those blocks.

INTRODUCTION TO COACHING FROM THE INSIDE OUT

Since we started using the phrase "inside out" in 1998, it has become much more common in the personal and professional development arena. But the concept remains valid, if not unique. This work in the human arena demands that the coach have experience in learning, growing, and living from the inside out. As a rule, people are taught instead to live from the outside in. They are not taught how to examine their own lives through the lens of fulfillment.

Growing up, we're taught how to fit in, be a good boy or girl, fulfill our parents' expectations, and make choices that create the fewest waves. In our 20s, we get busy building a career, and sometimes those choices, too, are made to fulfill other people's purpose for us rather than our purpose for ourselves. In our 30s, most of us continue in career building and often in family building, and we're often too busy with both of these to take time to ask, "Am I fulfilled? Am I on the right path?" Then, in our 40s and 50s, we may find ourselves burned out or in the midst of a midlife reexamination. In our experience, many clients hire life coaches for exactly this purpose: to reexamine earlier choices and to consider redesigning their life or doing a life makeover.

Pat Williams, for example, had a client who was a lawyer in her mid-40s. She hired him ostensibly to build her legal practice and to become more successful in her three-partner firm. During the third or fourth coaching call, when she was reviewing the Wheel of Life (see Chapter 8) and considering life purpose questions, Pat asked her when she first noticed her passion to become a lawyer. She said, "It was always my father's dream for me. My brother is a lawyer, and my uncle is a lawyer." She ended up saying, "I never really wanted to be a lawyer." She began to examine how her career could begin to reflect her life purpose. She did want to make a difference in people's lives and be a positive influence. But she said that she would rather be a teacher, trainer, or consultant than a lawyer, and that's what she began to explore.

The Inside Out chapters are critical to coaches as well as to clients. Coaches need to do their own work on life purpose and explore the very same themes they will ask their clients to explore. Coaching is a profession that demands that the coach be living a purposeful, examined life.

We will ask in these chapters for you to do exercises to examine your own life. These become opportunities for exercises you may want to assign to clients. At ILCT, we say that students use their lives as a *practice field* for the Inside Out work. Why? Coaches need to be *models* for their clients. It increases the coaches' authenticity, which is key to life coaching. Coaches ask clients to probe deeply into their lives: their values, priorities, goals, and obstacles to fulfillment. Coaches must have done—and continue to do—the same work themselves.

This is your opportunity—and challenge—to focus on yourself, your life purpose, and how well your own life works for you in all dimensions. The exercises in these chapters will ask you various questions, such as: "What do you want for yourself in the future?" "What obstacles and challenges need to be addressed?" "How do you get in your own way?" "Where are your strengths?" and "How can you express your gifts more fully in your coaching and in your relationships with others, with yourself, and with your spirit?"

The earlier sections of this book focused on particular coaching skills, strategies, and techniques. This section focuses on *you and your life*—not on your skills, your clients, or your future clients. Take the time to do each exercise with intention and care. Your participation in the Inside Out process will maximize the benefits you receive from these chapters by adding richness and texture to your learning. Your participation also ensures that your whole being, not just your intellect, is involved as you read. Bringing yourself fully to this learning experience translates into bringing more of yourself to your clients.

So commit to doing the exercises with full attention. You will learn how people use life fulfillment coaching to create fulfilling and balanced lives—by practicing it on yourself.

THE IMPORTANCE OF PARTICIPATING FULLY

Great coaches know that coaching is as much an art as it is a skill. They have committed themselves to fully mastering the *way of being* that they coach their clients to attain. They are models of what it means to fully learn, to be fully effective, and to create a fulfilling life.

In this respect, it is much harder to be a model coach than to be a model therapist. A therapist's commitment as a model for clients is to be functioning normally, without "dis-ease."

As a coach, on the other hand, you are committed to modeling how it is to either be living a fulfilling life *or* be on the path to creating that for yourself. Your way of being is as critical to the way you coach as are your skills. This is the responsibility you carry: to model what you coach others to do and to be. Living this commitment will stretch you, which is why coaching is *interdevelopmental*. It develops and grows both you and the client.

UNCONSCIOUS BLOCKS TO LEARNING

Eric Hoffer (1951) recognized how easy it is for us human beings to get in our own way. We fall in love with our past learning and expertise, and

157

stop growing. As experts, we expect ourselves to know it all. We act as if we are static creatures—as if doing something once or hearing something once makes it old stuff and not worthy of further consideration. We resist going back to the receptivity and openness that characterized us when we were beginners. As beginners, we easily took in new data and practiced doing and thinking things that were unfamiliar. We were willing to get outside of our personal comfort zone in service of learning something interesting and important to us. This *beginner's mind,* as some describe it, is essential for coaches and their clients to recognize and cultivate.

Hoffer was a man ahead of his time. Pat William's father gave him a copy of *True Believer* (1951) to read as a young teen. Pat remembers his father paraphrasing Hoffer as saying "Our greatest pretenses are built up not to hide the evil and the ugly in us, but our emptiness. The hardest thing to hide is something that is not there."

That's why coaching requires us to be curious and work with clients to be curious about everything we believe, feel, and think we understand. Coaches strive to take nothing for granted and to remain nonjudgmental and curious about their clients and about life itself. Coaching requires that we become truly open, flexible learners. We require those characteristics of both ourselves and our clients. The Inside Out chapters of this book engage you in learning that is *deeply personal*—about your gifts and talents, your needs and desires, the blessings and challenges in your life right now. If you give yourself fully to the exercises and teachings of these chapters, you're sure to extend yourself beyond your comfort zone.

An easy way to resist this expansion is to say, "I've heard this . . . done this . . . known this . . . before!" Human neurobiology predisposes us to be habit focused. The human mind tends to want to conserve energy, so it resists thinking when automatic responses will do. We all know how this works when we find ourselves driving, having noticed nothing about the road or other drivers until we reach our destination. We are on autopilot. It works for driving and many other things. However, the tendency toward habituated action inhibits awareness and doesn't welcome new learning.

As you work through the Inside Out chapters, you will undoubtedly encounter things you've heard about, learned about, and perhaps even mastered previously. When this occurs, you'll be faced with a choice: to stay in expertness, outside the learning conversation, or to see the invitation that these chapters offer an opportunity to stretch yourself and open yourself to the next step in your life, whatever that may be.

Educated and experienced professionals may find they have erected many barriers to learning. We have found at ILCT that both our students and often their clients find it difficult to embrace the condition of being a learner. Some of the ways that we can recognize this resistance to embrace learning are:

- We find it difficult to admit that we don't know how to do something or haven't mastered it yet. We let our disappointment about our situation stop us.
- We want to be clear all of the time, about everything. Consequently, we lose patience with the ambiguity and messiness—even the chaos—required for great learning to occur.
- We may live in a permanent state of judgment. We judge ourselves and our adequacy, this book and its adequacy, the book's authors and their adequacy. We find it hard to simply stop judging and start appreciating people (ourselves included) and opportunities for what they can offer.
- We don't often grant others the authority to teach us or coach us. Instead, we tend to make them wrong and inadequate. The choice we could instead make is to see them as having a unique perspective—and to allow ourselves to be the beneficiaries of their uniqueness.
- Often the need to look good (perfect, right, sensible, smart) keeps professionals reactive to life instead of responding to possibilities. Response implies choices.

159

Ask yourself:
What are the obstacles I create that hinder a full engagement with my learning? How might they appear during the Inside Out chapters?

Chapter 7

The Power of Purpose

This chapter is about *life purpose:* how to work with clients to discover theirs, how to maximize the usefulness of life purpose, and how to use it in life coaching with particular clients. First, we focus on what life purpose is and how to discover life purpose. Later in the chapter we focus on how to refine a life purpose and how to use it with clients.

LIVE FROM A DEEP PLACE

Rainer Maria Rilke, the 19th-century German poet, wrote to a young would-be poet to "live from a deep place." Only then, Rilke said, would his writing become great.

It's not easy for clients to find their deep place when their lives are cluttered and busy. It requires becoming still and quiet, focusing on beginning the work that we describe below, and making a commitment to themselves—putting themselves at the top of the to-do list. There are no slogans, no easy shortcuts. This is a process of getting to know oneself fully.

Supporting clients to find their *deep place* begins with discovering their life purpose. When they know their life purpose, they have access to incredible power to make choices and to act.

That's what it did for Terry Fox, a young man from Canada. Terry was an athlete who was stricken with cancer, lost one of his legs, and was naturally depressed about his situation. He had lost his sense of a viable future. Some months into his recovery, after being fitted with a wooden leg, Terry did the serious work of reconsidering who he was. He discovered a *lively vision* (see page 163): that people in his area would care enough about cancer to contribute money to find a cure for bone cancer. Then he found his own life purpose: he would be the carrier of the message that if communities contributed, a cure could be found. Shortly thereafter, his *mission* surfaced: he would run across Canada, from coast to coast, bearing personal witness to the strength of the human spirit and the need for a cure.

Terry's run across Canada was filmed and made visible to many people; however, it doesn't matter how public clients' vision, purpose, and mission are. What is important is that they articulate them clearly, commit themselves fully, and use them to create meaningful work and a satisfying life. This will serve them in knowing how to live, work, and be "on purpose."

LIFE PURPOSE

Each of us looks for fulfillment and authentic happiness in our own way. Sometimes the yearning for fulfillment becomes a call so loud and so intense at midlife that we cannot help but step off the path we are on and devote ourselves to the search for fulfillment. As many midlife questers discover, fulfillment often means returning to deep sources of satisfaction that we may have had glimpses of many years ago. At that earlier time, we may have lacked the courage to follow the call, or we may have allowed life's stresses and serious pursuits to cover up the glimmer of what we knew to be true.

This pattern takes place in the lives of so many people because each of us has a life purpose that, we believe, has been with us since we were very young. At moments when we experienced a profound sense of being in the flow—being in the right place, at the right time, using our gifts—we are likely to be living out our life purpose. Life purpose *calls us forth.* It may be a calling we answer, something larger than our small selves, that deeply connects us with others, with what is larger than ourselves. Gregg Levoy (1997) eloquently illustrates how discovering one's life purpose often begins with a sense of experiencing a calling.

Bookstore shelves are filled with information about our contemporary search for meaning. We know that life purpose has become an important focus for many people: *The Purpose-Driven Life* (Warren, 2002) has become the biggest selling self-help book of all time. A common definition of life purpose is a calling, an overall theme for your life or intent

161

that transcends your daily activities. A quick search indicates that the word *purpose* means many different things to different writers. A variety of spiritual leaders and traditions have said that the ultimate purpose of our lives is to remember who we are and to whom we owe our lives, and to feel *joy.*

Ancient writers wrote about this topic. An ancient Tibetan text states that a life purpose is "for the benefit of self and for the benefit of others." Below are four quotations relevant to the issue of life purpose that we give to ILCT participants, asking them to reflect on what the quotes mean to them. These four seem to be particularly meaningful quotations that move students toward introspective thinking about the importance of life purpose and the variety of ways to describe it.

> *When we are motivated by goals that have deep meaning, by dreams that need completion, by pure love that needs expressing, then we truly live life.* (Anderson, 1997, p. 36)

> *We can define "purpose" in several ways. For one, when we know our purpose, we have an anchor—a device of the mind to provide some stability, to keep from tossing us to and fro, from inflicting constant seasickness on us. Or we can think of our purpose as being a master nautical chart marking shoals and rocks, sandbars and derelicts, something to guide us and keep us on course. Perhaps the most profound thing we can say about being "on purpose" is that when that is our status, our condition, and our comfort, we find our lives have meaning, and when we are "off purpose," we are confused about meanings and motives.* (Lynch & Kordis, 1988, p. 42)

> *The first principle of ethical power is Purpose. . . . By purpose, I mean your objective or intention—something toward which you are always striving. Purpose is something bigger. It is the picture you have of yourself—the kind of person you want to be or the kind of life you want to lead."* (Blanchard & Peale, 1988, p. 44)

> *A purpose is more ongoing and gives meaning to our lives. . . . When people have a purpose in life, they enjoy everything they do more! People go on chasing goals to prove something that doesn't have to be proved: that they're already worthwhile.* (Johnson, 2002, p. 23)

THE IMPORTANCE OF KNOWING LIFE PURPOSE

In industrialized countries, 21st-century culture has become obsessed with accumulating just for the sake of accumulating: information, goods, material objects, and more.

The paradoxes of our time have been summed up well by His Holiness the Dalai Lama (2002):

> We have more conveniences, but less time. We have more degrees, but less sense . . . more knowledge but less judgment. More experts, but more problems. More medicines, but less healthiness.
> We have been all the way to the moon and back but have trouble crossing the street to meet the new neighbor.
> We build more computers to hold more information that produce more copies than ever before, but have less communication.
> We have become long on quantity, but short on quality.
> These are the times of fast foods but weak digestion.
> It is a time when there is much in the window but nothing in the room.
> (p. 77)

As we live with these paradoxes, we have lost sight of the importance of *being* in life. Many people in the United States misguidedly believe that the only way to have what we want is to work hard and long.

There is an alternative: *be* who you are first. When you focus on being first, this lets you *do* what you want to do, which lets you *have* what you need. We need to allow ourselves to *be* first; the rest will follow. Discovering our life purpose focuses our attention on the essence of who we are—our *be*-ing.

WAYS TO DISCOVER LIFE PURPOSE

Create a Lively Vision as the Context for Life Purpose

Clients' visions are statements about the world in which they want to live. They don't need to consider the whole planet unless they want to— just their personal world of friends, community, work colleagues—the world that touches their everyday life.

163

We suggest using the following process to help clients create their vision.

1. List the top ten things you love to do or have always done and loved. Name several things you have consistently made part of your life, regardless of the circumstances. Examples might include networking with like-minded people, your faith or spirituality, your creativity at work, your heartfelt communications, or your ability to take action under pressure.

2. Identify the characteristics of the context or environment that support your list from Step 1. List the qualities of people you want and need to be around to accomplish your top ten. Draw a series of concentric circles on a blank piece of paper, and write "ME" in the center circle. Each circle represents a group of people who are important to you. Put the names of those closest to you, who affect your life most, in the circle next to you. Then continue to draw your circles outward: family, friends, work colleagues, professional groups, community, and so on. In each circle, write a few words that describe the qualities this group must embody to support you in just the way you need and want.

    Then identify other resources that are essential to you: peacefulness, time in nature, other creative people, and so on. Ask yourself, "What are the essential supporting features of the world I want to live in so that I can be at my best?"

3. Using the phrases you generated in Step 2, write one to two sentences that express your vision of the world you want to live in. This is the path of least resistance for you, the world you flourish in and want to create for yourself through purpose-full action. Crystallize the essence of your vision. For example, "My vision is that all people of the world will be able to live their lives by *choice*—in a way that matters to them." This vision expresses the fact that choice is essential for the writer.

Examine Past Experiences to Discover Purpose

Our purpose serves us in many ways. It is our compelling reason for living. It gives meaning to our work and our life. It guides our choices.

Some people describe their purpose as their "calling." Whatever we call it, it profoundly shapes the direction of our life.

Career counselors and coaches have known for quite some time that working with past experience is a way of discovering personal strengths and patterns. Clients who want to change careers make lists of their best successes and then examine these to identify the skills and resources they have learned to use effectively at work. Coaches use this strategy, too, examining past experiences to uncover life purpose. The steps below draw on clients' past experiences to create a grounded sense of life purpose. This is a powerful and effective way for clients to source their life purpose because it is based on the reality of their life—what they have already experienced and what they know about themselves from many years of living—not on what their intellect alone tells them to want.

Clients' purpose statements are unique to those clients. Whether or not they are conscious of it, they have already been living out their purpose in some way. Because of this, they can plumb their past to find their purpose. Ask your clients to the following exercises.

165

1. *List a dozen or more examples of times in your life when you knew you were* on purpose. That is, you had an intuitive sense of being aligned with the exact reasons why you are in the world. Some people recognize they are on purpose because they are "in the flow"—psychologist Mikhail Csikszentmihalyi (1990) has written eloquently about the satisfaction that comes when people are in a *flow* state. Selecting these intuitively is important because you may not be able to articulate rationally why you felt on purpose during this time. Let us give you an example: One of Diane Menendez's experiences of being on purpose occurred during a vacation to Costa Rica with her husband. She was on the side of a hill, looking out over a valley and on to the Osa Peninsula ocean below. As she admired the view, through the valley flew 100 blue jeweled macaws. They swooped through the valley and alighted in the tallest trees to her left. At the time, this was the only experience she identified of this kind—the sole one that occurred outside of work, community service, or friendship. Yet, as she worked through the the five exer-

cises described here, this experience had the elements that were common to her life purpose: recognizing the universal divine in the present moment, admiring the sheer beauty of the world, and connecting the two.

Most recently, Pat Williams had an experience of being *on purpose* while delivering the keynote address in Brisbane, Australia, to 400 delegates in a theater-in-the-round setting at the ICF Australian conference. He felt in the flow, loving the opportunity to speak to the delegates about his passion for life coaching, the profession of coaching, and the impact that it can have in the world in other ways. Pat was aware that he was in Australia, clear across the globe from where he lived, getting paid to be in a foreign country speaking to people about the passion and the power of life coaching. He was living his dream of a global village in that moment.

We advise you to start your list of examples very quickly; don't stop to analyze why you are choosing them. The examples may be from any part of your life, even as early as childhood. Many people have amazing childhood experiences related to purpose, perhaps because they occur prior to the time when analytical thought is possible. The experience makes a keen impression, and only later can the adult reflect upon why. Make sure that the examples span the entirety of your life, including two or three from each decade and, if possible, more from the past 5 to 10 years.

2. *Write briefly about each of these examples.* For each of the experiences you listed, write a few bullet points, phrases, or sentences about the experience. Include what you did, where you were, what the outcome was, and how you felt. Your writing should also answer these questions:

   What was essential to my sense of being "on purpose"?
   What about this experience was richly satisfying?
   What was of value here for me?

3. *Highlight key words and phrases.* Once you've written your paragraphs, highlight the key words from each experience. Copy all of the

underlined words onto a separate page. Examine them to identify the commonalities and themes among them. You will use these words and phrases to build your statement of purpose.

4. *Draft a brief statement of your life purpose in two to four sentences using the key words and phrases of your life purpose.* Because every person has a unique purpose, no one else's statement will fit yours. How does a purpose statement sound? Here are some examples:

My purpose is to support and partner personally and professionally with leaders to create organizations where the human spirit thrives.

My purpose is to work generously and to live in service; to manifest love through connecting and caring for self and others; and to support the development of inner wisdom and inner peace in myself, my colleagues, my clients, and my community.

My purpose is to build and lead organizations that model the best practices in our industry, are profitable financially and viable long-term, and offer dedicated workers meaningful work and sustained employment.

The purpose of my life is to proclaim the good news that married couples live very holy lives, and that all of life is holy.

The purpose of my life is to create a world of love and empowerment, by loving and empowering myself and others.

Don't expect yourself to get it just right in 1 hour. Let your draft incubate for several days. Getting it 85% right is enough for now. Read it to others and get feedback.

To refine your purpose statement, read it aloud a number of times very slowly. As you do, listen for the particular words that resonate with you as you read them—as if you and the purpose are tuning forks that resonate together when you are in sync with each other.

5. *Test your purpose.* A good purpose statement pulls you toward it. It engenders energy—like the wind in your sails. You know where you are headed when your purpose is clear. Does your statement help you clarify what you'll do in your work and in your life?
Here are some clues that you've connected with your purpose:

- You feel a strong connection with the purpose you've described.
- You have a desire to fulfill it.
- You feel deep pleasure when you act in concert with it.
- You interests naturally gravitate toward fulfilling it.

Whatever your clients' unique life purpose, however big or small it may look to others, it's their true path and the one that gives their life meaning. When clients identify their life purpose, they have taken a powerful step toward manifesting it and creating a fulfilling life for themselves.

Encourage your clients to refine their life purpose statement until they feel an internal *yes* that lets them know they've captured the essence of their life purpose. They might also benefit from taking time to journal about how this work on life purpose has impacted them.

Refining the statement may occur over several coaching sessions or a longer period of time. It is important that the clients realize that this statement is only for them. It is not a promotional statement and needs to speak and inspire only them. They will never have to share it with anyone else. As the coach, your role is to help the clients clarify the statement until it is succinct enough for them to remember it and, when the clients speak it to themselves, they have the intuitive sense that they are resonating with it. We often use this metaphor of resonating, as if the clients and the purpose statements were responding like a tuning fork does. On several coaching sessions, Diane Menendez has actually used a tuning fork, demonstrating how it vibrates when struck. This helps clients understand the relationship they have with their purpose statement, once it has been refined.

BEING PURPOSE-FULL: WORKING WITH LIFE PURPOSE

A favorite quote about the power of life purpose comes from a well-known U.S. president, Woodrow Wilson, who said: "You are not here merely to make a living. You are here in order to enable the world to live more amply, with greater vision, with a finer spirit of hope and achievement. You are here to enrich the world, and you impoverish yourself if you forget the errand."

Wilson's quote reinforces the value of life purpose work: When our purpose, our power, and our passion intersect, we find personal fulfillment *and* enrich the world.

As you work with clients on life purpose, you'll find that sometimes they confuse *life purpose, vision,* and *mission.*

Life purpose is our calling—the underlying reason for being that gives meaning to our life. It is the purpose an individual enacts throughout a lifetime. Spiritual traditions often describe a *universal life purpose* for all human beings. For example, when asked what he believed to be the meaning of life, the Dalai Lama said, "To be happy and to make others happy." Within the universal life purpose for all human beings, individuals still must find their own life purpose.

Mission is the particular way or ways we choose to fulfill our purpose at a particular point in our life. For example, individuals whose life purpose is to "honor and evoke the highest and best in myself and others" might fulfill that purpose through many different kinds of work and actions over the course of their life.

Vision refers to a specific, compelling image of the future that an individual holds. Earlier in this chapter, we included an exercise for clients to consider their vision for the world in which they want to live. In Chapter 8, we'll describe an exercise for creating a vision for each of the 12 life areas.

When you work with clients, you want to assist them in distinguishing between life purpose, vision, and mission. Most clients will need to examine all three.

Ways to Work with Life Purpose
Coaches and their clients have many options for working with life purpose. We've included a list of books at the end of this chapter, each of which includes suggestions for helping clients identify life purpose.

169

In the coach training at ILCT, we use the method drawn from career counseling that we described above. This exercise accesses clients' cognitive, intellectual, emotional, and intuitive capacities. We also use a structured way of creating life purpose that is described in *Human Being,* one of the texts in our training course.[1]

Sometimes the clients' first reaction to sharing their purpose statement is, "Oh, it sounds so grandiose!" A rich purpose statement should, in fact, be big and inclusive, enough so that it compels the clients to expand. As Marianne Williamson said so eloquently, "Your playing small serves no one." A good purpose statement creates the energy to play large.

A purpose statement is a private thing, unlike a company's vision statement that hangs on the wall. It is something we use privately to create our goals and our life. Make sure your clients understand that no one besides themselves and their coach ever needs to know their life purpose unless they choose to share it with others. This information usually elicits a sigh of relief.

The clients' purpose is not necessarily something they discover in midlife. In fact, it probably has been with them for quite some time, even though they may never have articulated it. That is why they will benefit from going back into their past and working with some real experiences of being "on purpose."

When we are on purpose, we live from our being, or our core self. When we have lost track and are living "off purpose," our life feels less fulfilling. Many clients discover that when they have chosen work or a way of life that does not feel fulfilling, it is because they have lost sight of their purpose. They have become a human *doing* instead of a human *being.*

Using Life Purpose with Clients
Almost all clients can benefit from life purpose work if they have adequate willingness and a capacity for self-reflection. Sometimes clients need to be taught the value of reflection in order to benefit from life purpose work. Using inquiries with clients, powerful questions that guide their focused attention and lead to introspection can be helpful in devel-

[1] *Human Being* is no longer in print, but you may order it on CD-ROM at www.life coachtraining.com.

170

oping the ability to self-reflect, as can meditation practices, journaling, and many of the other tools we use in our role as helping professionals. Some clients come to us with a strong need to reexamine life purpose. Clients may seem to have lost their way, to be "off purpose" in their life. If they were a boat, we'd say that they lacked a rudder and were adrift in a sea of circumstances. The clients may feel as if they are surviving, but only with a struggle, or they may be striving to achieve but don't feel much satisfaction in their accomplishments.

Sometimes in the natural cycle of life, clues emerge that suggest life purpose work may be called for:

- A client in midlife feels listless, fatigued, and disenchanted.
- The client has experienced losses—deaths, job losses, or health issues—that make the old way of living no longer possible.
- The client is overwhelmed with life and is asking, "Is this the life I really want to lead?"
- The client has undergone significant life transitions—children have left, retirement is near, divorce has occurred, and so on.
- The client feels a serious mismatch between current work and/or roles and the deep desires of the self.

171

Notice that these situations might also prompt a client to seek the services of a psychotherapist, if clinical depression or extensive anxiety is present. On the other hand, life purpose work can be very therapeutic. It can be done using a coach approach either by you or by referring to a coach who specializes in life purpose coaching.

Life Purpose Work and Deep Change

In our private lives, as well as in our professional lives, getting back "on purpose" may require some startling changes. Living from a deep place is not easy to maintain in 21st-century life in the United States, where speed, multitasking, and constant noise make lack of depth a fact of life. Living from a deep place may require a client to undergo deep change. As Robert E. Quinn (1996), the organizational behavior and human resource management expert and consultant, wrote:

Ultimately, deep change . . . is a spiritual process. Loss of alignment occurs when, for whatever reason, we begin to pursue the wrong end. This process begins innocently enough. In pursuing some justifiable end, we make a trade-off of some kind. We know it is wrong, but we rationalize our choice. We use the end to justify the means. As time passes, something inside us starts to wither. We are forced to live at the cognitive level, the rational, goal-seeking level. We lose our vitality and begin to work from sheer discipline. Our energy is not naturally replenished, and we experience no joy in what we do. We are experiencing slow death . . . We must recognize the lies we have been telling ourselves. We must acknowledge our own weakness, greed, insensitivity and lack of vision and courage. If we do so, we begin to understand the clear need for a course correction, and we slowly begin to reinvent our self. (p. 78)

The truth is that almost any moment offers us an opportunity to live out our life purpose. By choosing work, relationships, avocations, creative pursuits, and other life elements consciously, we can find the most fulfilling ways to experience our purpose.

Life purpose work can also help clients begin to sense and/or to live out a higher level of consciousness. In Chapter 3, you read about the work on levels of consciousness. As you consider working with life purpose, consider the level of consciousness that clients seem to be embedded in or moving to.

What level of consciousness do these people seem to be at?
Is there a transitional stage, an urge toward transformation of consciousness that is at work in their life?
How might life purpose work be of assistance?

An Example of Life Purpose Work
Consider the case of Andy, a 38-year-old coaching client, who is a teacher and workshop leader. Andy is happily married, has two children, and is considering whether or not to start his own business. He has been a high school teacher and counselor during his entire career and says he finds himself "sort of itching to make a big change in my work."

172

Andy's Life Experiences of Being "On Purpose"

Andy turns in the following random list to you as fieldwork:

- Staying with my grandmother for 2 months after her husband of 63 years died unexpectedly
- Being the only child in a blue-collar family to graduate from college
- The birth of my two sons
- Adopting two babies from China
- Committing to completing a master's degree in counseling to enrich my work as a high school counselor
- Working successfully as a counselor at the high school
- Creating a special support group program for young unmarried fathers at the high school
- Moving in to care for my father, a widower, for the 6 months before he died

Andy's Life Purpose Themes

As Andy shares the experiences with you, you note the following words and phrases recurring time and time again throughout his stories. These become his purpose themes.

173

- Connecting to self, others, and the whole
- Fun, different every day
- Friends and connections
- Peace
- Creativity
- Challenges
- Persistence
- Learning
- Believing in myself and my capabilities
- Coming into my own
- In the right place, doing the right thing
- Committed, conscious, courageous

A Life Purpose Statement for Andy

The life purpose statement Andy drafted after this work was the following:

> My life purpose is to create connection between myself, my clients, and all those I contact to the universal whole of life, through joyfully living and transforming our life challenges into sources of creativity and learning.

Using Life Purpose as a Guide

The real benefit of knowing one's life purpose comes when clients use it as a guide to make choices and decisions that lead to greater, more authentic happiness and fulfillment. Life purpose work leads clients to discover new choices, as well as to become clear about directions to pursue and choices to release. In later chapters we explore how clients use values and life design considerations to these ends, as well.

Helping professionals regularly encounter clients who have been living out roles, values, and commitments that were assigned to them early on by their family of origin. Clients often seek coaching because those old ways don't work for them anymore. Once they discover their individual life purpose, they may discover, with sadness or with elation, that the roles they have chosen to play and the line of work they have chosen have never fit them well. This discovery often leads to a realization that they feel called to live out a different purpose—one that is uniquely their own and may have nothing to do with their family's desires or agenda.

This happened to a client who had spent 20 years working as a divorce lawyer, never feeling a sense of fulfillment from the work. When he did the life purpose work, he chose only one of his 25 *on-purpose* examples from his legal career. Most of the examples he chose came from his church work, his volunteer work as a Big Brother, and his 10 years of service to the board of education in his township. Recognizing what these choices meant to him about his fulfillment at work, he felt deeply sad about this situation and needed to do some grief work before moving forward with his life work. He gave himself time for grieving, and then was able to articulate his life purpose in this way:

Through intuitively catalyzing people and ideas, I create understanding, awareness, and connections that enhance people's lives.

Imagine that he asks you this question: "Is there any way that I could live out my life purpose in my work as an attorney?" What changes might he consider that would create a better fit between his purpose and his current professional role?

OTHER WRITTEN RESOURCES

As coaches, we often suggest our clients read something about life purpose. Other resources on how people have discovered and lived their purpose include:

Carol Adrienne, *The Purpose of Your Life: Finding Your Place in the World Using Synchronicity, Intuition, and Uncommon Sense*

Teri-E Belf and Charlotte Ward, *Simply Live It Up: Brief Solutions*

Laurie Beth Jones, *The Path: Creating Your Mission Statement for Work and for Life*

Barbara Braham, *Finding Your Purpose: A Guide to Personal Fulfillment*

Stephen Covey, *The 7 Habits of Highly Effective People: Powerful Lessons in Personal Change* (Covey focuses on principles, but the intent is the same. If you offer this resource to clients, be sure that they understand the difference in terminology between Covey's and what we offer here.)

Fredric M. Hudson and Pamela D. McLean, *Life Launch: A Passionate Guide to the Rest of Your Life* (Hudson also has published a short pamphlet for clients called *Planning on Purpose: Discovery Guide.* Order from www.hudsoninstitute.com.)

Richard J. Leider, *The Power of Purpose*

175

Chapter 8

Design Your Life

LIVING A FULFILLED LIFE

It is no secret that countless Americans complain daily that they are too busy, too rushed, have lost track of friends, and have lost track of themselves. Many clients hire coaches because they want to find ways to make their lives more satisfying and fulfilling. At heart, they want to feel more *alive*. As we wrote in Chapter 7, the high level of stimulation in life in modern industrialized societies deadens people. Writers describe this as a trance, similar to a hypnotic state. Bill O'Hanlon, a student of Milton Erickson, the father of hypnosis, shared this view of *life as trance* with Pat Williams in a personal conversation.

Most of us go about our lives in an unconscious or semiconscious, robotlike manner. This has its benefits: the human brain conserves energy when it doesn't have to think consciously about each action or choice. However, when our lives aren't bringing satisfaction, the autopilot needs to be changed. That's particularly true if clients are being driven by habitual choices and ways of coping that were developed as young children and have remained unchanged. When adults' coping habits outlive their usefulness, they may turn to a coach, seeking help to reshape their life. Redesigning their life will require them to develop new habits of thinking and behaving. This requires a personal breakthrough. Nadler and Hibino (1998) described this well: "Otherwise intelligent people take the same self-limiting thinking approaches every time without realizing they are stuck in time-worn ruts on the road to mediocrity" (p. 72). Coaching clients generally clearly state that they want to get beyond mediocrity. They often are less clear about the ways that their habitual thinking and coping habits are limitations to moving beyond their current life choices.

In coaching we sometimes talk about the *life purpose* and *life design* work being *tranceformational.* People become conscious of their unconsciousness. We can't always be totally conscious at all times. Our desire is that people design their lives purposefully. We want to form new ways of being that are positive and purposeful—new good habits and daily practices, and a new way of being. These then become a *new trance,* like an operating system that operates in the background of their lives.

We have all seen the legitimate ways that hypnosis is used to assist people in stopping smoking, losing weight, calming anxiety, and overcoming phobias and fears. In its simplest sense, hypnosis isn't "watch my watch and fall into a deep trance." It is the use of language and storytelling to take people inward to reflect on the images and senses the language calls forth from them. Hypnotic inductions work through embedded messages. When people use hypnosis to change habits, they are given new messages that become filtered through their unconscious. These create positive habits that replace the unhealthy or unwanted behaviors. So, designing a life can be *tranceformational* in the most positive sense. Practitioners of neurolinguistic programming would be familiar with this, since much of their practice is based on Ericksonian theory and technique.

We are not saying that coaching is hypnosis. Our point is that human beings are creatures of habit who put themselves in trances all day long. Anyone who knows the effects of television or routine noise is familiar with the ways that humans semi-attend, falling into a sort of autopilot stupor. Coaching uses the principle of examining a client's everyday life habits, determining which ones are habitual and the assumptions that underpin them. The coach works directly with the client, exploring cognitively and emotionally ways to change habits and create more purposeful behavior that is in line with the client's desired life. As we describe in this chapter, the coach and client engage together in designing a new life for the client and then crafting a life that matches this design.

Oriah Mountain Dreamer's (1999) poem "The Invitation" created a stir because it speaks to this longing to feel more alive. Circulating for months on the Internet, the poem struck a chord with us and thousands of others. We learned later, at a coaching conference in Vancouver,

177

Canada, where Oprah spoke, that her son was initially responsible for passing it around the Internet. Its impact caused people like us to spread it around the world. We passed it along to friends, who in turn passed it along to other friends. Ultimately, it became so popular that she wrote a book by the same name, which easily found a publisher. Her poem speaks eloquently to the need to feel *alive:* to inhabit our lives fully, to risk, to share, to see beauty, and to connect ourselves with a source greater than our individuality—to build our lives around a worthy core. This is in keeping with the research from positive psychology, which finds that the strongest route to authentic happiness is to use one's signature strengths in service of something greater than oneself. We encourage you to find "The Invitation" in a bookstore or on the Web, where it is reprinted on a number of sites. The poem speaks to clients who are ready to consider that they are the authors and designers of their lives.

This chapter focuses on life design. Most of us did not grow up thinking we could design a life. Design a picture, maybe, or design a room, as an interior designer does. Something small, maybe—but not our lives!

What do you associate with the word *design? artistry? craftsmanship? architecture? quilting?* Webster's Dictionary offers these definitions:

Design: to create, fashion, execute, or construct according to plan
Devise, Contrive: to conceive and plan out in the mind; to have as a purpose
Intend: to devise for a specific function or end; to make a drawing, pattern, or sketch of; to draw the plans for

As coaches, we take the role of design very seriously. We coach our clients to become the interior designers of their lives in an integral way— body, mind, and spirit. Through our work, our clients realize they can make choices about their lives. They can consciously design a way of living that will bring them deep fulfillment. *Fulfillment* means "a feeling of satisfaction of having achieved one's desires, or the act of consummating something" (American Heritage Dictionary of the English Language, 2000). Coaches help clients to discover what they as individuals desire and want to bring into actuality, to completion. Is anyone ever totally fulfilled? Of course not. Even the popular notion of mindfulness, represented well by Tolle (1999), allows for the fact that mindfulness is a temporary state to which we return, hopefully more frequently than when we are unconscious of it. Generally people experience fulfillment in the moment. Life brings new challenges and learning opportunities. What we want our coaching clients to learn is that in being more purposeful—in consciously choosing and designing their experience—they have opportunities to experience moments of fulfillment more frequently. We find that clients often choose these moments of fulfillment as the sources for their work on life purpose, described in Chapter 7. Understandably, clients would want more of whatever feels fulfilling. Living purposefully and living with design allows people to be more conscious of their choices, actions, and mind-set.

The basic premise of life design is that human beings *can* create the life of their dreams. Eleanor Roosevelt said, "The future belongs to those who believe in the beauty of their dreams" (1937). Coaches know that this belief is necessary but not sufficient.

To create the life of our dreams, we also need to have the courage to create. As L. J. Cardinal Suenens said, "Happy are those who dream dreams and are ready to pay the price to make them come true" (2006). Cardinal Suenens's quote emphasizes the cost of courage. As coaches, we also know of the high cost of *not* living the life of our dreams, of not leading a fulfilling life.

Life design exercises are an excellent way to support your clients in exploring the life of their dreams. We recommend that you instruct clients to give themselves several hours to complete the exercises. Also, they'll get the most out of the exercises if they take off their rose-colored glasses and are as honest as possible.

LIFE *CAN* WORK

Many of us need to be reminded that we create our own lives—through our intentions, our beliefs, our courage, and our ability to link our desires with our actions. Yet, as singer-songwriter and former Beatle John Lennon

179

knew, the real art of life is in balancing—in living in the present with an ability to focus on the future. He wisely said, "Life is what happens when you are busy making other plans."

Many coaches use some version of a tool called the Wheel of Life. It's very common, and no one seems to know its original source. We teach our students to use the Life Balance Wheel (see Figure 8.1), which we sometimes call the Coaching Mandala, referenced in *Therapist as Life Coach* (Williams & Davis, 2002). When Pat Williams teaches it live, he asks the audience, "Why do you think we call it the Coaching Mandala?" When the participants fall into a weighty silence, Pat relates humorously, "Well, it gives it that magical, esoteric quality!"

Figure 8.1

Life balance wheel (coaching mandala)

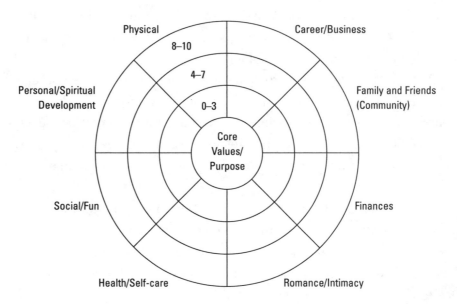

Instructions for the Client

The hub represents the clients' core values and life purpose. Clients may have worked on this separately, or may not yet have the exact language to express what belongs in the hub. Each area is interrelated in an ideal life. For each of the mandala areas, ask the clients to give a score (1–10) and shade or color the space accordingly in terms of their current level of satisfaction with this particular area *right now.* Use this mandala as a way to assess the current level of life satisfaction in each area. The clients may score it numerically to measure the improvement desired, or they may use it to have a coaching conversation about gaps between where the clients are now and where the clients would like to be.

At ILCT, we recommend students use this tool early, even in the first conversation with clients, as a way to begin the conversation about gaps in their life. It allows the coach to ask the clients, "Where do you most want coaching to focus?" The clients score their level of satisfaction in each area of the wheel, giving them a numerical comparison for the various areas of their life. This becomes a simple way for clients to see where coaching might benefit them most. For example, coach and client might explore together what it would take to move from a 4 to a 10 in an area of the client's life. In a first session, the coach and client are apt to discover many or most of the areas to be less satisfactory than the client wants. So the challenge here is to help the client select several areas to start on. The client will soon see that it's all connected. This fits with our philosophy of teaching a whole-person, integrated approach to coaching. Changes in one area will inevitably impact the client's satisfaction in other areas. The wheel is not linear; it is just a starting point for coaching conversations.

The beauty of this tool is that it can be used in *coaching check-ups* at various intervals during the coaching relationship. The client might complete the Wheel of Life at 6-month intervals, or even quarterly, to give both coach and client a current snapshot of the client's satisfaction. These snapshots can be compared to the initial scoring. We also think it is important for clients to update their wheel if a change in their circumstances occurs that impacts an area. For example, both Pat Williams and Diane Menendez have experienced the death of a parent and the subsequent need to become the remaining parent's caretaker. These events radically impacted satisfaction in several areas. Loss and caretaking require time and energy that must be drawn from other areas. This is just one example of how life changes require the client to reexamine satisfaction and redesign.

181

THE TRADITION OF THE WHEEL OF LIFE

The symbol and the term *Wheel of Life* (Figure 8.2) did not originate with coaching. In fact, its origins come from the Middle Ages and from a grimmer view of life's possibilities than we hold today. In the Middle Ages, life was short in comparison with our current longevity, and it also was quite difficult for most people. The Wheel of Life was often carved into the stone walls of cathedrals. People who viewed the image received figurative instruction about life's inevitable change process.

Figure 8.2

The wheel of life (From www.lessons4living.com)

182

At the top of the wheel (where 12 o'clock would be on a clock) sits a well-dressed, smiling, kingly or queenly person. This person is located in the position of *Happiness.* Things are normal and going well. The wheel turns in a clockwise direction when change occurs. In the 3 o'clock position, the same person is now upside down, falling through space with a look of distress. This is the position of *Loss.* As the wheel continues its movement, at the bottom of the wheel (where 6 o'clock would be), the individual is now naked, stripped of possessions and everything he or she found valuable, and pulled along through the muck and mire of life. This is the position of *Suffering*. When the wheel turns again, toward the 9 o'clock position, the person is once again clothed and has arisen to the position of *Hope*. He or she anticipates with hope the possibility of once again reaching the position of Happiness.

The wheel's lesson is that there are only four positions in life: happiness, loss, suffering, and hope. We are always in one of these positions.

The Wheel of Life offers wisdom for us as coaches and for our coaching clients. In fact, the four positions are similar to Frederic Hudson's *cycle of change,* presented in Chapter 3 (p. 93).

Happiness is our desired position. Everything seems normal. Whatever we are doing is succeeding. Our routine works. We are comfortable.

Loss is where the happiness of routine begins to fall apart. A variety of events signal change, and we are challenged to let go of the routine that worked. When loss arrives in our life, we want to return to our previous happiness as quickly as possible. We want to regain our equilibrium by making the wheel move in reverse. However, the wheel only moves forward, in a clockwise direction. To regain happiness, we must follow the wheel into suffering.

Suffering, the phase of transition, is located at the bottom of the wheel. The Latin root word for *suffering* means to "experience or allow." Suffering asks us to go through and fully experience our loss. We cannot avoid this process and still hope to achieve our goal. We cannot go over, under, or around the transition phase. We must go through it—with all the hard work of planning, implementing, and revising that it entails. This is often an unpleasant process that involves true suffering: tension, stress, anxiety, worry, frustration, anger, conflict, and sadness. It is only through suffering—fully experiencing our pain—that hope arises.

Hope emerges when our plans begin to work. We notice progress and begin to feel competent. We hold a vision of a return to happiness and normality. Naturally, the new normality will be different from the old. When the process of change is effective, the elements of our life

183

come together in a new configuration. We find happiness in a new state of equilibrium.

The medieval philosophers saw human life as a cycle: the wheel always turns. Happiness is rarely a permanent state. Change will reliably come as we journey around the wheel into loss, suffering, and hope—a continuous process through our lives.

The Emotions of Change

As a consequence of this natural cycle, we repeatedly experience the natural emotions of change. As we sense that loss is coming, we feel anxiety, apprehension, and worry. When loss arrives we feel sad, angry, irritated, and frustrated. Grieving needs to be done. Along with the experience of suffering through change, we may experience stress, depression, burnout, helplessness, and even hopelessness.

Eventually hope brings a renewed energy, optimism, and enthusiasm, and happiness brings a sense of satisfaction and contentment. The Wheel of Life teaches that we cannot be happy and stay happy forever. Change is a natural part of our lives. It brings growth and is inevitably accompanied by the emotions associated with change.

We introduce clients to this classic view, part of a long human tradition, as a way of examining the assumptions they hold about suffering and joy. Recognizing, experiencing fully, and accepting or surrendering to emotions help clients work through and align with the natural process of change.

We Can Turn the Wheel

The Wheel of Life is an important model for coaches to know about because some clients initially resist doing life design work. They believe their Wheel of Life process brings them as much suffering as it does happiness. The truth for coaches is that life design work doesn't keep change and the turns of the wheel at bay; it does, however, offer clients the opportunity to put their hands on the wheel and turn it at a speed that returns them more quickly to happiness. This is the possibility that conscious coaching offers. We help clients discover that they *can* have their hands on their Wheel of Life. They can manage their lives through phases of pain so that they can navigate these times as smoothly as possible, emerging more resilient and less drained. They can fully experience loss in order to move through it. They can design their lives in the spirit of hope so that authentic happiness occurs more quickly, more easily, and more frequently.

If you have clients who are suffering greatly, you might share the medieval Wheel of Life with them. It offers a perspective on natural changes in human life. Pain in life may be inevitable. Coaches assist their clients to experience and move through that pain as elegantly as possible.

USING THE CONTEMPORARY WHEEL OF LIFE WITH CLIENTS

Master coaches have many different ways to help clients examine and assess their lives. As we said earlier, the Life Balance Wheel is often used at an early session. There, the coach and client examine the ratings the client has assigned. Through discussion, they examine what is behind the client's ratings. This is a relatively informal and conversational process, the goal of which is to help identify early areas for the coaching focus. Other tools, like Frederic Hudson's *Cycle of Renewal* (Hudson, 1999; see p. 93), assist in determining if there is an additional cycle occurring, one that is leading the client to a need for renewal in some life area. The Cycle of Renewal and the Life Balance Wheel are both useful during times of transition for the client. This is a major emphasis at ILCT because we recommend tools that lead to conversations about the whole of the client's life.

185

Sometimes clients come very reluctantly to the task of getting specific about *what is* and *what could be* in specific life areas. They may bring many "shoulds" with them. They can become embarrassed or ashamed about how they've been living, or barely managing, their lives up until now. We believe—and they discover in the context of the coaching relationship—that "the truth shall set you free."

We coach clients to tell the truth and to discover, perhaps for the first time, what they really want in various areas of their lives. In doing so, we use most of the strategies from Dave Ellis's "Ways to Know Yourself" (Ellis & Lankowitz, 1995, pp. 44–45):

1. *Be specific.* Instead of analyzing their lives in a global manner, ask clients to focus on the details of eight to twelve life areas. They often discover that some specific parts of their lives are working very well, although they may not have appreciated this fact because other parts seem powerfully lacking.

2. *Collect the facts.* The satisfaction levels we ask clients to assign, from 1 to 10, allow for comparison and measurement. Over time, clients can track changes in their satisfaction levels, which provides them with feedback about how "on track" their lives are.

3. *Listen to others.* Clients who are working through the life design process often share their work with significant others in their lives, asking for feedback on possible ways to close the gaps. When working with couples, each individual can create a Wheel of Life separately. Then they can share their visions and create a joint vision for their life together.

4. *Evaluate.* The success of life design relies on our ability as coaches to work with our clients to assess how their habits, beliefs, and behaviors may need to be altered in order to close the gaps we have identified.

EXERCISE 8.1
The life design process: Are you thriving or surviving?

1. Ask the clients to describe the current state of life. For each of the life areas listed below (or others that are appropriate for the client), assign a satisfaction rating. Use a scale of 1–10, with 10 as high, 1 as low. Some coaches prefer scales that use 1 to 7, the classic Likert scale, because it has a midpoint. We suggest you use the same scale that you used with the Wheel of Life diagram so that you and the client can refer to it during this exercise.

    "10" means that the clients are absolutely satisfied with that area of their life—that they are *thriving* in it.

    "1" means that the clients are absolutely dissatisfied with that area—that they are *not thriving* in it. They may even be *suffering*.

    The clients can choose areas that they have not addressed on the Wheel of Life. This is their opportunity to be even more specific. For example, the Wheel of Life lists "Family, Friends, and Community" as a category. We encourage the clients to break down that category into three or more categories. For example, if the clients have children as well as other family

EXERCISE 8.1 (continued)

members to consider, they may want to create additional categories, such as one for children and one for parents and/or siblings. Their level of satisfaction may be very different with their parents than with their children or siblings.

_____ Appearance

_____ Family

_____ Finances/Money

_____ Friends and Community

_____ Fun and Play

_____ Health and well-being

_____ Home and Environment

_____ Personal Development and Growth

_____ Primary Relationship (spouse, partner, most intimate relationship)

_____ Spirituality

_____ Work/Career

2. For each of the areas above, ask the clients to write two to three bullet points indicating the key reasons for their rating. Example: "You gave a rating of "3" for "Fun and Play." Why?"

   • Working 6 days/week, 10 hours/day; too tired when I am finished to play with kids

   • Canoe needs repair, so we can't use it and have stopped canoeing

   • Little time to just have fun with my wife and two small children

3. Ask the clients how they want to be. Ask the clients to take four 8 1/2 x 11" sheets of paper and fold each one so that it is divided into four separate areas. Write the name of one life area in each section. If the clients prefer, you may also use 3 x 5" index cards for this purpose, with the main area of focus in the middle of the card and the desired state below it. Leave space on the card so the client can record planned actions and priorities that develop later through coaching.

   Ask the clients to describe *what they really want* in each of the areas of their life from Step 1—that is, what a "10" would be in each area *in the next 12 to 18 months.* This activity is a way of doing visioning with clients and making a vision concrete. Choose an end point far enough out so that the clients can use the interim to realize the vision. This becomes a working document that can be referred to and adjusted as needed.

> ### EXERCISE 8.1 (continued)
>
> Ask the clients to begin the work by addressing the four life areas with the lowest scores. Treat each area separately. The client will end up with a number of bulleted lists, each of which focuses on one area of their life.
>
> Ask the clients to write a *brief* bulleted list—like a vision statement—that addresses each of the areas, using these guidelines:
>
> - Pick a time frame—the next 9, 12, or 18 months. Make sure the clients set a specific time period within 2 years so that they can make this a concrete set of goals and not simply a mental exercise.
> - Ask the clients to focus on what fulfillment would look like and mean for them in each life area within the specific time period. A "10" means they are absolutely satisfied with the area and are thriving in that dimension of life. Ask the clients focus on what they really want, and also to include their vision of what is possible during the time period. What kinds of fulfillment constitute both a deep desire *and* a realistic goal during this period of time? We want clients to dream big as well as to be able to identify realistic steps that will lead them there. It is not our job to judge whether it is realistic or not—that is the clients' determination. The coach's job is to stress the *both-and,* not *either-or,* in this exercise, emphasizing dreams and visions as well as the practical steps needed to attain them.
> - Ask the clients to use present-tense verbs for the bullets or paragraph. Write *as if* they already have that area working just the way they want it.
> - Align the clients' life design work with their work on life purpose. Ask them to refer to their life purpose statement (discussed in Chapter 7) as they do this work. They will ask themselves: "What would fulfillment look like in this area if I were truly living my life purpose?"
>
> It may help the clients to use visualization to imagine more vividly how this area of life would look. They can do that independently of the coach or within a coaching session if needed.

Example 1

Figure 8.3 illustrates how this life design process exercise might look. It is drawn from work Diane Menendez did in midlife. At that time, both of her parents were alive and living in Florida and she lived in the Midwest.

Her parents were in their mid- to late-70s, and her mother had recently experienced a series of small strokes, as well as two hip replacements within a 4-month period. In the example below, Diane uses full sentences in the present tense (not in the future tense) and personalizes using "I."

Figure 8.3

Sample life design exercise

Work/Career	Finances/Money
Primary Relationship	**Family** 1. I consistently support my father as he cares for my mother. 2. I talk to my cousin and his wife at least once a month, and we find ways to support each other. 3. I feel an abiding sense of love for each member of my family, and gratitude that they are a part of who I am in my life. 4. I am fully connected with my sisters-in-law, and we freely share our lives, emotions, and thoughts. 5. My dad and I have found a place for him and my mom to live in Cincinnati that will meet all of our needs for the next 1 to 3 years. 6. I do this willingly and effortlessly, and feel love.

This life design exercise uses the classic coaching strategy: *identify the gap* between what clients have and what they truly want. After working through Steps 1 and 2, the gap between what your clients have now and what they want becomes vividly real. Done well, the visions they create for each area of their life will draw them forward toward them. Your clients will have created a compelling vision of the life they most want for themselves that is achievable in 9 to 18 months.

USING LIFE DESIGN WITH CLIENTS

So far, we've illustrated the key steps that constitute the clients' fieldwork, as they identify key areas, rate level of satisfaction, and then create a +/−12-month specific vision for fulfillment. We recommend coaches ask clients to do the fieldwork in increments, over a period of several weeks, or so that they don't become overwhelmed with the task. It can seem overwhelming to clients to be creating specific visions for a dozen areas of life. On the other hand, many clients get inspired and can complete the visions for all areas within a week or two.

To break down the task over several coaching sessions, ask the clients to do the following, using the worksheet below (Table 8.1), which includes key items and indicators, as well as space for "How I could create it." Tell the clients:

1. Identify two or three life design areas to work on.
2. For each area, write down the three to five key bullet points that you definitely want to have represented in that life area. These might be tangible things, relationships, people, ways of being, ways of doing, and so on. These are either the bullet points or even more specific details drawn from the work in Step 3 above.
3. For each of the three to five items or indicators, identify three to five ways you could choose to create it for yourself.

Table 8.1

Worksheet

Life Design Area #1

_____

Key Items and Indicators

1._____

2._____

3._____

4._____

5._____

Item 1: How I could create it

a._____

b._____

c._____

Item 2: How I could create it

a._____

b._____

c._____

Item 3: How I could create it

a._____

b._____

c._____

Item 4: How I could create it

a._____

b._____

c._____

Item 5: How I could create it

a._____

b._____

c._____

Life Design Area #2

_____

Key Items and Indicators

1._____

2._____

3._____

4._____

5._____

Item 1: How I could create it

a._____

b._____

c._____

Item 2: How I could create it

a._____

b._____

c._____

Item 3: How I could create it

a._____

b._____

c._____

Item 4: How I could create it

a._____

b._____

c._____

Item 5: How I could create it

a._____

b._____

c._____

Ask the clients to pick one of the life design areas where they have a gap they want to close during the next few months. Ask the clients to describe the gap as they see it now (Table 8.2). Then identify some first steps the clients will take to close the gap—steps they can take within the next several weeks. (Make sure clients don't overwhelm themselves by having to describe *all* of the steps.)

Table 8.2

Closing the Gap Worksheet

Life Area: Family

Describe the gap(s) you want to close: (for example)	**First steps you will take to close the gaps:** (for example)
Talk to my cousin and his wife regularly for support. Currently we speak rarely and inconsistently.	• E-mail my cousin and describe what I think would be really desirable: speaking every 1–2 weeks on the phone when we can both relax and there is no crisis. Set up a time for the first of these calls.
I am fully connected with my sisters-in-law, and we freely share our lives, emotions, and thoughts. Right now we don't always get to talk when my husband calls them.	• Make a specific request of my husband— that he place the calls when I am there so I can talk to his sisters after he is finished. (I know he'll say yes; I've just never asked!)
My dad and I have found a place for him and my mom to live in Cincinnati that will meet all of our needs for the next 1 to 2 years. Right now he wants to come, but there are no plans.	• I will ask my dad next time we talk about his parameters for a good place: monthly costs, as well as other considerations. Then I will start researching places so that when they come up this summer we can look at some.

192

FREQUENTLY ASKED QUESTIONS: LIFE DESIGN

Coaches often ask these questions about working with the material from Chapter 7 ("The Power of Purpose) and Chapter 8 ("Design Your Life"): *How do we integrate the life purpose work the clients does with their work in life design?*

We said earlier that fulfillment in life is derived from living from one's primary values and life purpose. This is how we achieve a sense of wholeness, satisfaction, and fulfillment. Consequently, clients benefit from considering this question as they first begin to create their vision and write specific bullets: "How would this life area look in the next 18 months if you were living out your life purpose fully in this area?"

Ask yourself:
How could you coach clients to incorporate their life purpose into the work around each life area? If clients were ignoring purpose, how could you help them consider it as important?

Does it matter whether the clients work with life purpose first? Or can they start with life design?

There's no one way that works best with all clients. Because life design is more specific, this work can be easier for some clients, particularly for those who like concrete, actionable work. It is fine to begin here. If so, the client may need to go back to reconsider their life design work once the work on life purpose is complete, to determine whether each area reflects purposefulness as well as fulfillment.

When midlife clients come for coaching and report extremely low scores on every area of a beginning Wheel of Life assessment, they may need to start with life purpose. The clients would be taking the most holistic and integrated view of their life in that way.

193

Ask yourself:
Under what circumstances would you want to do life purpose work first?

Can you work with clients over a period of years with life design?

Absolutely yes! Because life design focuses on a specific time period, clients will need to update it periodically. As circumstances change, clients will need to change their vision for that life area. Coaches can use this material to create life design visioning retreats with clients, individually or in groups. Many coaches do annual retreats with clients, examining current satisfaction with life areas and designing for the next year or period of time. This is a rich way for coaches to stay connected to their clients over time. The process provides the clients with new energy and perspective. We also suggest that coaches take time each year to review their Wheel of Life and life design, examining and re-creating specific areas to better fulfill their life purpose.

Ask yourself:

Consider the situation of a client who wants to retire in a year. You have been working with him for the past 9 months. How would you use life design to assist him in planning his retirement?

Chapter 9

What Gets In Your Way?

Once clients have identified their life purpose and created a compelling view of what they want for each of the important areas in their life, they are on the path to creating exactly what they want. However, the path may not be an easy one to follow. They may encounter blocks to progress in creating the life they truly want. Ultimately, these hinder them from living a fulfilling life.

What kinds of blocks do coaching clients typically encounter? The most common obstacles are:

- energy drainers: *psychic vampires* (such as clutter) that suck the vitality out of each day
- unmet, and sometimes unacknowledged, needs
- fears, which will be explored in depth in Chapter 14.

Let's begin by exploring the top two blocks—energy drainers and unmet needs—by first knowing how to identify them and then addressing them.

ENERGY DRAINERS

In Chapter 8, we presented a life design exercise in which clients rate their level of satisfaction in each of the areas of their life and identify what would constitute full satisfaction in each area. One strategy for creating more fulfillment is to:

- identify the obstacles, both big and small, that stand in the way of satisfaction;
- figure out what those blocks cost the clients in terms of energy, time, focus, and so on;

- find ways to eliminate, minimize, or effectively manage the blocks, all of which are variations on *do it, delegate it, delay it,* or *dump it.*

This process leads clients to manage their life in a different way.

Blocks to satisfaction are things that drain our energy—things we put up with and endure. They usually come in a variety of sizes.

Category 1. The Little Annoyances—Life's "Gnats"

These are the small things in life that we handle. We usually just brush them off, as we do gnats at a picnic. We ignore them, unaware that these annoyances tax our attention and energy. If they felt more like bees or even mosquitoes, we might do something about them. Mostly, we just deal with them.

Gnats are things such as messy closets and work shelves that keep us from finding things, a crowded garage, an unfinished marketing brochure, a car that needs a tune-up, a broken lock, and dry cleaning to take in for winter storage.

Most of us tend to tolerate these things until they accumulate and *really* bug us. Then we get so annoyed that we finally do something about them. Unfortunately, they may have grown to quite a massive size by that time, just from the accumulation of so many little things. At that point, they may have moved into Category 2.

Category 2. The Big or Chronic Complaints—Life's Sufferings

These issues create tension and crowd us. We are conscious of how they diminish the quality of our life. We probably just accept them as normal because we don't know how to effectively handle them.

Sufferings might be related to long work hours as we start our new business. We cannot delegate because our staff is not well trained. Our demanding clients call us at all hours. Our daughter is upset and says, "You don't ever come to my soccer games, Dad!" We do not take vacations. We don't have time to talk—to share deeply—with our spouse. We have stopped exercising. Our 83-year-old forgetful mother needs more attention than we can afford to give her.

Although gnats and sufferings are a part of life, we don't have to be helpless or passive in the face of them. As the Buddha said, "Life is 10,000 joys and 10,000 sorrows." Every human being must expect to participate in both. In fact, the first Noble Truth of Buddhism is "To live is to suffer"—sorrow is the universal experience of mankind. This teaches us that we don't need to create suffering—there will be plenty of it. The goal is to accept it, embrace it, and move beyond it because that is where growth occurs. Every coaching client can benefit from learning about gnats and sufferings, and doing the following exercise to gain control of, or eliminate, them, which creates more satisfaction.

Step 1. Sit down and identify your personal gnats and sufferings.
List as many as you can right now. Most people's gnats and sufferings come in the areas of work, family, home/environment, and community. Start with these, or return to your life design chart and list your gnats and sufferings for each area of your life.

Step 2. Count the cost.
Anything you tolerate has a cost. It may cost you time, inconvenience, or frustration. The cost may be your own or others' disappointments, or it may be a loss of well-being and vitality. Identify what each gnat and suffering costs you. Ask yourself whether enduring this issue and bearing the cost is worth it. The cost you are paying is probably way too high. If you want fulfillment and balance in your life, you cannot afford to give up pieces of yourself in this way.

Some people acquire energy from suffering and from enduring difficult circumstances. Feeling like a martyr energizes them—handling heavy loads, feeling oppressed, sacrificing for others. Sometimes it even makes them feel heroic to manage suffering and to be miserable. There are better ways to live life—ways that are much more nourishing for both the martyrs and the people in their lives, but these ways are invisible until people stop putting energy into the gnats and sufferings, and start making space for more nourishing activities.

197

Step 3. Do something about each gnat and suffering if the cost is not worth it to you.
There are basically four ways you can swat the gnats and eliminate the sufferings.

- Find a strategy for eliminating them. Create a plan for eliminating each one completely by handling them yourself. That might mean spending a Saturday cleaning up the garage, organizing a garage sale and discarding unsold items, setting a realistic completion date for your brochure and marking it on your calendar, deciding to delegate, or hiring a graphic designer or a writer to complete your brochure.
- Allow the gnats and sufferings to disappear on their own. Once you decide not to have them in your life, some gnats and sufferings will just naturally disappear. They seem to realize that their time is over and just take care of themselves without any effort on your part. These times are a great illustration of the power of intention.

If there is no clear action that can be taken, we sometimes suggest to our clients that they consciously *park* or put aside an issue they are putting up with, to get it out of their focus. Then they work on something else. Lacking the energy that focus brings, the issue often just disappears. This builds on the common idea that *what you resist persists.* Dropping resistance means that the issue stops persisting.

A common example might be people who hate winter and live in Colorado. What they know is that Colorado weather is very changeable. After a few cold and blustery days, the sun comes out. They recognize that their mood changes. They realize then that they can intentionally recognize that "this, too, shall pass." In saying that to themselves, they accept what is—the cold weather—and also focus their attention on what will be. However, if they lived in Nova Scotia, the "this, too, shall pass" strategy might not work for them. This way of thinking—surrendering to what is and anticipating what will come—is effective for things that truly are out of people's control—weather, taxes, and so on. Allowing them instead of resisting them uses the strategy of consciously choosing to *delay.* We don't mean denial here. The choice is to take our focus elsewhere.

- Neutralize them. In order to do this, you look for a compromise—a short-term solution that will take the emotional charge out of the situation. Acknowledge that you cannot do everything at once, and get real about your expectations. Establishing a realistic date for completing your brochure, for example, will take the sting out of it hanging over your head.

- Convert gnats and sufferings into learning opportunities or gratitudes. Some things, such as your 83-year-old mother who is in decline, may be unchangeable facts in your life. What you can change is *how you respond* to these situations. As discussed in a previous chapter, this situation is an opportunity to coach clients to *respond* (to take time to examine choices), as opposed to *react* with a habitual, instantaneous emotion or action. Clients in this situation, for example, might choose to think of how long their mother took care of them: she probably invested at least 16 years of her life in a nurturing, protective, and supportive relationship for their growth. They might choose to be grateful for the opportunity to give something back, or look for the lessons in this challenge.

  A colleague, Michael O'Brien, teaches clients to ask, "What is life calling for here?" as they choose a response. The clients focus their attention on something larger than their own skin when they ask that question. It puts the situation into perspective for them. The clients might choose to be thankful for whatever time they have left with their parent. They might arrange as much support as they can for themselves and seek out opportunities to learn from the situation. They may need to do a life redesign in order to accommodate their situation.

199

Update your list of gnats and sufferings periodically. Revisit your list every 60 days. Add new items and eliminate those you have accomplished. Consider the areas in your life where most of these gnats and sufferings collect. Most of us have a few areas that are especially prone to gnats and sufferings. If you find, for example, that they are mostly at work, take action.

Do not let new ones accumulate or multiply there. One gnat attracts others, and soon you will have a swarm.

Get clear with yourself about the real costs to your vitality. How long are you willing to put up with these annoyances? Set a "termination date" for each of your gnats and sufferings. Put it on your calendar and become a Terminator of the things you have been tolerating. Remember Arnold Schwarzenegger's character who stopped at nothing? Use that kind of energy to handle your gnats and sufferings.

Sometimes gnats and sufferings are linked to how clients meet their needs or live their values. We'll revisit the issue of gnats and sufferings in Chapter 10, which focuses on values. For the current discussion, the following worksheet on energy drainers is a useful tool to use with clients. We teach the importance of this simple tool as a way for clients to get down on paper the things that drain them of energy. This allows them to systematically begin to check drainers off the list. The magic that often happens is that when clients take care of two or three of the items, others tend to disappear as well.

Worksheet 9.1 can be an early fieldwork assignment with new clients. It can be used to focus a sample coaching session with prospective clients. Many coaches also use it as the basis of a short speech or workshop they give to market their services. Clients complete the sheet and experience a coaching session. The conversation may be very brief—maybe just 7 to 10 minutes—but the clients experience the coaching conversation and sees how it focuses them on what they wants in their life.

WORKSHEET 9.1
The energy drainer worksheet

We put up with, accept, take on, and are dragged down by people and situations that we may have come to ignore in our lives rather than address proactively. Take this time to identify those things that drain your energy from positive activities. As you think of more items, add them to your list.

ENERGY DRAINERS AT WORK

1. _____

2. _____

3. _____

ENERGY DRAINERS AT HOME

1. _____

2. _____

3. _____

```
                    WORKSHEET 9.1 (continued)

4. _____      4. _____

5. _____      5. _____

6. _____      6. _____

7. _____      7. _____

8. _____      8. _____

9 _____     9. _____

10. _____     10. _____

11. _____     11. _____

12. _____     12. _____

13. _____     13. _____

14. _____     14. _____

15. _____     15. _____

16. _____     16. _____

17. _____     17. _____

18. _____     18. _____

19. _____     19. _____

20. _____     20. _____
```

Which of these are gnats? Which of these are sufferings? Go back and mark each with a "G" or an "S" to indicate their magnitude.

Which of these can you address right away? Put a star next to two items you can do something about within the next 2 days.

The Energy Drainer Worksheet is a strategy to help clients be conscious of what is added to and can be taken off the Energy Drainer list. The clients begin to experience the energy that can be reclaimed that was attached to the item, chore, or issue. Coaches can request the clients to make a similar list of Energy Gainers, things that impact their life in a positive way, things they love to do (Williams & Davis, 2002, pp. 33–34). When coaches ask clients what they love to do, the clients often find that they have not set aside time for these activities on their calendar. The clients who identify that walks in the park, listening to favorite music, spending time in nature, and going to the theater and museums are energy gainers can use the reclaimed energy to consciously put these activities in their life. Then life begins to change.

IDENTIFYING NEEDS[1]

In most of the modern world, and definitely in the United States, we have collapsed any real distinctions between *having needs* and *being needy.* We say things like, "He's so needy! I just can't stand being around him." "She's letting her neediness ruin that relationship!" How many times have we found ourselves running the other way when we heard someone described as "needy"?

The truth is, we all have needs. They are a normal and natural part of human existence. The trouble comes when we don't acknowledge that our needs exist. When we believe that it is not okay to have needs—when we are so embarrassed about our needs that we deny that they even exist—we drive our needs underground, where they gain power and begin to run our life.

Maslow's Hierarchy: A Classic View of Needs

Most of us grew up afraid of being labeled *needy.* American psychologist Abraham Maslow proposed that every human being has a hierarchy of needs, ranging from security to self-actualization. Figure 9.1 is a recent depiction of this hierarchy.

Some years after he developed his original hierarchy, Maslow added several levels to it. He added *transcendence* as the top level, in 1971, and in 1988 he added *aesthetic needs* and the *need to know and understand,* as precedents for self-actualization.

202

[1] A good portion of this material is drawn from an article by Diane Menendez and Sherry Lowry (2006) that was originally published on the e-zine *The SideRoad.* The full text article may be found at www.sideroad.com/seamless.

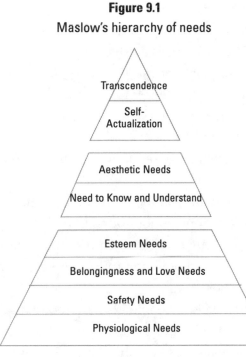

Figure 9.1

Maslow's hierarchy of needs

Transcendence

Self-Actualization

Aesthetic Needs

Need to Know and Understand

Esteem Needs

Belongingness and Love Needs

Safety Needs

Physiological Needs

203

Maslow defined the aesthetic need as the need for symmetry, order, and beauty; self-actualization as the need to find self-fulfillment and realize one's potential; and transcendence as the need to help others find self-fulfillment and realize their potential.

Maslow believed that as we become more self-actualized and transcendent, we develop wisdom and automatically know what to do in a wide variety of situations. This is consistent with the research on emotional intelligence, which suggests that emotional intelligence scores rise over the decades as we age.

That information should have made it acceptable to have needs, but most of us learned to pretend that we had it all together. We could meet all of our own needs just fine, thank you. Our popular heroes—Superman, Wonder Woman, Sheena, John Wayne, and Rambo—were the die hards of the world: they did it alone or the hard way, and didn't seem to need anyone or anything.

A Coaching View of Needs

The construct of self-actualization developed by psychologist Abraham Maslow in the 1960s and 1970s is a relevant and useful contribution to coaching. Maslow's approach moved psychologists beyond the disease model when looking at how a person functions.

In 1968, Maslow redefined self-actualization as the ability of people to do the following (Jon Bellanti, personal communication, March 10, 2005): to bring their powers together in a particularly efficient and intensively enjoyable way and as a state in which people are more integrated and less split, living more fully in the here and now, more self-supporting, more self-accepting, more open to their experiences, more idiosyncratic, more perfectly expressive and spontaneous or more fully functioning, more creative, more humorous, more ego-transcending, and more independent of their lower needs.

Through self-actualization, people become more capable of activating their own potentialities by becoming more truly and fully aware and accepting of their total person with all their gifts and concerns. Therefore, self-actualization is not an end point or destination, but rather a manner of traveling. To become more fully functioning and more fully authentic requires self-actualizing thoughts, visions, awareness, and acceptance not only of who we are but also of who we are becoming. We are not just humans being—we are also humans becoming, constantly in a state of change. To the degree to which we are aware of these changes and take responsibility for them, we are freer to become more of who we are capable of becoming.

Why is Maslow's research important to coaching? Coaches work with mentally and emotionally healthy individuals; we say we work with clients' gifts, their unique creative windows to the world, and their signature strengths. Coaches partner with individuals and groups to develop greater awareness, ownership, and actualization of their gifts as they apply them to their wants, objectives, and life goals for their everyday life. In this, coaches follow the lead of Maslow and his cohorts.

Abraham Maslow was the first to study healthy persons. His model changed the way we view human beings. Maslow's research findings suggested that there are basic biological needs beyond "being" needs—

beyond the basic needs for survival, safety, security, love, and belonging. For example, people placed themselves in risk-taking situations not because there was something *sick,* he believed, but because there was something *sought.* He discovered that individuals had higher-order needs: the needs for self-esteem and esteem from others, as well as self-actualizing needs such as the need to seek truth, goodness, creativity, spontaneity, individuality, and beauty. Maslow also discovered that when basic needs are fulfilled, individuals move up the hierarchy. Although they function at all levels of the hierarchy all the time, their primary awareness is at one or two levels.

Maslow (1971) wrote a delightful chapter titled "High, Low, and Meta-Grumbles." If you listen to what people complain or grumble about, it is easy to understand at what level on the hierarchy they are functioning. People who come to a coach mainly complaining about drivers running traffic lights, concerns about whether they'll have a job the next morning, and concerns about the brakes on their car working properly are functioning at a different level than people who complain about students snapping the branches off a newly planted tree on Main Street, the validity of most diet plans, whether their shoes match their clothing, or how adults are being good role models for our youth. These concerns not only shift the conscious level of personal needs—they also suggest other differences in more fully functioning persons. Therefore, as coaches listen to a cluster of complaints, we obtain a sense of the level at which clients are primarily functioning at their stage in life. This information is relevant to our coaching work since our goal is to make a difference in our clients' lives, and we need to know where they're currently at before we can know how best to be of service.

Maslow discovered that people who function at higher levels on the need hierarchy are more *time-competent* and more *inner-directed.* He defined *time-competent* as the ability to live primarily and effectively in the present and to experience the past, present, and future as a continuous whole. Today is the yesterday of tomorrow. To the coach, change is always in the present and in planning for the future. If we don't live effectively in the present, we can very easily become a prisoner of our past. We can become stuck in how we *have been* rather than focusing

205

on how we *can be.* Coaches work with clients' strengths in the present to design pathways for change that are more consistent with clients' core values and wants.

Maslow defined *inner-directedness* as clients' abilities to rely on their internal gyroscope when making decisions. The more inner-directed, the more the clients are living a life of responsible awareness. Being responsible is, in our language, being *response-able,* possessing the ability to respond and seeing oneself as the author of one's choices. When individuals develop into more responsible people, they soon discover the opposite of the cliché, "There cannot be any freedom without responsibility." They discover that the more response-able they become, the more freedom they possess. Coaches invite clients to become more proactive to discover the freedom and gifts they have and make use of them to take charge of their lives. They take charge by making choices that get them what they want in life and that are consistent with the greater good of others.

Self-actualization is a lifelong developmental process that is consistent with the process and goals of coaching. Since self-actualization requires clients to work with their human needs at various levels of development, coaches need to have a working definition and principles for working with needs. These are simple but can be quite different from how other professions view needs.

> *Definition:* Needs occur at every level of Maslow's hierarchy, and when insufficiently met they keep clients from being their best. Coaches want clients to be working toward being their best. It is not enough to be simply functioning.

Following are several principles we use when working with needs in coaching:

- Needs are situational. They can appear because something in clients' lives changed, so that suddenly a need is not sufficiently met. Whenever clients are undergoing any sort of transition, new needs may appear. For example, in her 30s Diane Menendez worked in a training and development organization at AT&T with many other career-minded women and men of her age. It was an environment in which she thrived. She loved the work, made many friends easily, and enjoyed the vibrancy of her colleagues. People came to the organization from all over the country and the world, which created a stimulating learning environment. Diane had never had so much fun at work. When she was offered a promotion to work in another organization, she took it. It was a small department, very quiet, where much of the work was done individually. After several months, Diane realized how important her need for affiliation was—because it was not being met. Where before the need had been met easily at work, Diane had not recognized it. At her new job, it became very visible. In her new situation, she needed to take steps to meet that need outside of work.

- When a need is insufficiently met, it drives a person. When it is sufficiently met, it goes away, drops back into the background of the client's gestalt.
- Needs are different from wants and desires; the latter are desirable but do not exert the driving force that an unmet need can create.

207

When we live a fulfilled life, we make friends with our needs. How do we do this?

- Acknowledge our needs—they exist; they are real.
- Identify the needs we now have.
- Discover how our needs are getting met and whether those ways nourish us.
- Find satisfying and healthy ways to meet each of our needs.

The reason we teach the importance of awareness of needs and addressing them is that, as we said earlier, needs can drive our choices and possibilities. If clients are unaware of their needs, they will be unconsciously driven to satisfy them. Although they may say that they want to achieve a particular goal, they will find themselves first doing things that satisfy the needs and only second doing things that address their goals.

A second reason for addressing needs, which we learned from Thomas Leonard, founder of Coach University, becomes clear if we look at needs metaphorically, like a green lawn that needs water in the summer. Many people who live in a dry climate install an automatic sprinkler system so that the grass is watered without them having to think about it. The yard needs water regularly, but because it is getting it, the need is automatically met and there is no scarcity. The goal for managing needs is similar: to recognize them and build in an automatic system to meet the needs.

For example, clients might have a need for recognition. Because it sounds egotistical to them, they deny having the need. However, the need is still there, even though they are unconscious of it. They meet it in a way that isn't effective for them. They appear thirsty for recognition. At work, they talk too much about any small success they have and appear competitive with teammates. Teammates describe them as boastful. A healthy way to meet the need for recognition might be to find alternatives, such as volunteering for a community service organization or a project they believed in. When a need is consciously acknowledged, it becomes much more possible to find healthy ways to meet it, which then can be systematized.

The following exercise, which expands on the above steps, is a good one for supporting clients in making friends with their needs. As the coach, it is important not to harshly judge clients' needs. While you may not have a need for dominance, for example, clients may express their need in this way. We believe that needs drive a person's beliefs, actions, and attitudes. They may at times appear neurotic, narcissistic, or misguided. However, in coaching we have found that when explored, the needs for dominance, power, and control are underlain by original unmet needs, such as the need for acceptance, recognition, or being valued. The point for the coach is to help clients find healthy ways of fulfilling needs that are in alignment with their purpose, values, and desires for their life. Whenever possible, we want the clients to build something into their life so that the need can be consistently sufficiently met. When that occurs, the need is no longer a driving force.

Step 1. Acknowledge That We Have Needs

Our needs are those things that are essential to us now in our life—essential to us doing our best, having our best, and being our best. When a need is fulfilled, we do not think much about it, much as breathable air is essential to humans but normally occurs without conscious thought or effort. Unless we are in danger of suffocation, we may not think about the breathing process. When we don't have enough clean air to breathe, our energy pours into meeting that need.

Most of us have enough air for that not to be a concern. At any given time, however, we may experience insufficiency in the areas of any of about 100+ other needs, including the needs for achievement, intimacy, excellence, results, companionship, and beauty, encouragement, allies, mentors, and so on.

How do we recognize a need? We can often identify needs by tracking some of our emotions. When a need is *not* met, we may feel frustrated, fearful, disappointed, hurt, and angry. When a need is met, we may feel pleased, excited, and motivated. When we track our emotions and discover patterns of difficult and charged emotions, we are on the trail of a need. This is explained in Step 2 below. These are opportunities to become awakened to our needs and begin seeking ways to fill them sufficiently.

An unmet need causes us to feel empty, incomplete, or less than whole. We have a nagging feeling that something isn't right. In contrast, when we *aren't* being driven by needs, we have the full freedom to be ourselves.

A need can be mistaken for a desire or a want. Consumer societies such as that of the United States teach children and young adults not to distinguish between needs and wants. Advertising, in fact, turns wants into needs in order to maximize sales. The way to distinguish a need is to notice if we can't live effectively or happily without it for more than a short time (hours or days—not weeks). If that's the case, it's probably a need. In the example of Diane Menendez's work, she began to feel lonely after the first several weeks at her new job, which was an unfamiliar feeling for her as an adult. The emotion of loneliness led her to recognize her need for friendship and affiliation with other women.

Let's use the example of the need for security. If it were simply a desire for security, we would want it and perhaps even work to obtain it, but life would be okay without it. The difference between need and desire, then, is one of intensity. If we feel a sense of uneasiness, foreboding, or discomfort with it left unfulfilled, it's probably a need.

Another indicator of a need is that we experience a feeling of relief when it is filled. If we simply desire or want security and then obtain it, we feel more of a sense of satisfaction, similar to having accomplished a goal.

One question coaches ask their clients is, "How would you know this need was sufficiently met in your life right now? That is, what would make the need stop being a driver of attention, behavior, or emotion?" Each of us will have particular ways to identify when a need is adequately met. We may recognize it through our thoughts, our emotions, or a physical sensation—or in all of these ways. In Diane Menendez's example, she recognized that her need for affiliation was met when she no longer felt lonely for friends.

210

Step 2. What Are Your Five Greatest Needs Right Now?
As you create a balanced and fulfilled life, it's helpful to recognize the needs you have right now. The following exercise involves creating a list of your top five needs.

You may find it easy to articulate your needs. You may already know what is causing you pain or tension. For example, you may already know that you want and need more affection from your spouse, more peace and quiet in the morning, more energy, or more evidence of business results.

Needs generally fall under one of four major categories:

1. *Needs for security.* For example: safety, protection, stability, information, duty, clarity, certainty, honesty, financial security, order, authenticity, commitment to meet obligations.
2. *Needs for power and influence.* For example: control, wealth, authority, management, morality, dominance, freedom, perfection, visibility, leadership, acknowledgment, praise, recognition, influence.

3. *Needs for achievement or attainment.* For example: to create, accomplish, achieve results, strive for, perform, excel, excellence, attain calmness and peace, be busy, be responsible, succeed, make a contribution, be useful, be of service.
4. *Needs for intimacy, relationship, and connection.* For example: to be listened to, needed, loved, touched, helped, included, cherished, appreciated, connected, central to a group; to collaborate and communicate, be connected with something greater than oneself.

If you have trouble identifying your needs, that might be an indication that you don't think it is acceptable to have needs. Perhaps you are ashamed of them or you have denied them for so long that you fool yourself about having them.

> ✎ *Write down your top 10 needs. If it would be helpful, start with a longer list and then narrow it down.*

My top 10 current needs are:

1. _____
2. _____
3. _____
4. _____
5. _____
6. _____
7. _____
8. _____
9. _____
10. _____

Review your list and place an asterisk (*) by the top three. Prioritize them, if you can, with your top need identified as #1, the next need as #2, and so on.

211

Step 3. Discover How Your Needs Are Met and Whether Those Ways Nourish You

Reflect back on the life design process in Chapter 8 (page 186). In Step 1, you rated the current state of your life in many dimensions:

- Work/career
- Finances
- Family
- Friends/community
- Primary relationship
- Home/environment
- Appearance
- Health
- Personal development and growth
- Spirituality
- Fun and play

Rate your needs as they apply to dimensions of your life. For each of the five needs you identified above, assign a rating, from +5 to −5, as it applies to the various dimensions of your life:

+5 = Need gets fully met in this dimension
 0 = Need does not show up in this dimension
−5 = Need does not get met at all in this dimension

Here is one client's brief list:

Need for inclusion:
Work: −3 (do not get invited to lunches)
Home: +5 (feel very included with family)
Friends: +2 (some invitations; want more)

List the ways you meet each of your needs. For example: You may try to be present at every work meeting because you want to be included. Your work may be suffering because you are spreading yourself too thin and cannot get everything done. Ask yourself: What is the exchange I make to get this need met? Is it worth it?

Look back at the list of gnats and sufferings you created earlier in this chapter. Are any of these present because you are trying to meet another need? For example, see if you wrote, "I have too many meetings at work." If so, consider the possibility that you might stop attending half of these meetings, but that you continue to attend in an attempt to meet your need for inclusion.

Step 4. Find Satisfying and Healthy Ways to Meet Each of Your Needs
Be scrupulous and take time when you examine your needs. Our actions are mostly unconscious—autopiloted by expectations based on what we think we want. Usually a deeper, unexpressed need is present. Becoming more aware of these underlying needs can help us make better choices and have more satisfying relationships. For example, we may seek attention when we really want acknowledgment. We may seek sexual companions when we really want intimacy. We may seek money when we really need security. We may seek answers when we really need assistance. We may seek power when the deeper need is for respect. We may seek distance when we really need freedom.

Ideally, you want to meet your needs to your full satisfaction now, and you want to do so in ways that are healthy—ways that allow you to create a fulfilled life. How do you do this?

1. Examine each need and ask: How can I meet this need easily and without great effort? Is there another dimension of my life where I can meet this need more easily and fully?
2. Make a list of at least three ways you can meet each need more easily, without a high cost, and in a more satisfying way during the next 2 to 4 weeks. Then take action based on your list. Experiment until you meet your needs—until they are fulfilled. Eventually, you will be able to remove each need from your list.

Case Study: Jerry's Needs
Jerry is an entrepreneur with a significant need for achievement. He looks to work to satisfy this need, but with a new business, he has not yet

213

received any accolades for his efforts. His need drives him disproportion-ately. It leaks into other areas of his life. He then tries to meet his need for results at home. He bosses around his family and makes to-do lists for them. He looks to an adult sister to take care of something when he could really do it better himself. His standards are very high, and she feels criticized. He overorganizes tasks to be done. He complains about a church committee that does effectively address a problem.

Here is what he could do instead:

At home, he could take on the job that he delegates to his sister, who simply cannot meet his standards. He could scratch the to-do lists for others and recognize that it doesn't work to set priorities for other people that are not their priorities. He could work with his family to design new priorities that align with everyone's needs—or he could do those tasks himself that are on only his agenda.

In his community, he could take on an active leadership role on his church board in order to have the satisfaction of short-term results. He could get other people involved who have influence. Together they could create and implement an action plan.

At work, he could start a new project to meet his need for achieve-ment. The project might include: upgrading his client list, asking more directly for feedback from key clients, retraining his staff, tight-ening up marketing, and starting a targeted marketing initiative.

Fulfilling Needs Is Critical to Clients

Clients cannot live a fulfilled and balanced life while their needs drive them. In fact, needs are like the dust on a diamond—they obscure the possibility of fully living our purpose and values.

Humans function better and live more satisfying lives when our work and our whole life express our core values. Your clients will gain great benefit from identifying and meeting needs in the key arenas of their lives. When you support them through this process, you move them forward on the path toward fulfillment and balance.

Additional Suggestions to Help Identify and Work With Needs

Needs are something people usually meet by striving to gain something externally or by contrasting current life and desired life. We learn more about needs by comparing or noticing how well we manage external actions and opinions, which are usually outside of our control.

For example, we may measure our need for approval by how often we are complimented or acknowledged publicly. When that happens frequently, our need for approval may sometimes be filled to capacity. At that point, it may no longer be a need. When it is filled, we may find that our self-esteem is sufficiently strong that we can rearrange our life so that this particular need no longer surfaces and is no longer an issue.

Maslow once said that if a need were at least 60% met, it would set us free, so to speak. Once this happens, we can put our energies into meeting a higher-order need. It is at this point that our values begin to draw our attention.

When our basic needs for a secure shelter, sufficient food, and a stable income are met, we may, as an example, meet our need to be more responsible by taking a time-management class. That experience may lead us to develop the new habit of spending time with a calendar/organizer for 10 minutes each morning, which supports a need to be responsible. We probably would not prioritize every day with a calendar/organizer if we were unemployed, could not pay our rent, or were starving.

Needs tend to drive us until we understand how to drive and direct them. When we reach this point, we establish ways in our life to meet our needs with less effort and expense. This is one of the goals coaches have for their clients: that their lives run more smoothly and that they are freed up to focus more attention on higher-order aspects of their lives, such as their values and their purpose. We teach that needs and values can be directly related to each other; in other words, once a need is met, it can become a value that a person prioritizes and lives by, such as peace and tranquillity. An underlying value can create a driving need. If people do not have peace and tranquillity in their life, it will operate as a need, driving them. When the need is met, they can then hold it as a value, living from it rather than being driven by it. We say more about this in the next chapter on values.

Chapter 10

Steering Your Life by True North

ALIGNING VALUES, ACTIONS, AND HABITS

Values function like compass points for us. A compass needle points toward true north and acts as a consistent guide for mariners and travelers. Travelers rarely get lost if they have a working compass. Our values serve us in a similar way, guiding us in determining the direction of our life. When we align with our values, they help us make critical decisions. They also function as key indicators that we are out of integrity, which is evidenced by our frustration, anger, or feeling off-center.

What Do We Mean by Values?

We've heard it said that one of the most important things in life is to decide what is most important.

Merriam-Webster's Collegiate Dictionary defines *value* as "something (as a principle or quality) intrinsically valuable or desirable." A thesaurus offers *worth* and *quality* as synonyms for the kinds of values we're considering here—those that are important to individuals. Values are beliefs, qualities, or philosophies that are meaningful to individuals, so much so that they are willing to shape their lives and actions to live by them.

Values are important in coaching because clients' core values, or personal value systems, lead them to make certain judgments and decisions, which prompt them to take certain actions that lead to certain results. By understanding clients' core values, we can predict their actions.

A value or belief is a trust or conviction—a feeling, idea, or opinion—about a principle, standard, or aspect of life that is considered to be true, desirable, and inherently worthwhile.

Whether or not we are consciously aware of them, every individual has a number of personal values. Values can range from the commonplace—the belief in hard work, self-reliance, and punctuality—to more psychological values, such as concern for others, trust in others, and harmony of purpose.

Coaches often find it helpful to consider three kinds—or levels—of values:

- *The Superficial "Shoulds"*—These are relatively superficial values we hold that come primarily from things we think we *should* believe, do, or act in accordance with. These kinds of values, which are frequently unexamined, often have their origin in messages we "swallowed whole" from parents, teachers, our church, or some other authority, usually when we were young.
- *Chosen Values*—These are values we hold and attempt to uphold because they resonate with us personally. We have selected them as important to fulfill, and we act in accordance with them as consistently as possible.
- *Core Values*—These are the three to five critically important personal values we hold. When we are not living our values consistently, we are likely to feel dissatisfied, depressed, embarrassed, and even ashamed. It's impossible to lead a fulfilling life that does not honor or that is out of alignment with our core values.

Values create energy toward their fulfillment through action and results. When we examine the lives of famous people, we often learn about important personal values that shaped their lives by guiding their actions and choices. These personal values propelled them to great achievement and success.

For example, one famous actor was motivated by his commitment to social justice, which caused him to seek out powerful acting roles related to that value. A famous business CEO was motivated by the personal value that computers should be easy to use for the average person. Regardless of the unique personal values that guided various famous people's lives, it was ultimately their commitment to implementation that paved the way to their great success.

Values, as determinants of our priorities, are the silent forces behind many of our actions and decisions. When we live according to our values, we are healthier and more satisfied. Research reveals that

217

personal values are key to physicians' job satisfaction. A study of family physicians found that job satisfaction is highest among those who identify benevolence as a guiding principle in their lives. Other significant values include a sense of independence and self-direction, as well as the opportunity to train medical students. The researchers concluded that physicians who identify and adhere to their own personal values in their work will be less vulnerable to burnout, and could help raise the quality of care (Medical College of Wisconsin Health News, 2000).

Working With Values Is Critical to Great Coaching

These principles assist us in coaching clients around values:

- *The power of values.* The deepest, most powerful, and most centering force for an individual, business, or society is its values. When we coach at the level of values, outer circumstances can change 10 times faster and have much more sustained impact than if we merely try to change things on the surface.
- *Values reflect the highest thoughts.* An individual's personal values are a reflection of the highest principles of mind and thought, and may even be part of the spiritual domain. Values release tremendous potential for success, accomplishment, and happiness.
- *A values-based life is a fulfilled life.* When clients live their life in line with their values, it engenders a sense of well-being, self-respect, and self-esteem. When they live a life that violates their values, it can lead to confusion, frustration, and depression.
- *Conscious work on values is critical.* Unless or until clients consciously explore, distinguish, and clearly delineate their personal values or beliefs, it's impossible to orient and create a personal or professional life around them.
- *Needs come first.* Clients can't live their values when they are driven by insufficiently satisfied needs. Addressing these needs takes precedence and eventually clears the path for clients to focus on and align with their values.

Most clients have not consciously worked with their values. In the 1970s and 1980s, schools and universities sometimes offered values clar-

218

ification courses, often based on the work of Sydney Simon (Simon, 1972). Both Pat Williams and Diane Menendez worked with undergraduates and teachers to help them clarify their own values and bring the work into high schools. Strangely enough, outside of education, the importance of values clarification seemed to wane. We believe this is one of the reasons why life coaching surfaced so strongly in the 21st century. Pat can distinctly remember being in a course at the University of West Georgia where he clarified his values. It was an affirming experience to illuminate why he had passion for what he did—and it explained the importance of aligning his actions with his values. In Diane's case, she combined her two key values, learning and supporting others, to create her first graduate program and course of study. For both of us, values have been a critical focus throughout our lives, and we consequently make values work a critical focus in ILCT's training.

Even those who have experience with this realm of their life may not have done the challenging work of assessing whether their life and actions are in line with their values. Clients frequently come into coaching because they are experiencing a radical rift between their current external or internal way of being and their core values. They may not recognize that this issue is central to many of the challenges in their life.

For example, imagine clients who value family, but who are working at a job that requires long hours, which precludes spending much quality time with family members. If those client's work situation mandates the violation of a deeply held value, they will likely experience serious inner conflict. If clients value respect, yet their opinions and views are not listened to at work, their life is in conflict with one of their values. The same is true of people who value health but do not make the effort to get regular exercise. These kinds of situations can cause clients considerable pain and confusion.

The superficial values (the "shoulds") clients hold may need to be challenged, developed, or worked with through coaching so that the clients do not use them as the basis for making critical decisions. Sometimes clients confuse other people's values with their own. They may have "inherited" values through their family or other early influences that, when examined closely, do not truly belong or fit and must be set

219

aside or outgrown. Also, values may shift as circumstances and priorities change.

Life coaching can help clients to explore and give credence to their unique set of values at any point in their life. Clients are able to be more self-directed and effective when they consciously choose which values have a high priority in their life—in other words, which ones they want to keep and live by as an adult. Clarity about values is particularly important when values come into conflict with one another. As clients work to redesign their life, they will make critical decisions based on the secure compass point—the true north—that a clear set of personal values provides.

Identifying Values[1]
Coaching clients seek a life that has value—one that satisfies a deep and authentic longing for meaning. When they align their work and life with their core values, they find the meaning they sought and satisfy the longing. Once clients have addressed their basic needs, their strongest motivators, and greatest sources of deep meaning and their core values—can become the primary drivers of their life.

Clients whose life and work aren't aligned with their core values may be getting results but not thriving or experiencing full satisfaction. They may be bored, on the edge of burnout, or just living in a comfortable rut. Aligning their life with their core values releases two things: incredible creativity, and a sense of immense satisfaction and well-being. When these are released, their potential for outrageous success is maximized.

Core Values Are Those We Naturally Want to Act On
Core values are those qualities that have intrinsic worth for an individual. When our behavior is aligned with our most deeply held values, our actions are desirable and worthy of esteem for their own sake.

Take, for example, the value of integrity. How do you know someone has integrity? If people hold integrity as a core value, they just naturally demonstrate it, don't they? And don't you just naturally recognize it? If

[1]The following is adapted from a work that appeared in several articles written by Diane Menendez and Sherry Lowry (2006) in the e-zine, *TheSideRoad*, at www.sideroad.com/seamless.

clients hold the core value of service to others, for example, helping someone in need is an action they'll naturally take because they believe it's desirable and worthy. It will feel good to the clients to honor that value by acting on it and making more of their life consistent with it.

Our particular set of values is unique to each of us. We may not expect others to do what we do or derive the same sense of self-worth from it. The coach must suspend judgment about the clients' values and help the clients identify and articulate their values. The values then become compass points—the true north—for directing the clients' life journey and choices.

Coaching around values helps clients make frequent *course corrections, both big and small.* This is like an airplane that is actually offcourse about 90% of the time, arriving at its destination through a series of course corrections, some minor and others major, due to weather, traffic, or turbulence.

It is our belief that most people look to others too much for validation and lack sufficient tools for looking inside to access inner validation. They don't know how to access or articulate their values. Clients may come into coaching with a felt sense that they are off course. Working with values gets them back on track.

We believe people naturally act in accordance with their values whenever they have the opportunity. But they can only do that when they are familiar with their values and consciously make choices based on values.

Knowing and Articulating Values
The real benefit in supporting clients to know and be able to clearly articulate their values is so that they can create more opportunities to honor themselves, increase their satisfaction and sense of meaning and worth, and find fulfillment. The coaching relationship supports clients to design their time and their life to maximize opportunities to live their values fully. Assist clients to find the language they need to describe their values in compelling terms to themselves and others. It is critical for clients to know what they stand for before starting to set goals around values and before working on life design.

Identifying Core Values

Most of us have three to five core values that are abiding. They may have been with us since childhood. We generally can trust that they'll continue to be our core values for many years. Identifying these core values through a variety of values exercises can help clients find inspiration.

We work with clients on core values using a variety of exercises, which we include below. We recommend that clients create a list of three to five items for each exercise. Then, putting all the work together, they can cross out any repeated items and select the words that have the most resonance for them. Like a tuning fork, they'll be able to feel an internal "ring"—like a vibration on a subtle level—when they say each of those words aloud. When they imagine living those values, the thought should bring them a great sense of satisfaction and joy. What if it doesn't? Then they may be listing *superficial values,* what they have been told they should do, should believe, or should value—not their own core values. If this is the case, they need to go back and start again. Living out a list of "shoulds" does not elicit a sense of joy and satisfaction.

You can choose from any of the following exercises with your clients. Coaches generally have preferences for which exercises work best with their particular coaching clients. Values work is generally not done in just one session. Sometimes it is useful to give the clients several exercises over several sessions as different means for identifying their values. Diane Menendez prefers to use a combination of Values Exercise #3 and Values Exercise #1 below, so that her clients have both a cognitive and an experiential path for identifying values. She finds that this works well with very intellectual clients who wouldn't turn first to their personal experience but might be guided more by what they think their values should be, given their roles or work. Pat Williams frequently starts with Exercise 10.2 because he likes to go back to the client's formative years when values began to appear.

EXERCISE 10.1
Values exercise #1

Identify your values from the list below, which is drawn from the work of researchers and experts in motivation. Read through the examples and circle 10 or more words to which you are drawn, or list your own. Select those that are most important to you as guides for how you act or as components of a values-oriented life. Feel free to add any values of your own to this list. Then use the three exercises below to help you whittle your list down to three to five core values.

From reviewing various writings on values, we believe that generally values are drawn from these three major areas of our lives:

- *Experiencing:* Values that are fulfilled through what you experience, through what comes to you and how you respond, through acting on the world outside of you, and through achieving.

  Examples of Experiencing: Discovering, questing, catalyzing, achieving mastery or excellence, teaching, entertaining, ministering, communicating, appreciating what is, playing sports, joining with others, inspiring others, leading others, showing expertise, sensing fully, participating, exploring, guiding, nurturing, being a model, dancing, experiencing pleasure, doing, and acting with speed.

- *Creating:* Values that are fulfilled through what we bring into existence through our unique selves.

  Examples of Creating: Clarifying, beautifying, innovating, ordering, creating, generating symmetry, ideas, discipline, novelty, originality, intuition, and designing, playing, and architecting.

- *Being:* Values that are fulfilled through our attitudes, our mind-sets, our emotions, and the qualities of our character.

  Examples of Being: Integrity, joy, love, peace, truth, uniqueness, loyalty, empathy, spirituality, authenticity, godliness, flow, and energy.

223

EXERCISE 10.2
Values exercise #2

Think back to the qualities you had as a child. List five to 10 qualities that were true of you between the ages of 6 and 12.

You've been naturally drawn toward certain things ever since you were a child, when some qualities were just naturally part of you. You may have been naturally creative or thoughtful, or a lover of nature or beauty. You may have been a natural helper of others or may have been drawn to things that were new or different. Or perhaps you were an experimenter or explorer. These qualities may be among your core values or may be clues to help you identify them.

Sit down and quickly list five to 10 of these qualities right now. Circle all of those qualities that are still a part of your life and that come naturally to you. Include anything you would be and do if your work, time, and life supported you in fulfilling them. Also include things that people cannot stop you from doing.

EXERCISE 10.3
Values exercise #3

Make a list of 10 to 12 times in the past 2 to 5 years when you were being and doing your absolute best. These are times when you felt you were living your "best self"—living your values.

(One of the exercises in Chapter 7 asks clients to make a list of times in their life when they were "on purpose." You may want to use that exercise as a jumping-off point by having clients ask, for each of those times, "What values was I displaying here?" Ask clients to write a word or two indicating the value that was being fulfilled in each example.)

EXERCISE 10.4
Values exercise #4

Ask three people who know you well to name your values. Sometimes our values are more obvious to others than they are to us. Our values show up, no matter what. Because our values are one of our key driving forces, they show up in the decisions we make, the work we choose, and the things that bring us pleasure (and pain, when we disregard our values).

Write down what you hear from these three people. Ask questions for clarity, but mainly just listen. Don't argue with what you hear—treat it as a gift and a potential window into your true self.

LIVING YOUR VALUES

Once clients identify their core values, they will benefit from exploring the extent to which their life is informed by those values. This exploration can create "aha" experiences as clients make deeper connections between their core self and the ways in which their life is and is not an expression of their core values. This exploration also opens the door to many coaching opportunities because it can reveal gaps between a client's actual and ideal life.

The following exercises are designed to support clients in exploring ways to live their values.

Live Your Values: Three Exercises

EXERCISE 10.5
Reflect on your values and your life for a week

Take a week to find out to what extent you are living out your core values. Track how you are spending your time. Each time you participate in something that gives you a full sense of satisfaction, record it on your values list. At the end of the week, you hopefully will have listed six or more examples under each of your core values.

When you've designed your life to be aligned with your values, the possibility for fulfillment is maximized. This translates as expressing your values through your choices and behaviors on a daily basis. Living your values isn't a thing you save for weekends or vacations. When your life is consistently aligned with your values, you are intensely creative and you experience immense satisfaction and well-being.

EXERCISE 10.6
Get clear about your top three to five values

Write them down and hang them on your bathroom mirror. Your values are the *habits of your heart*. You can only live your values if you're clear about what they are and are conscious of them every day. When you clearly identify your core values, you'll feel an immense sense of relief at articulating what's most important to you.

EXERCISE 10.7
Pick one goal that will allow you to demonstrate one of your values

Create a goal that will allow you to measure and observe how well you demonstrate one of your core values through acting on it. Identify any blocks you'll need to eliminate in order to free your energy to live the value.

225

Case Example

A client explored her core values of creativity and living with passion. When she looked at her life, she saw that her needs for structure and detail were getting in the way of living from those two values. She set a goal of turning first to her intuition when she was making decisions. In other words, before she analyzed her situation and put a structure in place for solving a problem, she asked herself, "What do I intuitively believe is the right answer or approach here?" She held herself accountable for doing this every time she had a business or personal problem to solve during a 30-day period. She wrote down her intuitive insights to make them concrete. Then she let herself use her other analytical skills.

As a result of this process, she found that her decision making was easier and more efficient. Her solutions were more creative because she was living her values as she worked and consequently allowing herself to thrive. Her solutions were also more satisfying and more an expression of her core self. The actual solution was more in line with her deepest desires because she listened to herself at a deeper level and accessed a deeper level of knowing.

Creating New Opportunities for Living From Your Values

A key principle that coaches bring to their work with clients is: look to yourself, not to the outside world, for satisfaction. That's another reminder of why we call this coaching from the inside out. Not all opportunities are created equal! Sometimes current projects or clients will not allow you to fully live your core values; you will thrive when you're living your values, but don't do it because you expect to be rewarded by others. The reward is your thriving.

Another example: An advertising client who had a core value of creativity was frustrated at work. He would create and present eight terrific ad options to his clients, yet the clients consistently chose the least creative options. He learned over time that the real joy was in the creation itself. As a result, he quit "overdelivering" to clients who couldn't appreciate this aspect of his creativity, and he eliminated his own disappointment in their lack of discrimination. Then he created a portfolio of all the extra jewels they didn't select and used them to market outside his current client base to more creative companies.

Aligning Life and Work Goals With Core Values

Many clients bring desires for greater life balance to coaching. Often one aspect of balance is that the clients' core values are out of alignment in their work. It can seem difficult to them to align their values with their work if it seems to them that their organization doesn't support this. This can be particularly true if the clients work in a large, bureaucratic corporation. Here are some exercises to support clients in aligning their life and work goals with their core values.

EXERCISE 10.8
Goals

Make a list of your short-term goals for the next 60 to 90 days. Then make a list of your long-term goals for the next 2 to 5 years. Examine these lists closely. For each of the goals listed, assess whether you can really live out your core values as you meet these goals. You may need to change the goals themselves, or you may need to change your plans for attaining them.

Say you're building a business that requires a great deal of solo work, yet you have a core value of being a close friend. You may need to reprioritize in order to stay connected with your close friends, or you might get your friends involved in your business by creating a *master mind group* (Greenstreet, 2004). A master mind group is a group that creates a synergy of energy, commitment, and creativity as group members meet to support one another in their desires and intentions. The concept of the master mind group was formally introduced by Napoleon Hill in the early 1900s in his timeless classic *Think and Grow Rich*. He wrote about the master mind principle as "the coordination of knowledge and effort of two or more people who work toward a definite purpose in the spirit of harmony."

For each of your three to five core values, create a list of ways you can live them regularly.

Brainstorm 8 to 10 ways, both small and large, that you can live out your core values daily, weekly, and monthly. These are your "values rules of the road," so to speak. It's not enough to have only a few opportunities to live out your values each month. A life that allows you to thrive is one where you live out your core values daily.

227

EXERCISE 10.8 (continued)

When this happens, you'll see the result—your energy is higher, your creativity flows, and your work and life feel almost effortless.

Examine your current week. Where are each of your values being expressed?

Take a look at your weekly calendar. Circle the places where you found you were living out a value. Find ways to increase those activities during your week. For the value of creativity, for example, you might do the following:

- Get outside every day. Connect with nature. Notice what's around you.
- Keep a daily journal. Write for 20 minutes every morning.
- Keep flowers, greenery, and other living things around you.
- Change the things around your desk so that you are stimulated by what you look at as you work. Get a fountain in the proximity of your desk.

Eliminate things that block you from living out of a core value.

Take another look at your weekly planner. Draw a square around the activities that are "blockers" for you—activities that act as obstacles to you living your core values. You may want to delegate these or to let them go.

Keep your values list in front of you at all times.

Write your values on a sticky note that you post on each day of your planner. Look for opportunities for fulfilling your values as you get calls, consider projects, and do your work. Remember: a life in which you thrive is one in which you live out of your values. Redesigning your life to make that possible brings endless rewards.

ARE VALUES DRIVEN BY PLEASURE OR PAIN?

When clients have identified their top values, they will be able to recognize both their significance and their ability to live through them or honor them more consciously in their daily life. In short, they can lead clients to a new perspective on what they will allow in their life from this point forward and what they will not allow.

Values work can also take clients to a different place with a different perspective. A key piece in this shift in perspective comes when the clients ask themselves: "Is this value driven by pain or pleasure?" The odds are high that *all* of the clients' values provide one type of benefit. Another valuable question for clients is: "Is this a value that helps me maximize pleasure and enjoyment, or is it one that helps me avoid pain or penalty?" A value driven by pleasure tends to increase the clients' motivation and joy when living it. A value driven by avoidance of pain suggests that the clients are less focused in present time and are directing attention toward the future. Sometimes this means that the clients are living lower on the hierarchy of needs than is desirable and fulfilling. This may indicate that there's some additional work that the coach can do with the clients to explore what is being avoided.

Let's look at a concrete example with the value of wellness. One person may live this value by having a weekly or monthly massage. However, if a chronic pain condition is the motivating factor, the massage may be a pain-driven value activity that serves to alleviate or prevent pain. In contrast, if a person in great physical condition elects to have regularly scheduled massages for the sheer joy of it, massage would be more of a pleasure-driven value for that person. We aren't saying that pain-driven values are not important or that they shouldn't be central to clients. The coach needs to look for patterns in the clients' values and engage the clients in reflection about them. Values work brings to consciousness the clients' values that might otherwise be out of the clients' awareness. Once the clients are conscious of them, values do act as a true north point of a compass, guiding the clients in a direction which makes their life journey less haphazard and more purposeful.

For each of the values clients have identified, have them ask themselves: "If I do not get to live through a pleasure-driven value for a week or month, will I feel the loss of generating a good experience? If I fail to live through or honor a pain-driven value, will I notice anything more than a sense of regret?"

The question to examine with clients is, "Do I want to have choice about whether my values are driven by pain or pleasure?" If they do want to have choice, they have an opportunity to implement their preference regarding the kind of values they want to make primary.

We have seldom found clients to have all of their top five values be pain-driven. Asking clients to reflect on values driven by pleasure versus pain is an important way of deepening their understanding about their choices and their life.

TEN HELPFUL HABITS

Our habits are really our values in action. When we look at our habits, we discover the attitudes and mind-sets that drive our life—our personal operating program. One way to create more fulfillment is to create habits that bring health, joy, and satisfaction. Based on the values work in this chapter, you can encourage clients to identify three to five helpful habits (daily or weekly) that they commit to implementing in the next 10 weeks.

We ask our clients to examine their daily calendar to compare the reality of how they spend their time as compared with the values they have articulated. For example, a busy executive might say he values family and personal balance. Yet his calendar shows only one evening at home eating dinner with his family, four evenings traveling out of state, and no play or exercise time. He also reports that he takes work home with him.

Once clients uncover their values, we ask them to begin blocking time in their calendars that reflects their values. The clients make friends with their calendars by blocking in daily self-care time, date nights with their spouses, or children's sports games. There is an old law that work seems to expand to the time available. Committing a values-directed activity to a calendar is a way in which clients hold themselves accountable for acting in accordance with their values. The calendar and the Palm Pilot are modern-day conveniences that can support this practice.

We suggest that clients take charge of their schedules instead of being controlled by them. In the above example, the client decided that he would not answer work messages after 8:00 p.m., which allowed him to have uninterrupted time with his children and wife in the evening. While 8:00 p.m. sounded late to his coach, it was a radical departure from being on call 24/7 to his phone's text-messaging system. The next radical departure for this client took place when he agreed to his coach's request to leave his computer home when he went on vacation.

DEVELOPING NEW VALUES

Sometimes we find ourselves at a time in life when we desire to adopt new core values. We may be moving a value up in importance, for example. This often occurs in midlife when a value such as spirituality, which may have been important but not on a person's top-five list, begins to take on more importance. Shifting values can also occur at times when a client is emerging into a new level of consciousness (relating to Kegan's work on levels of consciousness presented in Chapter 3). At these times, certain values become more central and others more peripheral.

To assist clients in developing a new value, we suggest that the clients first go back and examine values that have been powerful and life-shaping for them. Ask the clients to think about two to five values that have shaped their life, the specific ways in which these values have benefited them, and the ways in which they were reflected in their choices, actions, and daily habits.

Then ask the clients to review a list of values, such as those included earlier in this chapter, and to consider which one or two new values they would like to implement in their life. Ask them to create a definition for each value, as well as to identify people in their life who demonstrate each value. These people can be personal acquaintances, people in the public view, or historical figures.

Once an operational definition of each new value has been created, the work can get very specific as far as the actions they might take in their own life to implement each of these values. Ask the clients to be very specific, and then come up with a specific action plan (with specific events, dates, and so on) to implement each of these values in daily life. Make sure the plan has a review process to evaluate how things are

231

going every few months. Encourage the clients to make values, including new values, the cornerstone of their life, contemplating them deeply and ensuring a values-focused life.

One additional step can be useful. Living according to one's values can have both benefits and potential costs—witness the price that Gandhi and Martin Luther King Jr., paid for living out their values. Ask your clients to reflect on how some of their past life-changing decisions might be made now through the lens of values that currently have a high priority. What would the cost of these decisions be? What would be gained or lost?

What we have shared in this chapter is crucial to our view of successful life coaching. Values work is at the heart of coaching from the inside out. It allows clients to explore the depth of change possible for them and to avoid superficial changes or simple problem solving. Clients who can articulate their values find fulfillment in the integrity of life from the inside and life from the outside.

Chapter 11
walk the Talk

In previous "Coaching from the Inside Out" chapters, we explored life purpose and the vision of fulfillment and satisfaction in each life area. We discussed how needs and values fit with the life clients want to create. This chapter focuses on what it takes to actually create that life by taking actions that are aligned with the clients' vision and values. We call this alignment *integrity.* Clients who are serious about creating that life need to "walk their talk." In other words, they need to do what it takes to turn their vision of a fulfilling life into a reality. If they do not act on their vision, it is just a wish—a dream.

PERSONAL INTEGRITY

Several years ago, two friends experienced a life event that illustrated the essence of integrity and alignment, demonstrating what happens when these qualities are lacking. The couple bought a house and had been living in it for about 3 months. It was a very old house that was situated on a hill. When they bought the house, the seller gave them a packet of information from an engineering firm that had inspected the house to determine whether the foundation was firm and the walls were in alignment. The firm apparently had said that the house had architectural integrity—in other words, that the foundation was firm, the walls were square, and the basement did not require any foundational supports.

Every room in the house was wallpapered, some with costly and expensive wallpaper that did not suit our friends' tastes. As they began to steam off the wallpaper, they discovered cracks in the walls. Almost every corner had big fissures that expanded as spring came. Also, two doors went out of alignment when the spring rains hit.

Despite the engineering firm's written report, the house was obviously not in good shape. When our friends contacted the seller, she refused to take responsibility for the cracks, saying she was not aware of them and had believed the engineering firm's report to be accurate.

Was this seller displaying integrity? If so, why was every room wallpapered?

Our friends investigated the situation with the engineering firm and learned that two pages from the back of the firm's report were missing. These missing pages contained an account of the existing cracks, as well as a record of the fact that the hillside had started to slip. The report recommended that another engineering survey be done in a year; otherwise, the house's structural integrity might be in jeopardy.

Our friends learned a major lesson about integrity: both in architecture and in relationships, integrity is essential.

Sometimes we consider taking action to only consist of the big actions. In fact, the small daily actions are equally critical because they create the foundation for something big to happen. Every day, we create our vision by consistently acting in ways that are aligned with our vision and our goals, or else we fail to create our vision by acting in ways that are inconsistent with our vision and goals, which gets us off track. Small habitual actions affect integrity. As the father of one of our ILCT participants said, "Integrity is the first chapter of the book of wisdom."

To paraphrase one of our colleagues, Madelyn Griffith-Haney, someone has personal integrity when what they do, who they are, what they say, what they feel, and what they think all come from the same place.

In recent years, we have seen scandals in formerly respected companies, such as Enron, where leaders lost their integrity at work. Many people deny the implications of their actions and their impact on integrity, as did the Mayflower Madam, who said, "I ran the wrong kind of business, but I did it with integrity" (Christy, 1986). Having personal integrity means taking responsibility for the whole.

Integrity is important enough for leadership and life that it is included in the models and assessments of *emotional intelligence.* In the 360 degree assessment, the Emotional Competence Inventory, published by the Hay Group, integrity is described as the competence titled *trans-*

parency. Cynthia Cooper is a contemporary example of integrity: she stood up and reported unethical business practices at World Com. Sharon Watkins was the *whistle blower* whose integrity and courage led to the recognition of the fraudulent business practices at Enron. Both of these women risked their work lives in order to live up to their personal integrity.

PISA: A TOWER AND ITS INTEGRITY

Watching a house, a city, or a life collapse is an emotionally challenging experience. Take, for example, the Italian engineers who tried to save the Leaning Tower of Pisa (Vuocolo, 2005). According to *Discover Magazine* (Kunzig, 2000), work on the tower began on August 9, 1173. The builders, contractors, engineers, and architects did not plan for it to lean. The tower was designed as an upright structure and was expected to point plumb starward.

However, tilting became a problem—a sudden and immediate problem. For centuries, the 177-foot-tall Tower of Pisa has looked as though it is about to topple. The combined weight of the marble stones has pressed downward into the soft, silted soils, squeezing water from the clay and bulging into the dense sand. The tower teetered on the extreme edge of disaster for 800 years. All 32 million pounds of marble constantly verged on collapse. Its 5.3-degree tilt is startling, even shocking—a full 15 feet out of plumb.

Computer models eventually proved that the tower was going to fall—sooner, rather than later—and a committee of engineers and scientists set about to right the tilting tourist trap. Thanks to some high-tech engineering, the Leaning Tower was stabilized during the decade between 1991 and 2001. Engineers removed bits of clay from beneath the tower through long, thin pipes at a rate of a shovel or two a day. By removing these small amounts from the right places, they were able to stabilize the tower for at least another 300 years.

Of course, it still leans a little, thereby preserving the tourist trade for the town and the surrounding region. This is by design. Bringing the tower into a perfectly upright position would kill the sale of thousands of ceramic replicas.

235

In order to correct the Pisa tilt, three important processes were inaugurated: extraction, replacement, and restraints. First, the bad soil needed to be extracted. Then a solid foundation needed to replace the bad soil. Finally, steel cables were added to hug the structure in order to assure that it would remain in place.

These same three elements are applicable to life coaching:

- To get our lives back in integrity, there may be things we need to *extract*—habits, people, work, and things to which we are attached.
- Then a process of *replacement* is needed and a solid foundation built—new habits, actions aligned with life purpose, and perhaps new people and practices that will facilitate and support solid choices.
- Finally, *restraints* need to be applied consistently. The steel cables that hug the tower's structure and keep its true function are analogous to the boundaries we set—the standards to which we hold ourselves accountable, the rules and guidelines by which we live, our spiritual practices and disciplines, and the ways we hold ourselves to the life design we create.

236

In coaching and in life, staying aligned and true to those things that are most valuable to us is important. We get off course when we are not aligned.

SIMPLE RULES FOR CREATING PERSONAL INTEGRITY

In recent years, a number of writers have popularized the simple life rules that indigenous cultures practice that preserved the integrity of individuals and thereby the community. Coaches use these as illustrations of principles and practices that create and maintain integrity.

Don Miguel Ruiz (1997) identified four Toltec practices that he called "a guide to personal freedom." His four agreements are four simple personal rules that foster integrity:

1. Be impeccable with your word.

2. Don't take anything personally. Nothing others say and do happens because of you.
3. Don't make assumptions.
4. Always do your best. And recognize that your best is going to change from moment to moment.

Borysenko (1994) attributed four guiding rules for life to Angeles Arrien, who may have derived them from Shaman Pete Ketchum's work:

1. Show up.
2. Pay attention.
3. Tell the truth.
4. Don't be attached to the results (Borysenko, 1994, p. 96).

Another example of the importance of integrity comes from Rotary International, in their four-way test, a guide for member conduct utilized since 1932. Its simple steps may assist the coaching community not only to practice ethically but to live with integrity. The four-way test provides a concise and easy reminder of the intent to live with integrity. Rotary members receive a wallet card with the test on it as a constant reminder to check their integrity.

237

The Four-Way Test of the Things We Say and Do,
from Rotary International
1. Is it the **truth**?
2. Is it **fair** to all concerned?
3. Will it build **good will** and better friendships?
4. Will it be **beneficial** to all concerned?

Taking a stand for one's integrity can be a cornerstone of a person's leadership and reputation. Leonard Roberts took over the CEO role at Arby's at a time when this fast-food franchise chain was struggling financially. He promised his franchisees more service and more financial and other support, and was able to turn Arby's around. However, Arby's owner refused to pay the promised bonuses, and Roberts resigned from the board in protest. He was eventually fired. He later became the CEO at Shoney's and was fired from that chain again because he held to his promises and refused to compromise them. Later he became the CEO at Tandy Corp because of his well-known reputation for integrity. "You cannot maintain your integrity 90 percent and be a leader," Roberts (National Institute of Business Management, 2006) said. "It's got to be 100 percent" (p.1). We don't know whether Roberts is a Rotarian, but he certainly modeled the four-way test.

Because of the importance of integrity to coaching, coaches need many ways of asking clients to consider the alignment of their actions with their goals and visions. Below we offer some of the exercises we frequently use with clients.

EXERCISE 11.1
Personal journal questions

The following exercise can be useful in early explorations of integrity. Using journaling, ask clients to reflect on integrity as they currently experience it in their life.

What is your definition of *personal integrity*?

What are the clues (physical, emotional, intellectual, spiritual) you use to notice when you *are* in integrity?

What are the clues you use to notice when you *are not* in integrity?

When your behavior does not match your words or your promises, you are out of alignment with your personal integrity. What are the two or three circumstances or situations that most frequently move you out of alignment?

- _____
- _____
- _____

Identify three to five places in your life where you are currently out of alignment, lacking sufficient integrity for yourself. For each one, identify the action you need to take to get yourself back in alignment (e.g., "I committed to complete X by Y date. It's beyond that time, and I'm only halfway through").

I am without integrity in . . .   What I need to do is . . .

1. _____   1. _____
2. _____   2. _____

EXERCISE 11.1 (continued)

3. _____ 3. _____
4. _____ 4. _____
5. _____ 5. _____

Do any of these examples identify the ways you break your "personal rules" (see below)?

What does each one cost you?

What are five personal rules you want to live by that will help you create the life you want and that will help you walk your talk (not "shoulds," but "I want tos")? What "personal rules for life" can you create that will help you live each day with integrity? What actions will align you with your five personal rules?

1. _____
2. _____
3. _____
4. _____
5. _____

Rule   Action to Take
1. _____
2. _____
3. _____
4. _____
5. _____

239

EXERCISE 11.2
The impact of loose ends

Many coaches and coaching articles describe the importance of eliminating clutter from clients' lives. Clutter is a distraction and an energy drainer, as we discussed in an earlier chapter. Integrity—a sense of wholeness—also comes from completing things, from tying up the loose ends of our lives.

How many loose ends do you have in your life? List below the top 20 things, both big and small, that you need to get closure on. What is incomplete or unfinished in any area of your life—finances, home, relationships, work, and so on?

1. _____
2. _____

EXERCISE 11.2 (continued)

3. _____
4. _____
5. _____
6. _____
7. _____
8. _____
9. _____
10. _____
11. _____
12. _____
13. _____
14. _____
15. _____
16. _____
17. _____
18. _____
19. _____
20. _____

Now, what do you notice about your list? Do the incomplete items seem to be concentrated in any one area of your life? How do these gaps direct you toward the actions you need to take?

THE IMPACT OF LOOSE ENDS

Back in the 1970s, Werner Erhard popularized the phrase, "Get complete." He may have borrowed the idea from Fritz Perls, the father of gestalt therapy, who made completing unfinished business the cornerstone of his therapeutic approach. Getting complete and finishing unfinished business are useful concepts for coaches and their clients. To achieve fulfillment, our clients may need to get complete with any number of things in their life:

- With their past—by getting over it, letting it go, or handling what needs to be handled.
- With people—by having courageous conversations.
- With projects—by finishing them, closing them down, or setting dates to complete them.

- With home—by achieving closure on where and how they want to live, by either taking action or letting it go (no pining or whining).
- With work—by finishing what's essential.

Coaching borrows the term *incompletion* from football, where an incompletion occurs when a receiver does not reach the ball. Metaphorically, clients have examples in life of incompletions, where something gets dropped and remains unfinished. In life, these loose ends operate like mental clutter: they are distracting and de-energizing. These are the things we are putting off and avoiding getting done. They may be projects or difficult conversations—anything unfinished that stays in our awareness. Having too many incompletions keeps us hovering between what we committed to in the past, what we feel we *should* do, and what we want to do in the future. We can't be fully present or fully focused when incompletions immobilize us.

What actions can we take to address incompletions? As Pat Williams often says, "Do it, delegate it, dump it, or delay it!" Stated more elegantly, we have four options:

241

- *Plan for it.* We can create a plan for completing it, establishing a timetable and a due date, and delegating as needed.
- *Let it go.* We can acknowledge that although we once made a commitment, we are withdrawing it. If we choose this option, we must have certain conversations (with ourselves or whoever else is involved) in order to officially terminate the commitment.
- *Get busy and complete it NOW!*
- *Create and implement workable systems* so that incompletions like this one don't pile up again.

SETTING PERSONAL STANDARDS: A WORKABLE SYSTEM

A standard is a criterion by which something is judged. People set and hold standards in areas in which it is important to create consistency. Standards are an acknowledged measure of qualitative value—a criterion against which people judge behaviors, worth, or merit. Setting standards is a practice that is widely recognized and employed because it creates a benchmark for excellence that, if made public, carries authority. People commonly speak of standard reference books, like *Webster's Dictionary.* Standards describe what is basically accepted, such as the gold standard against which we measure economic stability. Coaches encourage clients to examine and set personal standards for their behavior, to ensure that choices and behaviors live up to what clients really want.

Personal standards are the principles we choose to live by—the rules we set for ourselves that we choose to obey. They are not the rules that others set for us. We hold ourselves accountable to our personal standards. They are freely chosen, unlike "shoulds." One reason people get out of integrity, we believe, is that they have not examined their personal standards and adjusted them to reflect their current goals and desires.

This is where the personal rules exercise from earlier in this chapter comes into play. When we work with our personal standards and rules, we examine what we willingly hold ourselves accountable for. From time to time, we need to reexamine, update, and adjust our standards. Breakdowns in our satisfaction can be caused by standards that no longer work. Here's an example:

> Diane Menendez does a lot of coaching and consulting work in organizations. Diversity is a strong value for her. Back in the 1980s, she set a standard of not allowing herself to participate in any conversation where someone was being stereotyped or where racism or sexism was present. That standard allowed her to disengage from the conversation.
>
> A few years later, she realized that disengaging from such a conversation wasn't enough—she needed to speak up. She raised her standards and expectations for herself. When she found herself in that kind of conversation, she implemented her new, higher standard by speaking up and saying, "I can't participate in this conversation and here's why," and requesting that the conversation cease.

Certain risks may be associated with the new higher standards we set. If we decide not to participate in any conversations where gossip takes place, we may risk losing some friends. However, the value of setting higher standards is in preserving our integrity.

242

We believe that personal standards are the mechanism through which we implement our values moment by moment and day by day. When our standards are serving us and working well, they allow us to complete things and to maintain our integrity.

One way to support clients to discover and set effective personal standards is to use their list of core values (discussed in Chapter 10) and have them ask themselves, for each one: "What standard must be in place so that I can live out that value, as my life is organized right now?"

EXERCISE 11.3
Values and standards

You can use the two-column chart below with clients to help them with this question. First, ask them to fill in the blanks in Column 1 with their core values. Then, for each item, ask them to identify a key standard they commit to meeting so they can be in integrity with their values, and write it in Column 2.

Column 1 I am a person who . . . (fill in values)	Column 2 And so I must choose to . . . (fill in standards)
1. _____	1. _____
2. _____	2. _____
3. _____	3. _____
4. _____	4. _____
5. _____	5. _____
6. _____	6. _____
7. _____	7. _____
8. _____	8. _____
9. _____	9. _____
10. _____	10. _____

Let's say that clients filled in Column 1 as below. What standards would you help them set in Column 2 so they can be in integrity with who they say they are?

Column 1 I am a person who . . . (fill in values)	Column 2 And so I must choose to . . . (fill in standards)
1. Respects others	Listen and not interrupt.

EXERCISE 11.3 (continued)

2. Cares for my friends	Initiate contact, be available, ask how I can help in difficult times.
3. Is honest	Tell the truth—but not brutally.
4. Maintains good finances	Limit my debt; keep good records.
5. Shows love for my family	Be cautious in overpromising at work, which impacts my available time and energy; when I come home from an on-site coaching session, greet my spouse with a kiss before I start work again; give each other a great hug every day—at least 6 seconds; write a love letter to each other monthly; when out of town, e-mail every morning and evening, sending a note of appreciation and love.

Sometimes when clients work through this exercise, they find it challenging. That's because the second column asks clients to consider what they must choose. If coaches hear clients commonly saying, "I can't," this can indicate that the clients need to recognize that saying "I can't" is fundamentally usually saying, "I choose not to." Rephrasing in this way assists the clients in maintaining personal accountability for their actions and recognizing that most things in life really come from their choices. Obviously, there are some things that clients really can't do: a 5'4" 50-year-old woman probably can't be in training for the National Basketball Association. But she could get into a local senior basketball league if she chose to.

EXERCISE 11.4
Life is in the details

Coaching is, in part, about the big picture—clients' vision, values, and goals. But the big picture hinges on the small picture—the day-to-day choices and actions that either support the big picture or don't.

At ILCT, we use Dave Ellis's out-of-print book, *Human Being: A Manual for Health, Wealth, Love and Happiness* (Ellis & Lankowitz, 1995), as one of our basic texts. While this book is no longer in print, it is available as an Adobe Acrobat CD-ROM. It can be purchased from the ILCT Web site at www.life-coachtraining.com. It is an invaluable source of exercises coaches can use with clients. Ellis comments eloquently about the importance of integrity in daily life.

> If you want to get real insight into a person, observe in detail how she performs the simplest, smallest activities of daily life. A person who keeps a neat closet is also likely to be well organized at work. The person who supports human rights organizations is likely to give up her seat on the bus for an elderly person. The person who exercises regularly is more likely to pay close attention to what he eats. In a way, small behaviors give us an imprint of the entire person, just as the chromosomes of a single cell provide the blueprint for an entire human organism.

We coach clients to reflect and become aware of their processes and choices, to develop the practice of taking time each day to observe themselves and their habits. That awareness can lead to more thoughtful choices that bring their life into greater alignment with their values. Small choices add up to big results. Moment-to-moment choices are the building blocks of momentous results.

One of our favorite exercises from *Human Being* asks the client to examine an everyday routine activity, as follows, to explore how it reflects the client's values and creates or limits integrity.

1. My routine activity is:

   One student's example: I let the dishes pile up in the sink after dinner and wash them when the sink is full.

2. What this reveals about how I approach other aspects of my life is:

   When there is something to do that I don't enjoy doing, I don't make myself do it until I have to. I do let things pile up. And then I get frustrated because all of a sudden I have a lot of time-consuming things to do that aren't fun or enjoyable.

245

EXERCISE 11.4 (contInued)

3. Identify a simple related behavior that you can and will commit to change immediately—one that might pave the way for larger changes in the future.

   I will start doing the dishes before the evening is over. And I will commit to starting in on unpleasant tasks before they pile up on me. I will also look for ways to make things like doing the dishes fun. I can play music, dance while I do them, and stop thinking about them as a chore.

EXERCISE 11.5
Making and keeping promises

Our commitments, including our habits, help us identify how we are living our values. That's how it seems to us from the inside. Outside of us, those who know us understand us through what we say. They hear us make promises and state our intentions and commitments. What we say to others defines our core values. Consequently, we can really know ourselves by paying attention to the commitments we make and the commitments we avoid making.

Our words and our behaviors must be aligned for us to have integrity. We have two ways of going about that: we can align what we do with what we say, or we can align what we say with what we do. Alignment of words and behaviors brings with it the experience of freedom and a sense of comfort. When there are no broken promises to distract us, we live cleanly and truthfully. We have no one or nothing to avoid because of having reneged on a commitment.

If clients tend to be reluctant to make commitments, or tend to make promises and break them, you can recommend that the clients put into practice some of the strategies below to help them keep promises and consequently maintain integrity.

- When you make promises, make sure that they are both challenging and realistic. Effective promises avoid being too extreme in either direction; they commit you to doing enough but not too much. A challenging promise asks you to stretch to your potential but doesn't set you up to fail.
- When you break a promise, use it as a learning opportunity. It provides feedback—results to learn from. Avoid punishing yourself unnecessarily. Take the learning and make more effective promises next time. We suggest that you examine the intentions you held behind the broken promises. Were they in your best interest? Were they in the best interest of the other persons? Was the promise the right one to make in this situation? We believe that clients who break promises can benefit from making amends—through apologies, conversations, or other acts of contrition. Alcoholics Anonymous knows the value of making amends,

EXERCISE 11.5 (continued)

which is one of the early 12 steps of their program. They ask the clients to take a moral inventory and then to identify those to whom they need to make amends.

- When others break promises to you, help them recognize the learning opportunity. Hold a courageous conversation with them, but do not harbor resentment.

- Before you commit, explore the consequences of making and keeping the promises you are considering. Try mental rehearsal. Especially look for unintended consequences that may occur. Think about the systems that these promises and actions will touch, and identify how these promises may precipitate other actions as reactions, both positive and potentially negative.

- Fernando Flores (1997) developed a useful way of looking at commitments, which he called the Cycle of the Promise. It invites people working together to look at the full cycle of a promise, from the request that someone makes to the agreement that another person makes to fulfill the request. Flores stressed the need for clear communication and for specific times to allow for clear and honest renegotiation when any breakdown, as he called it, occurs. People who promise or who receive others' promises can expect breakdowns. That's just life. How we handle them, on the other hand, is the measure of who we are. When you experience a breakdown that jeopardizes your commitment, talk to others early on, perhaps even when you anticipate the breakdown before it has occurred. This allows for renegotiation and gets you back on track.

- When you make a commitment, put it down in writing on a list so that you remember it. E-mail can be helpful in this regard. If you are someone who dislikes details, developing a specific action plan for how you will accomplish the promise may be necessary to keep your commitment on track. Keep a written list of your promises for a month, like a to-do list of your major commitments. Review the promises daily and record your progress. This chart can be used to explore with your coach any patterns of unanticipated breakdowns that you experience. These may require you to develop new systems or habits.

- Really big promises in human life usually are accompanied by a ceremony or ritual. Think about marriages, bar mitzvahs, and other kinds of big promises that we make to others. Often these take place in public and we create ceremonies to honor them. Many indigenous or native cultures have ceremonies for life's promises. Consider developing a ritual or ceremony to accompany your promise. For an entrepreneur, this may, for example, be a ceremony to honor the bonuses that follow an excellent business year.

This chapter has focused on how integrity emerges from the alignment between what we say and what we do. Like all of our chapters in the "Inside Out" section, we believe that the coaches' work is to help clients connect head and heart. As someone said, the longest distance we ever go is the 12 inches between our head and our heart. Coaches become models of integrity for their clients when clients are doing this work. Both coaches and clients need to pay exquisite attention to *walking their talk.*

Chapter 12

Play Full Out

Peter Block (1999) was right when he said, "If you can't say 'no,' your 'yesses' don't mean a thing." Imagine what a waste it would be to own a beautiful piano, with all of its octaves, and be restricted to only using two of the octaves. Yes, you could play most melodies, but the music wouldn't be rich and sonorous. The instrument wouldn't be well used. What a disappointment that would be to anyone who knew the full potential of a piano and the gorgeous sounds it was capable of creating.

In coaching, we are the instruments. That's also true of our clients— their lives are their instruments. When we look at self as an instrument, our commitment becomes to live and to use ourselves as fully and richly as possible. That's what we mean by *playing full out* (Ellis & Lankowitz, 1995). We don't want to restrict ourselves to only half of our range, like the piano keyboard limited to two octaves.

To play full out requires us to make great choices and stay conscious while we make them. It also means taking responsibility for the choices we make and those we have made in the past. Through exercising our power of choice, we create the kind of life we want.

BEING AT CHOICE

Early on in the development of coaching as a profession, the phrase "Be at full choice in your life" began to appear frequently in writing and teaching. In coaching, we believe that to be at full choice in our life means that (a) we examine our choices fully, (b) we are deliberate—we are choosing consciously, and (c) we are being *responsive*, not *reactive* to what is going on. When we are at choice, we are not choosing by default since avoiding a decision is not the same as choosing consciously.

Consider this question: What role does choice play in the situations where we play small versus the situations where we *play full out*?

We use the word *play* in two ways. To play full out means that we play the game of life—or whatever we do—fully and richly. We bring *all* of ourselves to it. We play big, like the dolphin. As someone once said: "The dolphin as a master of games behaves as if there is no competition, no loser, and no winner—only fun for all."

In *Tuesdays with Morrie* (Albom, 1997), the author's English professor and mentor, Morrie, played full out. He drew his philosophy from Mark Twain's statement, "Live like there's only today, love like you've never been hurt, and dance like nobody's watching." *To play* also means to have fun, to be joyful, and to take ourselves and others lightly. The Dalai Lama exhibits this kind of playfulness—a quality of lightness and joy. Despite the fact that the Chinese devastated his monastery home and practiced genocide on many of his people, he forgives them. He is light and even giggles frequently.

The story of Rose, which follows, is a reminder that playfulness and joyfulness create blessings for all.

The Story of Rose[1]

The first day of school, our professor introduced himself and challenged us to get to know someone we didn't already know. I stood up to look around, when a gentle hand touched my shoulder. I turned around to find a wrinkled, little old lady beaming up at me with a smile that lit up her entire being.

She said, "Hi, handsome. My name is Rose. I'm 87 years old. Can I give you a hug?"

I laughed and enthusiastically responded, "Of course you may!" and she gave me a giant squeeze.

"Why are you in college at such a young, innocent age?" I asked. She jokingly replied, "I'm here to meet a rich husband, get married, have a couple of children, and then retire and travel."

[1] Versions of this story circulated around the Internet sometime in June 2000. We hope that the author, whose name we cannot find, will someday be identified so we can acknowledge and say thanks for a great story.

"No, seriously," I asked. I was curious as to what may have motivated her to take on this challenge at her age.

"I always dreamed of having a college education, and now I'm getting one!" she told me.

After class, we walked to the student union building and shared a chocolate milkshake. We became instant friends. Every day for the next 3 months, we would leave class together and talk nonstop. I was always mesmerized listening to this "time machine" as she shared her wisdom and experience with me. Over the course of the year, Rose became a campus icon and easily made friends wherever she went. She loved to dress up, and she reveled in the attention bestowed on her by the other students. She was living it up.

At the end of the semester, we invited Rose to speak at our football banquet. I'll never forget what she taught us. She was introduced and stepped up to the podium. As she began to deliver her prepared speech, she dropped her 3 x 5 cards on the floor. Frustrated and a little embarrassed, she leaned into the microphone and simply said, "I'm sorry I'm so jittery. I gave up beer for Lent, and this whiskey is killing me! I'll never get my speech back in order, so let me just tell you what I know."

As we laughed, she cleared her throat and began.

We do not stop playing because we are old; we grow old because we stop playing. There are only four secrets to staying young. One is being happy. Another is achieving success. You also have to laugh and find humor every day. And, you've got to have a dream. When you lose your dreams, you die. We have so many people walking around who are dead and don't even know it!

There is a huge difference between growing older and growing up. If you are 19 years old and lie in bed for one full year and don't do one productive thing, you will turn 20 years old. If I am 87 years old and stay in bed for a year and never do anything, I will turn 88. Anybody can grow older. That doesn't take any talent or ability. The idea is to grow up by always finding the opportunity in change.

Have no regrets. The elderly usually don't have regrets for what we did, but rather for the things we did not do. The only people who fear death are those with regrets.

She concluded her speech by courageously singing "The Rose." She challenged each of us to study the lyrics and live them out in our daily lives.

At the year's end, Rose finished the college degree she had begun all those years ago. One week after graduation, Rose died peacefully in her sleep. Over 2,000 college students attended her funeral in tribute to the wonderful woman who taught, by example, that it's never too late to be all you can possibly be.

Remember, growing old is mandatory—growing up is optional.

WHISTLE WHILE YOU WORK—OR PLURK!

Rose knew how to *plurk,* a term used by coach Teri-E Belf and Charlotte Ward (1997). They define *plurk* as "play while you work." Belf has even passed out buttons at conferences that say, "Ask me how I PLURK!" Remember how the seven dwarfs sang "Whistle While You Work" as they marched off to work? Yes, it is possible to be playful and joyful in all we do, says Belf. How would our lives be different if we *plurked* instead of just worked?

Children are masters of plurking, and watching them—or better yet—participating, brings out that quality in us. Coaches and other helping professionals often report both for themselves and their clients that Fun and Play are two of their lowest-rated areas on the Wheel of Life. Why is this so? Perhaps it is because work has taken over many professionals' lives in a way that leaves little time for fun and play. We have become human *doings* instead of human *beings.* We also speculate that the kind of work people do has a pervasive influence on their attitudes. Psychologists, counselors, nurses, and other helping professionals often work daily with people whose situations are dire. After spending 8 to 10 hours focused on what the Buddha called the 10,000 sorrows of life, it is easy to forget the other half of the Buddha's statement: "Life is 10,000 joys *and* 10,000 sorrows."

It requires real excellence at saying no to be able to make time for play. This applies equally well to our clients and ourselves. Consequently, if our Fun and Play quota is low, a good place to start in addressing the imbalance is to examine the places in our life where we are saying yes when saying no might be more beneficial to us and the life we want to live.

PLAY AND BEING AT CHOICE BOTH REQUIRE GOOD BOUNDARIES

Every time we say yes when we want to say no, we're jeopardizing our ability to take life lightly and to play, which are the roots of resilience in life. When we do this, we're compromising our boundaries and allowing things into our life that shouldn't be there. Those things sap our energy and zap our commitment to our priorities. (This material is drawn from Menendez & Lowry, 1999.)

Boundaries are the borders we create around ourselves by the limits we set—limits around time, limits around whom we let into our life, limits around the activities that we allow to take up our attention and time. They are the imaginary lines that tell people how close they can come to us and what they can expect from us. Good boundaries allow us to spend our time and energy wisely. We don't waste anything on what's not good for us—people, activities, or food. Boundaries put us in charge by allowing us to consciously choose what we allow inside our life.

For example, an executive client of ours decided that she would no longer take work home and do it after supper. Instead, she wanted to use that time to help her children with their homework and to simply enjoy being and playing with them. She decided that she was willing to stay a half hour later at the office so that she could be free and focused at home. Her decision not to take work home meant that she was drawing a boundary around her home life, which kept work from leaking into it.

Boundaries Create Safety and Protection

Boundaries are a fundamental tool for keeping us safe and supporting our well-being. We all learned how to set boundaries as a child—to say no to strangers, to turn away people who wanted to touch us inappropriately, to stay away from kids who had measles or who weren't good playmates. If we were parented well, we learned how to make our boundaries tight and steadfast, and to resist people who were boundary invaders. We learned how to keep ourselves safe and well.

253

Good fences make good neighbors.

—Robert Frost

Two-year-olds know the power of saying no. When things happen that children don't like, they will immediately scream "NO!" Saying no helps children feel powerful and able to set limits—it's the natural foundation for independence. Saying no and establishing boundaries give us power.

So why as adults are we often afraid to say no? Probably because when we first heard our parents say "No!" to us, it meant, "Stop immediately—you have no choice!" "No" was a signal that we were either unsafe at the moment or that what we were doing, and who we were being, was unacceptable. "No" was a sign of rejection, a signal that we weren't okay as we were. When we were young, rejection meant being cut off from the love and caring that sustained us. We could lose everything we had.

Saying no and maintaining good boundaries are hard when we think it means giving up someone's approval. We become afraid to say no—afraid of losing a client, being rejected, or being disliked. When we avoid saying no once, it seems like a small thing. When it becomes a habit, we're in trouble.

Keep Tight Boundaries

Whenever we say yes when we should say no, we're letting someone or something invade our boundaries. That is, we're interpreting someone else's *request* or *need* as a *demand.* We're telling ourselves that we have no choice about the situation because we can't run the risk of rejection or loss.

When we say yes to the demand, we're really saying no to ourselves. For that moment, we're making the other person more important than the commitments we've made to ourselves. Worse yet, when we say yes to something to which we want to say no, we're cheapening our word. As Peter Block said in the quote at the start of this chapter, our ability to say yes is only as good and as viable as our willingness to say no. That's because saying no means that we're very grounded. We know exactly the firm ground we're willing to stand on, and we're clear about what we are willing to do.

People usually respect those who are grounded and clear. If we say no gracefully and share the reasons why we won't say yes, for the most

254

part we'll be respected by others. But gaining the respect of others is not the reason why being grounded is important. Most important is that we'll regain respect for ourselves.

People don't always respect others who set clear boundaries. We need to make a point of paying attention to whether people in our lives support our autonomous choices regarding what's best for us, or whether they just want what they want and don't care how they get it. If they just want what they want, the situation is an opportunity to set a boundary and disengage from them. We're *choosing* to do this. It is our responsibility to recognize the people and situations that do and don't nourish us, and to take appropriate action. We can't ever expect another person to be fully looking out for our best interests and take care of us—that's OUR job. If we don't do it, it's not going to get done.

Once we recognize our need for healthy boundaries and once we create them, we are better able to respect other people's boundaries. We have acquired a distinction that we may not have had earlier in our life. So, we apply that distinction to ourselves as well as to others. We're better equipped to recognize that everyone, not just us, has a right to their boundaries.

When we're working with coaching clients on issues related to boundaries, we use several metaphors that we used to use with counseling clients. One common metaphor is that boundaries are like the moat around a castle. If clients want to connect with someone, they lower the drawbridge to let the person into their space. If not, they keep the drawbridge up, and the moat prevents access, just like boundaries do. When clients know that they are in a safe, nurturing environment, they may choose to keep the drawbridge down, metaphorically speaking. Other metaphors we have used include: the alarm system on your house (what are your personal alarms?) or border guards who maintain the gate between countries; you need a passport to be admitted (how do you admit people into the territory that is yours?).

We work with coaching clients on boundaries from these perspectives:

- Boundaries are the limits we set around who and what we allow to get close to us. They define our "safety zones," so to speak,

255

delineating what is out of bounds for us and unacceptable, and what is inbounds and acceptable.

- Boundaries define *who* we are and how we live. They define who we are and who we are *not*.

- When we have tight, strong boundaries, we attract people who have similar boundaries and consequently can maintain them well. When our boundaries are weak, we attract people who also have weak boundaries. They can show up as needy people who deplete our energy and whom we eventually tire of.

In order to be able to give generously, clients must have good boundaries. Remember, we said boundaries create freedom. Many spiritual teachers and quotations point to the truth of this—that in order to give, you must be sufficiently full yourself. One line we've heard is to compare giving as if from a pipe or a cup. Don't give like a pipe: it's open at both ends and never remains full. Give like an overflowing cup. The cup never runs out, but the overflow is available to be given to others.

As Pat Williams and Lloyd Thomas wrote in their book, *Total Life Coaching,* "When you establish healthy boundaries, you feel more secure. Your level of anxiety lowers and you strengthen the trust you have in yourself, in others, and in the world" (Williams & Thomas, 2005, p. 55).

Clients who want to have a fulfilling life must be able to make choices freely and fully, to play full out so that they do not feel the need to overprotect themselves from others or from events. We believe that in order to fully choose and to play full out, we need to have three things in place, all of which are related: (a) good boundaries, (b) high standards, which when combined and done well, help us (c) create our integrity.

EXERCISES ON BOUNDARIES

Most clients need to set tighter boundaries and higher standards in order to give themselves more room, more freedom, and more choices in order to create the life they really want to live. Playing full out can mean different things to different people: it can mean pursuing excellence,

256

having a sense of urgency, taking risks, keeping things in perspective, working smarter instead of harder, or consciously choosing how hard to play.

Journal Inquiries

- What are one or two places in your life where you are "playing small" instead of "playing big?" What is that about?
- What are the "rules of life" you learned about "work" and "play"?

For many clients and ILCT students, rules about play and work are tied together. Many say, for example, that play can occur only after work is done. In a 24/7 environment, where clients are continually accessible by instant messaging and cell phones, work may never end. Consequently, clients need to be vigilant in setting good boundaries to ensure that they get to play.

Play Full Out

The following exercise is used with ILCT students and their clients to encourage an experience of the interplay between hard work and having fun (Ellis & Lankowitz, 1995, pp. 127–136).

In order to balance the interplay between working hard and playing hard, consider that playing hard requires letting go. It requires us to examine our lives, notice what we can change, and accept what we can't change. Playing, to some extent, means going with the flow. If clients can detach from the need to win and the fear of losing, they free themselves to play full out. They can compete fiercely, but in a spirit of play and flow.

Letting go and lightening up require clients to examine their roles—work, family, community, and so on, and to commit to putting their soul before their role. That is, happiness can be independent of most of the things that people in industrialized societies get attached to. We are more than our roles, more than our behavior, more than our bank accounts, our credit cards, or our possessions.

In the first part of the exercise below, clients are asked to rewrite their personal equation for happiness so that they can move beyond whatever their current equation is, such as defining their happiness by possessions or their role. (*My happiness = my car; my happiness = being a perfect parent.*) We want them to rewrite the equation as: *My happiness = my happiness.* We first encountered this exercise in Roberto Assagioli's book, *Psychosynthesis* (Assagioli, 1965).

EXERCISE 12.1
Journal exercise

- Write a list of those things that are important to you.
- Then write the sentences as attachments and let them go, using the following form:

  I have a beautiful home, but I am not my home.
  I have a Mercedes, but I am not my Mercedes.
  I am married, but I am not my marriage.
  I have a beautiful body, but I am not my body.
  I have an overweight body, but I am not my body.
  I have a great job, but I am not my job.
  I have a _____, but I am not my _____.

Through this journal exercise, clients discover and work with limiting beliefs. They can emerge from the exercise with the awareness that they used to believe that their happiness depended on those things on their list. They learn that happiness is simply a choice. They can choose to be happy by separating from all they have. Happiness is a way of being; it does not depend on having.

258

EXERCISE 12.2
Taking a risk: Costs and benefits

This exercise asks clients to identify something they have been attracted to, something they would love to do but have chosen not to because they are afraid. They may fear looking foolish (for example, going to a dance when they feel they have two left feet). They may fear giving presentations to groups they don't know. They may fear wearing a particular kind of clothing even though they love the fabric and the cut. Singles may fear dating because they antici-pate being rejected.

- In the space below, identify first what you would love to do. Then list both the benefits and the costs of choosing not to take this action. (For example, the benefits of avoiding the dance might include not feeling uncomfortable or embarrassed. The costs might include not meeting new people and being bored at home.)

EXERCISE 12.2 (continued)

"The action I have chosen not to take is . . ."
"The benefits of choosing not to take this action include . . ."
"The costs of choosing not to take this action include . . ."

• How might making the choice to take this action help you to play full out?

Identify two situations or people in your life that you experience as disempowering. For each situation, identify the consequences of your feeling of disempowerment.

Situation   Why Disempowering
1. _____   _____
2. _____   _____

A good place to begin working with clients on the topic of boundaries is to have them reflect on the following questions and journal about them.

One of the ways to create more room for choice is to set clear boundaries. List three to five places in your life where you need to set better (stronger, tighter, or clearer) boundaries. Examples might include your time, your health, your relationships, your finances, and your spirit. These might be places where you need to say no to someone else so you can say yes to yourself.

1. _____
2. _____
3. _____
4. _____
5. _____

259

EXERCISE 12.3
Setting a tighter boundary

Do the following exercise, using one of the situations you listed as disempowering. When doing this exercise with clients, we have found that it works best in a live coaching session, not as a written exercise.

Step 1. Name a boundary that you now hold that you could tighten.

_____

Step 2. What would a tighter boundary look like, and how would it function?

_____

EXERCISE 12.3 (continued)

Step 3. Examine needs and values issues around setting this boundary.

What *need* is behind the old, loose boundary? In other words, what need is being met by keeping the boundary loose?

_____

What are two other ways you might meet that need?

_____

If you set a tighter boundary, would it conflict with your values or be more true to your values?

_____

Step 4. What standard would you set for yourself to make that tighter boundary work?

_____

Step 5. What part does this new standard play in helping you maintain your integrity?

_____

Keeping Boundaries Tight Around People

We recommend sharing the following guidelines with clients who are working on tighter and clearer boundaries.

- *Be clear about your limits.* A good rule of thumb is: *Allow no one to make demands of you.* Allow people to make *requests* of you, ask for your help, or say what they need from you. However, no one has the right to make demands of you as long as you are not causing harm or breaking the law.

  If you hear a request that makes you uncomfortable, your discomfort is likely to be a signal that this is an attempt to invade your boundaries. The person may not recognize this as an invasion, but you know it—your body knows it. Whatever you do, don't say yes under these conditions. This is a time to say no and really mean it.

- *Exercise your freedom to choose.* When you can't choose to say no to others, or when you take on other people's troubles, you probably are not free to make choices in any part of your life. Start today to exercise your choice muscles.

- *Set tight boundaries and attract great people.* Remember that good boundaries attract good people. Tight boundaries keep out needy and demanding people.

- *Say no when you mean no.*

- *Be willing to hold a courageous conversation if needed to rein-force your boundaries.* Often we need to have these conversations with people who have violated one of our boundaries. The goal is to teach them to respect your boundaries. The key steps of rein-forcing boundaries require you to be willing to hold several conversations to reinforcing the boundary.

1. Inform them that their behavior is violating a boundary or limit of yours. Tell them it's not acceptable. It is likely that the person may not have any clue that they've violated your boundary.
2. *Request* that they stop. Invite them to figure out alternatives for getting their own needs met.
3. If they still persist, require that they stop.
4. Terminate the relationship if the boundary violation continues. You don't need people in your life who continue to violate and disrespect your boundaries.

A PRIMER ON SAYING NO GRACEFULLY

On a day-to-day basis, most of us violate our own boundaries by saying yes when we really want to say no. We're awkward around saying no—to everyone but ourselves.

We can say no gracefully. If we're not yet seasoned practitioners of the art of *the graceful no* or if we're having trouble being consistent, these reminders can help:

- Saying no to trivial requests gives meaning to the things we say yes to, both for ourselves and for others who make requests of us.
- Saying no allows us to set and keep good boundaries in order to honor our commitments to ourselves and others.
- Finally, saying no wisely creates space and time for us so that we have the energy to create what we really want for ourselves.

saying "no" to this is my gift to whoever says "yes."

—Travis Twomey

261

Stephen Covey knew this really well. As he said, "It is easy to say 'no' when there is a greater 'yes'" (1989, p. 156). Saying no is key to staying on track and on purpose.

Saying the Graceful "No"

Cultivating an ability to say no is not the same as becoming one of those people whose first answer to every new idea is "No." We never have to take any chances if we always say no. In contrast, we all benefit by giving ourselves the time and freedom to generate new ideas of our own and to create new ways of being and doing. We support this process by saying no to others whose requests are not in our best interests right now.

Below is a bouquet of suggestions about how to say no with grace, preserving the relationship with someone who hopes we'll say yes. Adapt them as you see fit in working with your clients. This list was developed by asking colleagues to share their experiences with saying the graceful "no."

In the material below, we have written these to you, the reader—as coach, as client, as colleague. Each of the sections presents situations where a "no" is appropriate, and suggestions about how to say it.[2]

How to Say No When Someone Suggests Something
You Would Like to Consider

Say: *"This sounds like something that may be for me, and I've just committed to sticking to three other priorities right now. Will you come back in 90 days and give me another chance to look at this opportunity with you?"*

This one works because it acknowledges your interest *and* keeps you from taking on more than you can realistically complete. If the other person is really interested in this, he or she will get back to you and ask again. Make sure that you're telling the truth and that you really *do* see an opportunity for yourself. *Don't* use this one when you really don't want to do what's being asked of you. You'll just have to say no twice. Worse yet, you'll have intentionally misled the other person.

[2] The first draft of this section originally appeared as Lowry and Menendez (1999). The situations are drawn from conversations and suggestions our colleagues made when this article was first written.

How to Say No When the Timing's Just Not Right
Say: *"I wish I could, but it's just not possible right now. Thank you for thinking of me."*

Your no is based on the timing of the request. Thanking the requester really helps in this situation. Be sincere. Because you've acknowledged your thanks, the person will think of you again when similar opportunities arise. You've said no to this one but not to other similar requests. The requester will be back with future requests. Make sure you want that to happen before you use this strategy.

Similar variations include:

"Thanks for thinking of me, but I don't think so right now."
"I hate saying no to you, but I really must this time."
"It doesn't work for me at this time."

Make sure that you just stop after any of these responses. Don't say more—there's no need to justify or give reasons.

If you don't have the time now but might want to say yes at some other time, say something like:

"I'd love to help you with this, but I just don't have the time. Please let me know next time this comes up, and maybe our schedules will be a better match then."
Or: *"I would like to help, but I'm already overcommitted. How else might I support you?"*

How to Say No When You Have Other Priorities
Say: *"This year my priorities are very few and very focused. I won't be able to squeeze this one in."*

Laura Berman-Fortgang, a friend and colleague of ours, is adamant about saying no in the right way and sticking to her priorities. She, like other well-known published writers, gets many requests for public appearances and speaking engagements. Using her values as a compass, she modeled for Pat Williams the importance of priorities based on values. Shortly after her first book came out (Berman-Fortgang, 1998), she appeared on Oprah. She was inundated with requests for appearances and speeches—to many of which she said no, since her priority at the time was a book tour. You'll be in good company if you say a graceful no because you have other priorities! You might say:

> "This isn't a good time for me to do that. I have other commitments. I'll let you know if I can spend time on it later."
>
> "What a wonderful invitation, but I'm just stretched too much to accept it."

Remember that you don't have to share your priorities with the other person. We suggest, in fact, that you don't. You don't want to get into a debate about whether your priorities are truly more important or valuable than what the other person is asking you to do. You have a right to your priorities—without *any* justification.

We suggest you practice saying each of these *graceful "no"* lines until you've become comfortable hearing yourself say them. Then, when the time comes, you'll be ready to respond gracefully.

Once you've mastered the basic ways to say no, you're ready for the "black belt" skills. When you're able to do these well, you will be a master of the graceful "no." Here are more examples of graceful and artful ways to say no that you can practice regularly.

How to Say No New York–Style

This one's a favorite, learned from a playwright in New York City who used it with actors asking for roles in his shows. It works best with people who seem to make endless demands of you with great persistence.

You say, "*Gosh, I really wish I could, but it's just . . .* (count silently to four) *. . . impossible.*" (Shake your head slowly.)

That usually does it, especially if you say nothing else. If, however, they ask, "Why?" do this:

Open your mouth as if starting to speak, then take a breath, and say, "*Well, it's . . .* (count silently to four, look down, and then say, almost under your breath) *. . . just impossible. I wish I could say 'yes,' but I simply cannot.*" (Look up at the person at the very end and smile wanly.)

Why does this work? The requestor has nothing to argue with. You haven't lied, and he or she will fill in the blank with whatever awful thing happened to you that they would have difficulty talking about.

Remember, you don't need to give a reason why you're saying no. The truth is, it usually isn't their business. Often, they won't hear anything after "no" anyway. We're often just trying to justify our decision to ourselves!

How to Say No if You're Asked to Do Something That Goes Against Your Values or Values-driven Priorities
The best option is to say no quickly. If you hesitate, even for a moment, the person making the request will believe there is a chance you will change your mind. Say no firmly. Just "no." No reasons.

A next best choice is to make a sincere comment about your commitment to the results you are focused on achieving, for example:

> *"I must commit all my time to _____. It's what is most important to me right now."*

265

Then reaffirm your commitment to the person: "Although I'm saying no to your request, I want you to know how much I value you as a colleague."

If you have time, you might spend a few minutes brainstorming with the person about other ways he or she can fill the need.

> Or: *"Sorry, I'm unable to do that."*
> Or: *"I'll have to say no to that, but might I suggest _____?"*

In the last case, you've given the person a gift of your creativity by suggesting another way he or she might handle the need.

How to Say No When You're Asked to Do Something for Free That You Usually Charge for Doing
You may be one of those people who is asked to speak or contribute your consulting or services for free. Sometimes that may work for you. When it doesn't, say something like this:

> *"I do pro bono work on a limited basis, and that time has already been committed for this year. Would you like to be put on the waiting list for (_____ months/years) from now? I can do that."*

Most people don't plan that far in advance. Consequently, they end up having to say no to *your* suggestion!

How to Say No When Someone Continues to Ask You Repeatedly for Free Advice

After an ongoing fee-paying relationship is over, you're essentially giving away your services. If you don't want to continue to do that, you might respond with something like this:

> *"I feel awkward helping you at this point because I feel that I'm being unfair to my paying clients. Let's put together a list of things I can really help you with and see how we can work together."*

That usually will end the "for free" requests once and for all.

266

EXERCISE 12.4

Where do you need to say "no" right now?

Identify the places in your life where you see the need to say no. These are places where you need tighter boundaries. Identify five to 10 "nos" you need to say. Then, for each one, ask yourself, "What would I be willing to say yes to in this case?" If there is something you're willing to do, say it. Choose wisely— only what you are willing to do and can do gracefully, without resentment.

This chapter has focused on the connection between maintaining good boundaries and the freedom to choose that comes with them. Choosing means creating the possibility of playing full out, having fun, and creating a balanced life. Many clients come into coaching around the challenge of maintaining life balance. They will need to examine and rework boundaries in order to attain balance.

Helping professionals often think that boundaries are dealt with in therapy. We have found that the most severe cases of boundary violations—situations involving abuse or trauma—do in fact usually require a therapeutic intervention. However, human beings need to reexamine and re-create their boundaries throughout their lives. Consequently, coaches need to be able to work effectively with boundaries. They also need to recognize when a client's old boundary issues may not have been dealt with sufficiently and require therapy. At those times, a referral is in order.

Chapter 13

How Wealthy Are You?

In the 80s and early 90s in the United States, the motto was, "There's no such thing as too much." Money, time, possessions —"more is better" was the mantra. That time marked the appearance of the bumper sticker, "He who has the most toys wins."

Many coaching clients lived through that period of frantic striving and now, in the 21st century, have returned to seeking a simpler life. When we try to simplify our lives, sometimes we bump up against our unconscious beliefs about how much really is enough.

A classic definition of wealth can be helpful here. The *American Heritage Dictionary of the English Language* (2000) has a multipart definition. One definition is the state of being rich or affluent, or "all goods and resources having value in terms of exchange or use." The last definition is: "a great amount, a profusion, *a wealth of advice."* As coaches, we work with clients to see that their wealth in life goes well beyond simply money. It extends to any area where having a great amount or a profusion of something is a source of fulfillment and satisfaction to them. We want clients to have a wealth of time, an abundance of joy, a profusion of friends.

In the coaching profession, coaches have come to describe being clear about how much is enough, and having more than just enough, as having a *reserve,* sometimes described as *being in reserve,* to emphasize that we work with the state of *being,* not the state of *having.*

PERSONAL RESERVE

Personal reserve is a bit like the Federal Reserve's Fort Knox, which always has a stash of currency and gold that remains unused and out of circulation. Because it's there—safe and unused—it guarantees that the rest of the nation's money can be freely circulated without worry. Because there's always money in reserve, it can be used to stabilize the currency if the economy changes.

Here's another example. If you're old enough to have driven a car back in the 60s and 70s, you may have had the good fortune to own or drive a Volkswagen Beetle. Instead of a gasoline gauge indicator, the VW Beetle had a gadget called the reserve tank. When you started to run out of gas, you wouldn't know it by a gauge. However, you never got caught without gas because your reserve tank held two gallons of gas. You always had more than enough gas to get to the next gas station. The reserve tank in the VW Beetle kept you from worrying about running out of gas and getting stuck somewhere. Most of us who owned one were, in fact, not very wealthy in terms of how much money we had stashed away. We were college students or were starting a first job. But the lesson of the reserve tank has stayed with us.

A real sense of personal wealth comes from knowing that we always have a reserve of whatever resource we're focused on. We never need to be afraid of running out, so we're able to focus our attention on other things. This is another example of how Maslow's hierarchy of needs comes into play around a client's sense of fulfillment. When survival issues are addressed, clients focus on higher-order issues. The role of the coach is to work with the client to examine any scarcity mind-set that prevents the client from ever feeling a sense of abundance.

HOW MUCH IS ENOUGH?

As we stated at the beginning of this chapter, people living in nations like the United States have become confused about what is really necessary for a fulfilling life. Many never consider the personal question, "How much is enough for you?" In a consumer-driven society, the sense is that people always need to accumulate more. That sense is interrupted at times when people see disasters such as Hurricane Katrina, which show that people in fact can lose many of their possessions and find a gratitude for life and relationships that exceeds what they had before their losses.

Yet, numerous examples illustrate a pervasive sense of lack of security. When the Merck Family Fund conducted a nationwide survey, it discovered that 1 in 5 of U.S. families with household incomes of $100,000 or more spend everything they earn on basic needs; and over 25% said they don't believe they have enough to buy what they really need (White, 1998).

A 1997 *USA Today* survey asked the wealthiest Americans—those whose net worth was $2.5 million or more—how much they would pay to achieve happiness by various means. While becoming President was only worth an average of $55,000, having a great intellect was worth an average of $407,000. True love was worth $487,000. They offered to pay the most for a place in heaven: $640,000, on average (USA Today, 1997).

Money equated with happiness means a great deal to children as young as 9. In a *Time* magazine poll, 23% of young children ages 9 to 14 reported that they would prefer to be rich even if it meant being unhappy (Time, 2000). This percentage was up from 9% when the same survey was conducted a year earlier, in 1999. Yet, in a survey conducted by the *Wall Street Journal,* Americans who earned $100,000 or more yearly reported that their problems managing time far exceeded any problems with money (Graham & Crossen, 1996).

270

This chapter examines our sense of wealth—in other words, the feeling of being wealthy in many areas. Real wealth comes from experiencing *more than enough* of whatever is at issue.

It's critical to this discussion to think expansively, not narrowly, about the term *wealth.* John-Roger and Peter McWilliams, in their book *Wealth 101,* describe wealth as "health, happiness, abundance, prosperity, riches, loving, caring, sharing, learning, knowing what we want, opportunity, enjoying and balance" (McWilliams & McWilliams, 1992, p. 7) This is quite a rich definition of wealth compared with most people's definition!

For some people, their sense of what it would mean to be wealthy is shaky. They don't seem to have an *internal* barometer that says when enough is enough. Instead, they look to *external* sources to tell them when they have enough money, a big enough house, or a good enough job. They mistakenly believe that they *need* to have a great deal to feel safe. When they get to whatever that point is, they generally raise the bar, believing that they need still more.

We believe that our sense of wealth is dependent on two things. The first is establishing our own *internal* sense of knowing what "enough" is. The second is to create a sufficient "cushion" for ourselves so that we know we do have enough. This is our safety net, our personal reserve.

LIVING IN A WORLD OF ABUNDANCE

Many spiritual writers would say that we have available to us an abundance of everything we need in the universe, but that our blindness keeps us from seeing that this is the case. Working with abundance in this way is a matter of mind-set, which is addressed in Chapter 14. People can believe in a world of abundance but not *do their part* to ensure that it is available to them when needed. This is one reason why abundance and availability can differ.

Many teaching stories and parables in spiritual writings emphasize that *readiness* and *preparedness* are critical. A good example is in the Bible's parable of women waiting for a bridegroom. Darkness had fallen, and some women had not prepared their oil lamps in advance. It's not enough to know where to get oil for one's lamp, for example—we have to place it in the lamp and have the wick trimmed in order to be ready to live our intentions and to open the doors to all that is available to us.

An example of how the world changes through abundance versus scarcity thinking is a story told by a Native American man about when he was a boy, living with his grandfather in a wooden house along the shore of a lake. In wintertime, the wind whistled through the chinks in the wood of their home. Life as the boy knew it was the grandest adventure of all time. He experienced unbounded happiness and joy in his daily living. He and his grandfather had everything they needed.

But then one day a white man entered his grandfather's home and pronounced the pair poor and in need of assistance. The storyteller stated that his young life (his whole life, really) changed in that instant. In one fell verbal swoop, abundance mentality was replaced by scarcity mentality. In that moment, the grand adventure that was his life began to feel tarnished.

Some would argue that the white man's words just introduced a note of reality and described things as they really were. We don't think so.

271

Viewing that same situation, stepping into that house on the shores of the frozen lake, we would have said that the boy and his grandfather were extraordinarily rich relative to people who own many possessions and have a lot of money in the bank or whose houses don't have any wind whistling through them.

The white man made a declaration that, from his point of view, the boy and his grandfather were poor; he did this without offering any definition of what it means to be rich. Had the boy been coached by one of us, we would have asked him to consider what he needed to have in reserve in a multitude of areas—to put his specific needs, wants, and desires within a context. Without specificity, we may always feel poor because we work without *clarity* and without *context*. To paraphrase Thoreau: The boy gathers his materials to build a bridge to the moon, and the middle-aged man uses them to build a woodshed. Both are rich. Their contexts and intentions differ. So, how much wood is enough for each of them?

We want you to work with your clients and the specific details here. "The angel is in the details," we sometimes hear people say. It's critical for you and your clients to know your standards around reserve, so that you, and they, can begin to create it, one small step at a time if necessary.

GETTING IN SYNC WITH WHAT WE WANT

As adults, we may need to shift the ways we think about money and wealth—how it gets created and how it works—if those beliefs no longer serve us. If we grew up believing that we needed to struggle, work hard, suffer, and exhaust ourselves to make enough money, our beliefs need some revision. In fact, we need to discover that those beliefs may actually deter us from achieving what we want because exhausted, depleted human beings do not attract richness, spaciousness, and openness to their life. In fact, they attract more exhausted, depleted resources.

How does this work? Dr. Werner Von Braun, whom many consider the father of the U.S. space program, was once quoted as saying, "One cannot be exposed to the law and order of the universe without concluding that there must be a divine intent behind it all" (Hill, 1976, p. ii).

Obviously, he possessed a tremendous understanding of the laws of the universe, and he understood just how consistent and precise those laws are. One of those laws is the *law of attraction*. Through this law, living things attract what they most need for their existence at any given time, based on what they are communicating. How it works, very simplified, is that everything in the universe is in a constant state of movement, of vibration. The impulses communicated by this vibration draw other moving, vibrating things that match in some way the impulses that are emitted. People and other living things resonate with one another. We are all composed of electrical and cellular impulses, and we resonate with what is similar to our being or what our thoughts are holding. You might say that the vibrations attract similar vibrations, much as a logical person often is drawn to other logical people or an emotional person often is drawn to other emotional people. We even use language that reflects the physics of this phenomenon—we say that two people are on the same wavelength. As coaches, we can harness the law of attraction to assist clients in examining and refining their intentions.

Bob Proctor, in his book *You Were Born Rich* (Proctor, 1997), uses an acorn as a graphic example of how the law of attraction works. Like anything else that appears to be solid, an acorn (like we as human beings) is really a mass of molecules at a very high speed of vibration. Within the acorn is a patterned plan that governs the end product into which it will grow. As soon as the acorn is planted, the patterned plan sets up a force and begins to attract everything that vibrates in synchronicity or harmony with it. It attracts all the necessary particles of energy from the ground and they begin to join up and grow. As it expands, little shoots grow out of the bottom, forming roots. They begin to grow upward and eventually break through the earth. These top shoots then begin attracting molecules from the atmosphere, continuing their growth until eventually they become an oak tree.

An even simpler example is to think of two magnets. If you flip them one way, they don't attract each other. If you reverse them, the opposing polarities when in close proximity have a strong attraction. That's why we say that some people have a *magnetic personality*. When we say someone is attractive, we often confuse attraction with their looks. What we really mean is that people are drawn to them.

The attraction principle works similarly in human beings. The human body is one of the most efficient electrical instruments in the entire universe. This is not new information, for many years we have been reading the electrical impulses of the brain (an electroencephalogram) and the heart (an electrocardiogram). In fact, the brain is really a vibratory instrument. Energy is palpable and is felt by us when we're in contact with it. Daniel Goleman's books on emotional intelligence, including *Primal Leadership* (Goleman, 1995, 2002), contain excellent, readable information about the ways in which our human neurobiology create *open loops* so that we are affected by one another and by all living things. Goleman says that our emotions are as contagious to other people as viruses are.

We've all heard people talk about "good vibes," "bad vibes," and vibrations, but the vast majority of people are not aware of the connection between their vibrations and what they create in their lives. It's very common to see people with "bad vibes" trying very hard to get good results, while at the same time their negative vibrations draw to them all manner of negative people and situations. You know how this works and how palpable it is if you've ever walked into a room filled with a group of angry people. Even if you are facing their backs and can't see their faces, you can clearly feel the energy of anger.

Unlike human beings, acorns don't have the ability to change their vibratory rate. Consequently, they can only grow into what they have been programmed to become—namely, oak trees. But we have the ability to change our vibratory rate and therefore to make choices about what we are creating. We do this through what we envision, how we hold our emotions, how we choose to meditate, and how we synchronize ourselves with something larger than ourselves.

If this sounds purely metaphorical to you, solid research exists on how it works.

Meditation, prayer, and spiritual practices are ways in which we affect our thoughts and our bodies, which affect the ways that our vibratory systems work. Recent research on the heart's vibrations conducted by Doc Childre's group, HeartMath, supports this assertion (McCraty & Childre, 2006). It turns out that a person's thoughts and visualizations affect the heart's ability to synchronize with the brain, and that when synchronization occurs, it is detectable by research and is apparent to others. This synchronization can be detected through biofeedback methods that are simple and reliable. And, of course, we notice it in the way we feel, as well. The simple practices that HeartMath recommends can alter the synchronization of the heart and brain.

The HeartMath research found that even when we're not consciously communicating with others, our physiological systems interact in subtle and surprising ways. Did you know that the electromagnetic signal produced by your heart is registered in the brain waves of people around you? Or that your physiological responses sync up with your mate's during empathic interactions? The heart's electromagnetic field is believed to act as a central synchronizing signal within the body, an important carrier of emotional information, and a key mediator of energetic interactions between people.

HeartMath has created research and programs for schools that focus on using HeartMath processes for character building and reducing the stress associated with math exams, as well as for teaching kids about love. Their Web site is located at www.HeartMath.org. One of their best research papers is called "The Appreciative Heart: The Psychophysiology of Positive Emotions and Optimal Functioning," which describes their research on how the heart rhythms associated with gratitude, appreciation, and prayer affect stress, health, and well-being. This and other research pages are downloadable as e-books from the HeartMath site.

It should be no surprise, then, that the goal or image that we plant in our mind by constantly dwelling on it is the patterned plan or nucleus that determines what we will grow into. It determines what we will attract to us and what we will repel.

In an orderly universe, nothing occurs accidentally. The images a client plants in his marvelous mind instantly set up a force that intentionally creates specific results in life. This means that we coach clients to intentionally get into harmony with what they want out of life rather than what they don't want. In that way, clients draw to themselves what they need to learn in order to create what they want. Clients often discover that this principle appears as if it is synchronicity at work, as Carl Jung wrote about extensively. Synchronicity works because clients draw to themselves what they need at any given time. Sometimes what they need comes in the form of key experiences that create significant learning and shifts that are necessary for forward movement at a specific time in their life.

MAKING IT PRACTICAL

How can clients create *more than enough* of what they need so that they never need to worry about running out? How can clients learn to manage themselves so that their emotions do not get in the way of creating? For most clients, the major challenge is to manage themselves around fears and anxieties. Some of these fears and anxieties are based in old learning, and others may come from television images or from the bombardment of political statements designed to create urgency through a sense of impending terror.

Some writers have said that babies come into the world with only two innate fears, one of which is a fear of falling. Without unnecessary fear, humans are free to create, to act, and to explore. When clients come to terms with unnecessary fears, most of them come to understand that scarcity is simply a habitual way of thinking. Scarcity robs clients of the ability to feel appreciation for the abundance they do have in many areas of their lives. When we coach clients, we focus on the importance of having a sense of abundance—a reserve or a sense of wealth—in key areas: *relationship (or love), time, vision, money, career,* and *contribution.*

Coaches can start clients in working with their reserve by asking them to consider and record their initial responses to these questions:

How would you know you had a reserve in each of these areas—relationship/love, time, vision, money, career, and contribution? What structures would be in place so that you would have more than just enough and could generously give to others?

The coaching skill of visioning can be helpful to clients as they consider these questions. After identifying what would be present, ask the clients to answer these questions:

How would you behave differently?
How would you give to others in this area?

EXERCISE 13.1
Examining reserve

Ask the clients to complete this exercise as a fieldwork assignment. We've found it best to have a strong alliance with clients already in place before doing work on reserve, as the coaches will likely find themselves challenging some of the clients' deeply held beliefs.

A reserve of time for me would be evident in this way:

How I would then give time to others:

A reserve of money for me would be evident in this way:

How I would then give money to others

A reserve of caring or love for me would be evident in this way:

How I would then give care or love to others:

When the clients return for the next coaching session, the coaching task is to help them develop a plan for creating a reserve in one of the key areas identified in the exercise. The plan should include specific actions, and the coaches should request that the clients complete at least one of the actions during the time between this session and the next one. Sometimes clients discover that in order to create a true sense of wealth for themselves, they need to simplify. For example, they may discover that to create a wealth of time, they need to have a smaller house with a smaller yard to mow. To create a plan for this may take more than one session, and it will not be accomplished necessarily in a short time. However, taking the steps to create the plan will bring the clients a sense of future freedom.

EXERCISE 13.2
Creating a reserve of time

The coach training program at ILCT includes an out-of-print text by Dave Ellis called *Human Being* (Ellis & Lankowtiz, 1995). Within the text are a myriad of exercises that coaches can use with clients in the areas of time, health, wealth, money, and relationships.

We commonly ask clients to explore through fieldwork how they spend their time by listing typical weekly recurring activities—not responses to crises but those things they currently allow time for. They often need to examine their work calendars, confer with a spouse, and examine children's sports schedules, as well as family requirements. Once the clients create the list, the coaches ask them to consider each of the typical activities and to identify to

EXERCISE 13.2 (continued)

what extent each one is consistent with or supportive of the clients' values and commitments, or the extent to which it conflicts with their core values and commitments.

At the next coaching session, the coaches work with the clients to identify ways to eliminate recurring activities that are not aligned with values, or to modify the way the clients do these activities to bring them more in alignment with core values and commitments.

EXERCISE 13.3
Choices versus obligations

Clients tend to feel a stronger sense of a reserve around time when they choose how to spend it instead of investing time in the obligations imposed by others. Obligations are part of human life, of course, but people often misjudge and minimize the extent to which they have control over obligations and consequently don't explore ways to create more choice in their life. Ask the clients these questions:

Are you satisfied with the way you currently spend time?

Are you doing what you've chosen to do?

How much time do you spend on obligations imposed by others?

How much alignment is there between what you want and what you do?

What is the most important thing I can do to bring your activities in line with your values and your vision?

Coach the clients, using the above exercises, to make informed decisions about how they spend their time. For example, ask them to do a planning exercise that includes predictable events, errands, unexpected events, time for recreation and other self-nurturing activities, and so on. Ask them to plan time around life purpose and other priorities.

Then ask the clients to find a blank weekly calendar form. The clients can use their computer calendar system, such as Outlook, to find this kind of form. The task is to plan an ideal week, determining how they would spend their time during such a week, given their current job, family situation, and so on. They can include the events from the previous planning exercise but will be making conscious decisions about all other unplanned available time so that the week will serve them as the ideal.

EXERCISE 13.4

The meaning of money

Clients have many deeply held beliefs about money that can interfere with their desires. As Deepak Chopra says, we call money *currency*. Consequently, there should be a *flow* as we earn, use, and spend money. Many quoted masters describe an attitude of abundance such that if money is used wisely, it returns to us. On the other hand, hoarding money is a misuse of money. Saving is good—hoarding is not.

Ask the clients to complete two lists about money. First, ask them to list on one side of a page their beliefs about what money *is.* Then, ask them to list on the other side of a page their beliefs about what money *is not.*

At the next coaching session, discuss the lists with them, looking for any patterns of thinking that sound childlike—that once may have served the clients well but no longer do.

For example, it might be difficult for clients to find fulfillment in life if they have any of the following beliefs:

Money is a measure of competence.

Money is a source of evil.

Money solves all problems in life or cures all diseases.

Money is a source of power and control.

People's money is an indication of their worth.

Money buys happiness.

Some healthy beliefs about money might include the following:

Money affects how people and organizations come together in relationship.

Money catalyzes people to work, take action, serve, and do things that organizations and others are willing to pay to have done.

Money is something that some people inherit, but only a few are born with extensive wealth.

Money requires management and takes a level of responsibility to manage wisely.

Money is a primary source of unnecessary anxiety and worry in many people's lives.

Money can be a way that people measure the value of their time, energy, and contribution.

Noticing how we spend our money can be a measure of what we value.

EXERCISE 13.5
Early beliefs about money

We have found it useful to ask clients, as fieldwork, to write down several of their earliest memories around money. Questions might include the following:

Ask the clients to write down two early memories, preferably from elementary school or earlier.

Ask the clients to list what they learned about money from each of their parents or other family members who were prominent influences during their elementary school days. What messages about money did they receive from these important influences in their life?

Ask: "When in your life have you had a sense of being 'really wealthy'?" Feel free to interpret wealth as beyond just money. What was occurring in your life at that point?

Some people believe that "money is condensed personality." If that is true, what does your relationship with money say about you?

For example, one of Diane Menendez's earliest memories included a kindergarten example. At that time, kindergarten was the first year of school, and Friday was banking day. During class, kids could bring in whatever money they wanted to bank. They received a savings passbook, and the savings contributions were recorded by the teacher in the passbook. The teacher had a student who served as the banker, making sure that the money was deposited in a metal box with a lock. Diane always volunteered to be the banker. It gave her practice in learning to count, which she had learned from her parents before kindergarten.

What this early memory meant to her is that savings were always important. No matter what, have something that you save regularly. It gives her pleasure to notice her savings.

From both of her parents, Diane learned that money came through working, and working always came before play. Diane needed to work to reprogram herself around this latter belief in order to create a fulfilling life for herself.

Other Exercises
From the *Human Being* text (Ellis & Lankowitz, 1995) we use at ILCT, we assign students these exercises:

EXERCISE 13.6
Take a first step about money

This exercise asks the clients to fill in the following sentence stems. We use it as a fieldwork exercise and then work on it with the clients in a coaching session.

When it comes to money, I usually feel . . .
My greatest difficulty with money right now is . . .
One thing I do well about managing money is . . .
To me, financial success means . . .
What I most want to change about my relationship with money is . . .
The career I want to have 5 years from now is . . .
The things I want to be doing in my nonworking hours 5 years from now include . . .
The biggest change I would like to make in my life regarding money is . . .
Managing money more effectively could help me make that change by . . .

The next part of this exercise asks the clients to examine their statements and to engage in reprogramming attitudes about money.
Fallacies:

Money is evil.
Money is sacred.
Money is complicated.
Money is scarce.
Frugality ain't fun.

Consciously choose which beliefs about money to keep and which ones to let go. Then write a new belief statement about money.

EXERCISE 13.7
Match values and money

This exercise asks clients to begin by monitoring what they spend. Getting the clients to do this first step itself can be eye-opening, as many people do not know how much they spend each day, each week, or each month.

Write your expenses from the past month on separate 3 x 5 cards.
Write fundamental values on separate 3 x 5 cards.
Sort the cards, trying to pair each expense card with a values card.
Assess how well your spending aligns with your values.
Write a Discovery Statement ("I discovered that I . . .") and an Intention Statement ("I intend to . . .")

EXERCISE 13.8
The Life Balance Wheel and money

Clients can be in reserve in areas of life beyond finances and money, coaches believe. Ask the client to refer to the Wheel of Life areas and to indicate in which of these areas they feel *in reserve*. The coaches can also just provide the clients with a list of areas to consider, such as these:

- ❏ Time
- ❏ Money
- ❏ Love
- ❏ Relationships
- ❏ Space
- ❏ Freedom
- ❏ Connections
- ❏ Possibilities
- ❏ Play
- ❏ Quality of Life
- ❏ Spirit
- ❏ Energy

Then, in a coaching session, ask the clients what principles or practices enable them to be in reserve in areas where they experience a reserve. Look for opportunities to apply similar practices and principles in areas where the clients are not in reserve and believe they would benefit from having a sense of *more than just enough* in an area.

Even though this chapter is titled "How Wealthy Are You?" it's not limited to the usual sense of wealth as money. Wealth, in the larger view, is about having a sense of abundance and wealth, and a ready reserve in all areas of life. A sense of wealth is unique to each individual and can be created thoughtfully in any area of a person's life.

Chapter 14

Mind-set Is Causative

The experience you have is a result of how you see . . . and how you see is a result of the experience you have. Your mind-set, your beliefs, and your body all work together.

As we begin to examine how coaches work with mind-set, you might take a look at a poem by Portia Nelson—"An Autobiography in Five Short Chapters" (Nelson, 1993)—and how it speaks to you about your work with your clients. The poem points out, in just five stanzas, both the importance and difficulty of changing how we observe, explain, create stories, take responsibility for our choices, and ultimately create new lives for ourselves.

An Autobiography in Five Short Chapters
I
I walk down the street.
There is a deep hole in the sidewalk.
    I fall in.
I am lost . . . I am helpless.
      It isn't my fault.
      It takes forever to find a way out.

II
I walk down the same street.
There is a deep hole in the sidewalk.
      I pretend I don't see it.
      I fall in again.
I can't believe I am in this same place.
        But it isn't my fault.
It still takes a long time to get out.

III
I walk down the same street.

There is a deep hole in the sidewalk.
　I see it is there.
　I still fall in . . . it's a habit . . . but,
　　My eyes are open.
　　I know where I am.
　It is my fault.
　I get out immediately.

IV

I walk down the same street.
There is a deep hole in the sidewalk.
　I walk around it.

V

　I walk down another street.

People's responses to events are *mediated.* In other words, when an event takes place, our responses—our behaviors—are shaped by (a) our *interpretation* of the event, which is a consequence of our beliefs, attitudes, and assumptions, and (b) the *feelings* generated by those beliefs, attitudes, and assumptions. Those beliefs, attitudes, and assumptions are the preexisting lenses we wear and look through, which determine, or at least color, our observation and interpretation of events.

This chapter focuses on mind-set—the clients' habitual patterns of thinking, feeling, and responding, which make it more likely that they'll continue in a certain pattern in the absence of a big interruption or disruption to call those patterns into question. Because our memories, learning, and consciousness reside in all *of* our cells, we include the body in our definition of *mind-set.*

One of the coach's key roles is to assist clients in learning how they habitually see the world. As Peter Drucker, the well-known business consultant and author, once said, "We don't know who discovered water, but we know it wasn't fish" (2003). Our own thinking—our mind-set—tends to be invisible to us, as water is to the fish. We don't know what we don't know—that's the basis for being unconsciously incompetent about something. Coaching helps with that and also helps clients create what they want through creating conversations about possibilities. We sometimes say that coaching is a *possibilities* conversation, not a *guarantees* conversation.

Many research studies illustrate the power of mind-set, including an often-cited experiment in shooting baskets. An experimenter divided a group of basketball players into two groups. One group was to practice shooting free throws. The other group was asked to just visualize shooting free throws: to look at the basket and visualize themselves making the shot. Each person then shot a series of free throws. The not-surprising conclusion, as many star athletes will tell you, is that the group that visualized made more free throws than the group that actually practiced. Why? Visualization—which is the mind-set at work—coupled with skill gives a better result. The opposite is also true. How many times have you seen an athlete choke because he was visualizing a negative result. He is afraid to miss the shot, swing the club, miss the pass. The very thing he is imagining and afraid of actually does happen. How many of you have played golf and know that you can hit a nice 100-yard shot—until you see water in front of you? Your mind-set is, "Don't go in the water, don't go in the water." You repeatedly tell yourself about the water. And, of course, you are focused on the water and your ball goes right there, in exactly the place you are focused.

It is because of this fact that we say *mind-set is causative.*

To change a mind-set requires two things: recognizing the need for change and being able to observe yourself and notice when you're thinking or paying attention to things in a way that characteristically doesn't bring you what you want.

As coaches, our task is to:

* Surface the clients' mind-set and name it with them: "I'm operating from fear," or "You're operating from fear." In other words, the coaches support the clients to notice how they notice—the lens through which they view life.
* Build in conscious choice. Ask the clients: "Does that mind-set support you in creating the future you want?" Probably not.
* Have the clients take action on a new choice of mind-set and practice acting *as if* they live from that mind-set all the time.

Here is an example from a participant in an ILCT class, a man who flourished in the military and then became a counselor. He reported how he changed his mind-set. He used to have the belief, "I need to take control." In a class we were leading, we asked him to say more about that: "What's the *because* that underpins that belief?" He responded, "Because if I don't take control, we'll flounder!"

Most long-held beliefs like this are deeply ingrained because the clients have thought them so many times that strong, mylineated neural pathways in their brain make it easy for the thought to run in that way: these are like *brain ruts.* In the case of the counselor with a background in the military, class discussion started him on a new path. With the teacher as coach, he decided that his first step was to learn to notice the pervasiveness of the mind-set of control and the places where his attention went in his everyday life. He learned to consciously catch himself and lightly say, "Okay, Joe, now you're being a control freak."

Since awareness on its own isn't enough, how did he change this pattern? His coach asked him to begin to notice people who held mind-sets different from his. He noticed what those mind-sets were and asked himself what it would be like if he held them. He noticed that one thing he might say to himself is, "I could trust that the best will always happen. I don't always need to *make* it happen." He experimented with this new mind-set for a few weeks, religiously, and then noticed what was happening. He discovered that when he held this mind-set, "other people stepped up to the plate and made things happen, too, because he let them."

Some readers who have studied phenomenology, which was part of existential psychology during the 1960s (Rollo May, R. D. Laing, Victor Frankl, and others), call this the *observing self:* the ability to observe what you do while you are doing it. When clients access their observer self, they notice the phenomenon of their experience in the moment and then ask themselves what they can learn from that. The observer self increases clients' awareness—as if from an outside observer frame— which thereby increase the clients' choices for action.

Pat Williams used to teach clients who were fearful of attending a family reunion, for example, to go and imagine themselves sitting outside themselves watching themselves participate as if in the show. They noticed whether the patterns played out as usual: was the usual drama going on? This third-party perspective helped them be neutral and to detach from their habitual emotional patterns. In the strategies from neuro-linguistic programming, this is described as "third-person perspective." A first-person perspective looks at the situation from the person's own eyes. A second-person perspective experiences the situation from the perspective of another person. A third-person perspective watches both (or all) of the people, as well as the situation. From a third-person perspective, you can see yourself as well as observe; it's a further layer of detachment.

Coaches assist clients in developing their skills at observing themselves and their habitual behaviors, thoughts, and emotions. Clients need to be aware of how to gain distance from and perspective on their thoughts, feelings, and behavior, and how to step outside automatic behaviors.

Becoming aware of the *observing self* requires us to detach from our experience enough to notice how we are seeing and explaining to ourselves and others what is occurring.

Our everyday way of observing allows us to see some things and causes us to disregard others. Consequently, our experience is shaped by the ways in which we characteristically and habitually observe, dwell in, and explain our world. Our habits of thinking, our habitual moods, our habits of using our energy, the ways we hold our bodies, and the stories we use to explain what has happened, what is happening, and what will happen—all of these habits and actions shape how we see and experience the world. They circumscribe our world and limit our possibilities.

We tend to notice only what our mind-set accepts. Depressed clients seldom notice the good things. They are too mired in the mind-set (and bodily experience) of depression to have anything else register in their awareness.

When coaches work with clients' *mind-sets,* they work with the greatest potential for the clients' development. Once clients have identified what they want to create, the major question becomes whether they have the mind-set—the beliefs, lenses, flow of energy, determination, and persistence—that it takes to bring their vision into reality. If they don't, your challenge as a coach is to support them in shifting their mind-set and clearing the path to their self-expression and fulfillment.

HOW MIND-SET IS SOURCED

When a mind-set becomes so familiar that it is habitual, we may lose sight of it as something we have adopted and mistake it for reality. When this happens, we may focus outside of ourselves and say, "That's just how the world is," unaware that we have choices. When this occurs, we are operating out of *core beliefs*—about ourselves, others, and the world—that tend to be pervasive across the contexts of our experiences. Core beliefs generally dominate thinking and lead to predictable behaviors. They also limit our lives because we can only experience what our mind-set allows us to perceive and predict.

Back in Chapter 3, "Coaching as a Developmental Change Process," we introduced Kegan's levels of consciousness as one way of describing how consciousness develops. At each level, a particular mind-set is likely to dominate. Clients struggle when what they want to achieve in coaching is blocked by a mind-set that is a holdover from an earlier level of consciousness. Or they struggle when they are blocked by specific experiences that were so intense that they have created *brain ruts;* that is, the habitual response is so wired into the clients' neural pathways that when the stimulus occurs, the neurons immediately fire in the habitual sequence. It will take many repetitions to create a new "brain trail" to replace the old one.

As clients are developing and growing, they are often in transition between levels. This is when coaches are most likely to see the clients struggling with issues of mind-set.

For example, let's return to the case we examined in Chapter 3: George the chiropractor, who is working with you on career issues. His plans and goals primarily reflect the *independent self* (Kegan's Stage 4). Perhaps he wishes to make a career change, which would move him away from a familiar 20-year career and which strays from others' expectations of him. He has not fully transitioned into Stage 4, as evidenced by his intense fears around being judged by others and being separated from others. These fears manifest as a lack of confidence in his ability to create a different career for himself.

George's fear is a signal that his current way of being and observing will not take him where he wants to go without addressing *how* he observes and interprets the situation and his choices. This is a perfect

288

opportunity for a coach to support George's development by providing him with tools for transforming his mind-set.

What does the coach do? Some self-help writers might say, "Feel the fear and do it anyway." As life coaches, we encourage clients to first become an astute observers of themselves—to observe the ways they consistently gather data, what they notice and what they ignore, how they make judgments about situations, and what data they use to make these judgments. We ask them to notice how they hold their body, how they breathe in situations where they feel fearful. We ask them to notice their internal dialogue and to notice which aspects of the situation they are taking in and which aspects they are ignoring.

As a coach, you work with George the chiropractor to assist him in becoming aware of the tendencies of his ways of being and observing, and in beginning to make distinctions about other possible perspectives and options. Once he has stopped to notice, can make distinctions, and can comfortably live with the fact that, "Yes, this is how I'm seeing the situation—and I recognize that there are other ways of observing it," he is ready to make a transformational shift that can be maintained.

Clients' mind-sets often show up visibly around their perceptions of their body, their health, and the ways they consider self-care. Superb self-care is critical to our clients as well as to us as coaches. Our integrity gets jeopardized when we encourage self-care for our clients and don't take care of ourselves well. These are common areas where human beings struggle. Sometimes the issue is that the clients are holding old or outdated, unexamined beliefs about body, health, and self-care (or other areas).

Matthew Budd (Budd & Rothstein, 2000) made a distinction that can be useful in coaching around mind-set. Budd and other philosophers, including Fernando Flores, believe that human beings often confuse their *assessments* with their *assertions.* An assessment is "a judgment that you make about the world in the interest of taking some action" (Budd & Rothstein, 2000, p. 138). For example, Diane Menendez might say, "It's a beautiful day!" She's in Cincinnati on the first day of spring, the sun is shining after weeks of rain and cloud cover, and it's 60 degrees outside. On the other hand, Pat might not agree at all that it's a beautiful day. For Pat, who spends a lot of time in the Rocky Mountains, a "beautiful day" would be a summer day where the sun is shining through a grove of aspen trees next to a mountain stream or a beautiful day might be a winter day when the weather is snowy, the sun is out, and Pat can snow-shoe through the woods. Our point here is that beauty as a quality is *not* in the day itself, but rather in the eyes of the person who makes the judgment about beauty using his or her particular standards for it. Assessments are not facts—they are interpretations and opinions. They may have once been informed by facts and standards, but the person who makes the assessment may no longer remember the standard at all.

An *assertion,* on the other hand, is a statement a person makes for which he or she is willing to provide evidence, and the evidence is something that can be measured—height, weight, size, event, and so on. A good assessment is grounded in assertions. The person can return to commonly agreed-upon standards for making the judgment that is the assessment.

When we coach clients around body, health, self-care, and almost any other area, what will emerge first is their assessments. Their assessments are windows into their mind-set. These may have been formed very early in their lives and not adjusted. They may no longer be based in facts—assertions—but instead on some memory of being the recipient of someone's judgments or of learning how something *should* be. This occurs frequently with young women, who take in their culture's assessments on how much a young woman should weigh, how she should look. In the United States, this has resulted in many young woman believing they are overweight without realizing that they have taken in the culture's and the media's assessments as their own without thinking about them. So one way of working with clients around this area is to ask them to list their beliefs about body, health, self-care, and so on, and then help them discover the sources of these beliefs. What assertions and assessments are holding the beliefs together?

Ask yourself:
What is your mind-set around your body?
Your health? Around self-care?

USING WILBER'S FOUR QUADRANT MODEL TO
MAKE DISTINCTIONS FOR OBSERVING

In Chapter 3, we introduced Ken Wilber's Four Quadrant model for identifying the factors that together shape the way an individual views a
situation. A person is often more aware of some quadrants than others.
For example, many physicians are highly skilled in the exterior-individual
quadrant and much less skilled in the interior-individual quadrant. The
two left-hand quadrants, the interior-individual and the interior-collective, generally are fertile places from which to ask clients to observe their
way of being and observing in the world.

When the coach asks George to observe his ongoing interior
dialogue, the coach is asking George to identify the running commentary
his mind makes on his experience. That's an interior-individual (Quadrant 1) approach to George's experience. George might discover how
pessimistic his internal dialogue is and how a common mind-set for him
is "It won't work!" whenever he considers new possibilities.

George, for example, may be ignoring how much his way of being
and observing has been shaped by the cultural (interior-collective) quadrant. In order to examine the impact of that quadrant, we need to look at
the cumulative impact of events on an individual at a particular time in
history or from a particular culture. You might consider steering George
to the Internet to explore this issue. One resource would be the Beloit
College Web site, which, for the past five years, has created and distrib-
uted what it calls a "Mind-set List" for each recent freshman class.[1]

Beloit created the lists as a reminder of the many ways in which 17-
and 18-year-olds entering U.S. colleges or higher education see the
world differently from their professors, coaches, and mentors. One of the
benefits of the lists is that they illustrate how situations are held as *truths*
when a person lives in a time when something has always been true. The
Web site says, for example, that "the 2003 entering students have grown
up in a country where the presidents have all been Southerners and in a
world with AIDS and without apartheid. Saturns have always been on the
street, the Fox Network has always been on television, and prom dresses

291

---

[1] See www.beloit.edu/~pubaff/mindset/02index.html for 5 years of U.S.-centric mind-set
lists.

have always come in basic black. The evil empire is not earthbound, the drug Ecstasy has always been available, and with the breakup of AT&T, nobody has been able to comprehend a phone bill."

A coach might ask George to consider what a *mind-set* list for his generation, his family, and his cultural background might have on it—since all of these factors are influencing him now and probably tie in to the fear he is experiencing as well.

In Figure 14.1, first introduced in Chapter 3, the Interior-Individual quadrant is the focus of most of the work done in the helping professions, including spiritual direction. This quadrant is rich territory for coaching. If you use the Enneagram in your therapy or coaching, you could say that each of the nine Enneagram types has a pervasive mind-set. The Enneagram is an ancient system of examining the preconditioned points of view of nine spiritual-psychological frameworks. Each of these frameworks has its strengths, and each one also has characteristic ways of blocking individuals from a sense of wholeness in the world.

Figure 14.1
The client and the context

Interior		Exterior	
Individual	I INTENTIONAL emotional, mental, spiritual: impulses, perceptions, sensations, levels of trust for self, other, world, values, belief, moods, etc.		IT BEHAVIORAL physical, neurological, body, brain, behavior, things encountered, neural patterns, physiology, etc.
Collective	WE CULTURAL relationships, community, service, morals and ethics, myths, social expectations and rules, world view country of origin		ITS SOCIAL systems and institutions: rules, patterns, machinery

When we work with clients to develop their abilities to self-observe, we can ask them to consider and notice where they may be holding their beliefs too rigidly. For the client George, then, it might be beneficial to invite him to think about rigidity by introducing him to the ideas of learned optimism and learned pessimism. You might ask him to read the article summary below, "Learned Optimism, Learned Pessimism," and then to observe which of the patterns (or a modification thereof) he is using that may be driving his career fears.

Learned Optimism, Learned Pessimism

Martin Seligman, a past president of the American Psychological Association, has devoted much of his career to researching various ways that the *observer* becomes rigidified. In a lecture we attended, Seligman linked the incidence of depression in teenagers to mind-set patterns that we can trace back to a disturbance in Wilber's Four Quadrants. Seligman's research indicated that depression is 10 times more common than it was two generations ago. In fact, the average age for the onset of depression in wealthy nations has dropped from 29.5 to 14 years old. Seligman (2003) attributed the drop to three causes:

> I/We Balance: *We have become rampantly individualistic, where our grandparents had larger entities with which to connect. Our grandparents had rich, comfortable spiritual furniture in which to sit—God, community and extended families to console them. These have crumbled. Our children have threadbare spiritual furniture to sit in.*

> Self-esteem Movement: *Thirty years ago, it was* The Little Engine That Could, *while today the emblematic books suggest feeling good about yourself no matter what you do.*

> Victimology: *It is legion in the U.S. to blame others. Seligman noted some of the benefits, for example, for alcoholics who can now say it's a disease and seek treatment without thinking they are terrible people, and for the Civil Rights movement, which acknowledged the capabilities of people while stating that many are victims of discrimination. Victimology disempowers people because it takes the focus away from what they can do and puts their focus on others. We know this from examples like that of Victor Frankl. Frankl survived Auschwitz, the World War II concentration camp, by focusing on a future he desired and using his day-to-day experience of suffering as a means of learning about human behavior. It would have been easy for him to embrace victimology: he was, in fact, an incarcerated victim of religious persecution. He did not succumb but instead took it upon himself to forgo the role of victim and play the role*

293

of a survivor. He took responsibility for his life. The major cost of victi-
mology is the erosion of responsibility, according to Seligman.

Seligman's research on learning indicates that individuals have a pessimistic or optimistic observer based on a pessimistic or optimistic way of thinking. In other words, optimistic individuals tend to see the benefits of events, have half the tendency for depression, achieve more, enjoy better physical health, sustain better interpersonal relationships, and also are less realistic. Here's how they do it:

When a setback or *negative* experience occurs, three characteristics of an optimistic individual's thinking come into play. An optimist's explanatory style, in contrast with a pessimist's explanatory style, is to perceive and experience the event as: (a) temporary rather than permanent; (b) local (to the event) rather than pervasive; and (c) attributable to external causes. This third characteristic is worth elaborating on: the optimist makes an *external* attribution, crediting outside contributing circumstances, as opposed to an *internal* attribution, crediting the individual's actions, lack thereof, or way of being for the setback.

Conversely, when optimistic individuals have a *positive* experience, they see it as permanent and pervasive, and make internal attributions—the same characteristics of the pessimistic style for setbacks! The pessimistic explanatory style, when a setback or negative event occurs, is a key contributor to depression.

Not all pessimists end up in therapy. You will find many coaching clients using a pessimistic explanatory style around specific areas of their lives, such as health, body, relationships, family, and so on. As coaches, we can help them by challenging their explanation—that is, raising questions that challenge and dispute their mind-set. This is different from simply affirming a different way of being or behaving.

Ideally, a coach can aim for assisting a client in developing *flexible optimism*. Seligman suggested in the same lecture, "When the cost of failure is high, use the pessimist's realism. When the cost of failure is low, use the optimist's realism. You don't want a pilot using an optimist's realism to decide whether he or she should de-ice the plane. You certainly don't want to use an optimist's realism to decide whether you should have an affair that could ruin your relationships with your family."

Optimism can be an important coaching focus. Much of the research on *emotional intelligence* done by Reuven Bar-On (1997) and by Daniel Goleman (2005) identifies *optimism* as a competency of emotional intelligence. Bar-On's self-assessment, the Emotional Quotient Inventory (or EQ-I), identifies two factors that are highly correlated with success: *optimism* and *happiness*. At ILCT, we have trained many practicing psychologists and licensed therapists, and consequently many students can readily use psychometrically valid assessments with their clients. The EQ-I is particularly helpful to coaches in working with client mind-set (Bar-On, 1997).

How can you use this to assist your client? Seligman has an optimism assessment available on his Web site at www.authentichappiness.org. At the home page, click on the link to the Optimism test.

Ask your client to complete it as a stimulus to self-observation.

WORKING WITH MIND-SET

In the following pages, we describe frequently used coaching methods for working with a client's mind-set or beliefs.

295

Disputing the Belief

A commonly used process to work with beliefs comes from rational-emotive behavioral therapy (REBT), one of whose famous practitioners is Albert Ellis. The ABC framework is used to clarify the relationship between an activating event (A), our beliefs about it (B), and the cognitive-emotional or behavioral consequences of our beliefs (C). A good site we found that explains this clearly for the nonclinician is www.counsellingresource.com/types/rationalle-emotive. While REBT was developed by a psychologist, it has been widely used in nonclinical settings, including schools. If a coach were to use this framework with the control-oriented client described above, the conversation might go like this:

A: *The activating event.* Joe finds himself at a church committee meeting, in charge of a major fund-raising drive for a new building. He is already heading up two other major projects for his church and is very busy at work. When the minister asks, "Who can lead this project?" Joe finds himself automatically thinking, "I have to do it—I have to be in charge of it. If I don't, we'll flounder."

B: *The belief:* "I have to do it—I have to be in charge of it. If I don't, we'll flounder."

C: *The consequences.* If Joe takes on this assignment, he will probably do it well. But he'll be overwhelmed and overloaded, and will feel irritable and somewhat victimized by the fact that nobody else seems to step up.

Once the client has surfaced the belief, the coach's task is to help Joe discover the alternatives. The coach can help him surface some evidence that contradicts this belief as a way of disputing the fact that this is the only way things can happen. The coach might ask, "What evidence do you have that this isn't always true?" Joe will probably have to stretch himself to find some examples. In this case, he reported that when he was laid up after surgery for 8 to 12 weeks, he was amazed at how his church, family, and work all seemed to do okay without him. The coach would help him identify specific examples that contradicted his belief and would discuss with Joe how other people stepped in when Joe was unavailable.

The next step would be to generate alternatives through coaching. The coach might ask, "Joe, what are other things you could say to yourself in situations like these?" and would help Joe identify some new options. Joe might say, as above, "I can trust that the right thing will happen and wait for someone else to step up. Things always do work out." This is a time to have fun with the client and help him take a different perspective. We sometimes ask clients, "What would Robin Williams say or do in this situation?" to jostle them out of a fixed mind-set. Generate several other alternatives with the client, asking how an objective observer might see the situation. For example, what do other people in Joe's congregation seem to be thinking?

The next step is to help Joe identify other actions he can take that grow out of this new way of thinking. For example, the coach might request that Joe wait at least 3 minutes before he volunteers for anything, to leave room for others to step up. Joe could also volunteer somebody else, he could mentor someone in the church, and so on. Any of these are new ways of acting based on a new mind-set. The client's task is to notice, surface, experiment, and then choose to act differently when appropriate.

The hard part, of course, is that many clients have become very successful with the mind-sets they are now trying to change. But often they come to coaching because these mind-sets are contributing to their success but not to their fulfillment. The coach can help clients visualize how they can be successful and fulfilled by thinking differently.

Affirmations

Many of us use affirmations to help ourselves and our clients make mind-set shifts. Since we constantly affirm our beliefs and values, and demonstrate our consciousness through our thoughts, speech, writing, and other actions, affirmations provide unique opportunities for clients to literally put into words, *with conviction,* what they intend to hold, maintain, create, and declare. A popular tool we use with clients is asking them to buy a daybook such as Joan Borysenko's *Pocketful of Miracles* (1994), which contains a thought that is a good mind-starter for each day of the year. These small statements of inner wisdom function to affirm a positive, connected, universal mind-set for clients. They are affirmations.

Affirmations are generally thought of as single sentences repeated frequently that people intend to adopt as a new way of thinking and being. Most affirmations are intention statements. The television show *Saturday Night Live* poked fun of this practice when Al Franken affirmed, "I am good enough, I am smart enough, and doggone it, people like me." Someone may affirm something and be surprised that nothing may happen. Or nothing may happen in a short time. Affirmations are not designed to dispute reality. They are designed as statements of intention, to increase the likelihood that the intention will come to pass. But they are also habits of mind. If the clients' minds have been repeating to themselves for 20 years that they are not good enough, it will take many repetitions of an alternative affirmation before the clients' habits of mind

297

change. they are creating new links between the cells of their brains, and the brain will tend to want to run in the old tracks instead of the new. So someone using affirmations must keep up the practice until the new way of thinking overtakes the old.

Pat Williams spoke with Bill O'Hanlon (personal conversation, 2001) about O'Hanlon's labeling of his brand of therapy as possibility counseling. O'Hanlon said that he doesn't like the terms *negative thinking* and *positive thinking.* Instead, he uses the rubric of possibility because possibility leads a person to a desired outcome via his or her intention. It doesn't guarantee that something negative or positive won't happen—it just makes the outcome more likely based on the client's desired intention. Just teaching someone to think positively isn't enough; there need to be actions that support the desired possibility, as well as an understanding that there is no guarantee. We wonder whether it might instead be called *probability counseling.*

This ties in with our discussion of mind-set in that we believe in living purposefully with a designed plan for change or creation, while also understanding that life happens and adjustments may need to be made.

Sometimes the work clients do with regular affirmations succeeds. At other times, to our dismay, it seems as though something seems to be working against the new mind-set taking root in the clients' life.

If you and a client discover that the new mind-sets are not taking root, we suggest you follow the process that Jeanie Marshall has described in the material on pages 299–302, "Five Types of Affirmations for Empowerment" (Marshall, 2006).[2] By choosing the appropriate affirmation from five possible types, you increase the likelihood of its effectiveness.

Five Types of Affirmations for Empowerment

Five categories of affirmations support you in manifesting powerful change. You may work with affirmations in every category concurrently, or you may focus on a different category each day or each week. It is important that affirmations you select resonate with you—that is, that they feel natural and appropriate. In order to experience this resonance, you may need to change words in the ones listed here as examples, or let these inspire you to create ones you prefer, or develop your own from scratch.

POPULAR AFFIRMATIONS

Many popular affirmations are beautiful; indeed, they are quite extraordinary! However, if you do not believe them, they are useless or even counterproductive. If you say an affirmation you do not believe, saying it repeatedly will not make you believe it. Actually, the repetition can build up greater resistance to believing it. Consider this example: Sam feels powerless. He has had many experiences he can point to that justify his feelings and his belief in his own powerlessness and unworthiness. Saying "I am powerful" is less likely to erase his feelings of powerlessness than to prompt an emphatic reaction, such as, "Oh, no, I'm not!" If Sam does not deal with the resistance, he carries it with him as he lives his life.

An empowering process emerges by using these five categories of affirmations in a systematic way to assist you in embracing an affirmation that you desire to believe but currently do not. If you have an intention and a desire to say and believe "I am powerful," start by releasing powerlessness, open to the possibility of being powerful, affirm an intention and readiness to live in your power, claim your power, and let the idea of powerfulness integrate into your life.

Following are the five categories of affirmations described briefly, with a few examples of each type.

300

1. RELEASING/CLEANSING AFFIRMATIONS

The purpose of releasing and/or cleansing affirmations is to let go of unwanted and unneeded stuff. They allow you to purify your system. These affirmations stimulate the release of toxins such as negative thoughts, repressed or suppressed emotions, old memories, negative bonds with others, bad karma, dark consensus reality, and illusions of all types.

Examples:

I rescind outdated vows of poverty, celibacy, struggle, silence, and unworthiness.

I release resistance.

I let go of old programs that keep me stuck in old patterns.

I let go of everything I do not want or need for my highest good.

2. RECEIVING/ACCEPTING AFFIRMATIONS

The purpose of receiving and/or accepting affirmations is to allow something to be. They allow us to receive goodness from the Universe. They also can neutralize the disproportion of energy—that is, they can reverse illness, karma, or other imbalance. In addition, they help us shift the attention from disempowering actions such as "getting" or "taking" to more freeing concepts such as "receiving," "allowing," and "accepting."

Examples:

I open to the gifts of the Universe.

I allow abundance to flow through me.

I accept support when I need it.

Dear God, please let me know what to do in a way that I can understand.

I accept peace and joy in all aspects of my life.

3. BEING/INTENDING AFFIRMATIONS

The purpose of being and/or intending affirmations is to ground your purpose, especially your higher purpose. These affirmations enhance conscious awareness of your intention about something or about your mission in life. In addition, these affirmations can deepen your understanding of your reason for being and/or acting, either in general or in a specific situation. They can be used to enhance any and all actions.

Examples:

I know that this is for the highest good of all concerned.
I deepen my awareness of the consciousness from which actions spring.
I live my mission.
My intention is to live free from struggle, fear, and hopelessness.
I remember.

4. ACTING/CLAIMING AFFIRMATIONS

The purpose of acting and/or claiming affirmations is to bring something into manifestation or to direct the energy of your intention to appropriate manifestation. These affirmations bring into physical being those ideas that you hold in your mind and/or heart. In addition, these affirmations help you to claim your power and establish boundaries in relationships.

Examples:

I act with high intention and purposeful awareness.
I step into the world to live my mission in every word and action.
I demand my good right now.
I make every act an act of love (or freedom, mastery, or hope, and so on).
I am powerful. I am worthy. I am loveable. I am free.

301

5. INTEGRATING/EMBODYING AFFIRMATIONS

The purpose of integrating and/or embodying affirmations is to allow the energy and meaning of the affirmations to merge with your consciousness. Affirmations and ideas that do not resonate drop away. Integrating/embodying affirmations support us in knowing more deeply—in integrating what we have learned, rather than introducing new information.

Examples:

I integrate trust into every aspect of my life.
I breathe love into my job, my body, and my relationships.
Yes to life!
Today is an opportunity for peace.
I breathe in abundance, letting my whole body feel its energy.

AFFIRMATIONS AS LIFESTYLE

As you work more and more with intentional affirmations—written, spoken, read, chanted, meditated upon—you will make them part of your lifestyle. Affirmations are *already* working for (or against!) you. It is your job to select the ones you want to live by. Remember, you are already using affirmations every time you think or speak! If your current affirmations are disempowering, you can intentionally change them to ones by which you choose to live.

Moods, Emotions, and the Body

Affirmations work primarily on a cognitive level. An affirmation is a new thought. Until it is repeated enough that it can develop a neurological connection in the brain, it will not become a habitual way of thinking.

Body and emotions are critical to observing and shifting mind-set, too. Using Wilber's Quadrant 1 (interior-individual), we can ask coaching clients to observe their personal pervasive moods and to compare them with the pervasive moods of Wilber's Quadrant 3 (interior-collective). Let's imagine that George finds, for example, that dealing with the chronic pain and complaints of his patients creates a mind-set of irritation, despair, and resignation in the culture of his office. He and his staff feel resigned to dealing with the litany of daily complaints and feel relatively powerless to step outside of the negative effect their patients have on them. George finds himself frequently feeling down, disempowered, and resigned to this way of life. He's not angry—just resigned that nothing will change.

We focus now on Quadrant 2 by asking George to observe and demonstrate now how he sits when he's feeling resigned—how he holds his body at the office. As he reports out to his coach what he experiences, his reporting will be from Quadrant 1 (interior-individual). He discovers that he tends to experience a great deal of tension, to hunch over, and to clench his forearms and lower legs. George is telling you that he's contracting his body, making it smaller. One possibility for working with George might be to ask him to deliberately hold his body in a different way and to notice whether that changes his feelings and emotions. A useful fieldwork assignment for him would be to identify how he holds his body when he is feeling open, flexible, and light, to practice holding his body that way in his office or at times when he experiences moods of resignation, and to notice what happens.

Working with the Judging Mind

Once a client begins to self-observe, many paths for working with mind-set open up. Many useful practices exist for working with or moving beyond a chronic tendency toward an assessing and judging mind-set, which may block a client from feeling and experiencing life (Menendez, 2000).

Managers and professionals get paid to become highly adept at making judgments: "What's a right investment?" "What's a wrong investment?" "Who's capable and who's not?" "What's the right plan?" "Am I good enough, capable enough, worthy enough?" These thoughts fill up their mental space with plans and stories that can interfere with their ability to experience the present moment. This is mind clutter.

Chronic attachment to a judging mind has a high cost. That's because the potential for change—the moment of choice—is always right now, in the present. When clients spend too much time judging, dwelling on the past, or imagining the future, they miss the beauty and power of the moment. Fulfillment comes when they focus on the here and now.

303

Clients experience joy and fulfillment when they let go of the *judge* and embrace the *learner* in themselves through the discovery of *beginner's mind.* They shift in consciousness from "It isn't enough, and here's what it could be instead" toward a recognition that "What's here is just right for now."

EXERCISE 14.1
Examine the judging mind

A judging mind sees the world in either/or terms—in black or white. A judging mind is reactive; it asks questions such as:

> What's wrong with this person, the situation, or me?
> What do I need to do to stay in control?
> Who is to blame; whose fault is it?
> How can I win?
> How can I look good?

Set a digital watch so that it sounds on the hour, every hour, between 6 a.m. and 10 p.m. When it sounds, write down the specific thoughts you were having at that moment. At the end of the week, ask how your habits of mind serve you and how they limit you.

EXERCISE 14.2
Practice beginner's mind

A beginner's mind sees the world with fresh eyes, allows for *both/and* terms and shades of gray, and responds flexibly to whatever it encounters. A beginner's mind asks questions such as:

> What is there to be appreciated here?
> What can I learn?
> What are the choices?
> What am I feeling and experiencing right now?

Set a digital watch so that it sounds on the hour, every hour, between 6 a.m. and 10 p.m. When it sounds, use beginner's mind. Write down what you experience in specific terms.

EXERCISE 14.3
Breathe consciously and focus on the present

Do a 4-minute meditation once per hour at work. Sit in a quiet place and focus your attention on your breath. Exhale fully from the deepest place inside your being. Just notice your breath. When distracting thoughts come, notice them and simply return to your breathing.

EXERCISE 14.4
8-4-8 breathing

One mindful breathing approach is to count and create a rhythm of inhale and exhale that induces relaxation. This can be done by inhaling to a count of 8, holding the breath for a count of 4, and exhaling for a count of 8. Many clients find the counting focuses their attention on the present and allows them to return to whatever they are doing in a more conscious, open way.

Fear vs. Trust

In its simplest form, we can identify a client's mind-set by asking whether it's based on fear or on trust. In the example of the client earlier who believed that he had to be in control and make things happen, his mind-set can easily be tracked on the four-celled matrix[3] (see Figure 14.2). Above the horizontal axis are cells representing beliefs that are positive, life-giving, and sustaining for most clients—in other words, beliefs based on trust. Below the horizontal axis are beliefs about insufficiency and danger that generate fear. The left columns are beliefs about the self, or "I." The right columns are beliefs about others or the world in general. Clients can use this matrix to observe how they are judging themselves, others, and possibilities, and to track any core belief to discover whether it is rooted in fear or in trust. Joe was focused outside of himself—on other people and on the environment, which would not readily give him what he wanted. With a new mind-set, others started to behave differently: they supported his actions, and he easily got what he wanted.

As another example, a client says to us, "I'm really afraid to step out and start this business." That statement might have undertones

---

[3] Diane Menendez learned this way of thinking about mind-set from Linda Ackerman and Dean Anderson, complex system change consultants whose Web site is www.beingfirst.com.

concerning a *belief about the self*—"I am not sufficiently worthy or skilled to do this." It might have undertones concerning a *belief about others and the world*—"There are not enough people out there who want this product, and there is too much competition."

We can use the matrix to help clients vocalize their fears. Listen to what the clients say, and then place each statement in the appropriate cell(s) of the matrix. The key questions to ask the clients are, "Is this belief helpful? Does it support you in creating what you want?" If not, explore together what beliefs would be more supportive of the clients, and then discover what it would take for the clients to begin to step into those new beliefs.

Figure 14.2

Belief matrix

I am . . . Enough Worthy Competent	You/Environment are . . . Supportive Enough Abundant
I am not . . . Enough Worthy Competent	You/Environment are not . . . Supportive Enough Abundant

Replacing Fear with Love and Trust

When clients learn to suspend judgment, they notice how the mind tricks them into feeling anxious by focusing on the future and making judgments. Research shows that human beings *naturally* fear only three things: falling, high places, and tight spaces. A judging mind creates fear by focusing on "what if" and imagining a terrible future. Fear causes muscles to contract and creates chronic tension in fearful clients. Energy that gets invested in contracting is energy the clients could be investing in growth.

When clients acknowledge the limiting power of fear and can let go, they release themselves from tension that clamps down on their life like a vise. They open up to trusting themselves, others, and experience in general. Here are some exercises clients may find useful (from Menendez, 2000):

- Examine the energy of your relationships. Who are the people around you with whom you feel most energized? Most calm? Most de-energized? What story do you tell yourself about them that is de-energizing you?
- Experience others. How skilled are you at connecting with others well? Can you be close and feel safely vulnerable? Can you maintain distance without feeling arrogance or anxiety? Rate each of your key work and family relationships using a scale from 1 to 10 (1 = distant, 5 = optimal, 10 = merged). What is your pattern?
- Find the root. When you are feeling blocked by fear, ask yourself, "What other fears are fueling this one?" Identify a root fear, such as the fear of pain, loss or lack, abandonment/separation/rejection, being of no value, being judged, or being meaninglessness. Root fears fuel feelings of being anxious, nervous, unsettled, unfocused. The trick here is that our brain links habitual thoughts. So one fearful thought has elaborate links to others.
- Opportunities for love. Situations that trigger fear are opportunities for love—in other words, for relationship and connection with others. Find out who or what you need to connect with and love, because love drives out fear.
- My teachers. See every person and every situation as a teacher. Ask, "What can I learn here?"
- Cultivate gratitude. Cultivate a sense of appreciation and gratitude for everything that shows up in your life. Practice wonder, reference, and awe on a daily basis. These are ways of expressing love. They relieve pain and connect us with joy. Each day this week, end your day by listing 10 things for which you are grateful. Do not name anything you named on previous days.

307

In this chapter we have focused on one of the most deceptively simple truths that has been known from ancient times. What you think determines what you believe, and what you believe influences your experience . . . and may even create your reality. This is one of the most powerful places for coaches to work.

Chapter 15

Love Is All We Need

Remember that famous statement by Freud—that "what's important in life is to love and to work"? For many of us, it's easier to work well than to love well and be loved well. That may be because intimacy is the area in most people's lives where there is the biggest gap between what they *express* and what they *want,* according to research done using the Firo-B, a psychometric instrument.

What we mean by love in this chapter is not the usual sense of love as romance or intimacy with a partner. The world's major spiritual teachers have said that there are only two real emotions: love and fear. We speak of love here in the sense that spiritual leaders and writers do. Love as an emotion is the absence of fear. Love is a potential we want to experience. Love is a state of being—a *love consciousness* our clients can access that allows them to be courageous, purposeful, and in harmony with their values. Love is experienced in the body as well. Experiencing love, our body feels expansive. We feel centered, grounded, energized, available, and in touch with our whole being— what some might experience as a state of bliss. This state is the opposite of fear.When we experience fear, our body contracts. Physiologically, fear causes our muscles to tighten and prepares us to run, fight, or freeze. We know from research that states generated by fear literally cause our field of sight to narrow, giving us tunnel vision. We literally experience our world as contracted, more limited, and more threatening. That's why we say *love is all you need.* When in doubt, come back to love as a centering point.

In common understanding, love is also the act of creation. So when clients are attempting to create in their life, love is the state that allows them to be creative. We create the feeling of love through connecting: to people, to the earth, to life itself, to something larger than ourselves. Whether we realize it or not, we are always connected. When we are conscious of this connection, love can occur. One basic issue that we encounter frequently in our coaching is that clients feel isolated, particularly in industrialized cultures like that of the United States. They may feel this as loneliness. We coach them to acknowledge the connectedness they live in. Connectedness is a quality of life for all human beings, and to be unaware of our own connectedness is to be unaware of love.

Because human life is a connected life, the quality of each of our lives depends on the quality of our relationships—with family, friends, community, a higher power, and ourselves. When one or more of these relationships becomes unfulfilling, our life becomes unfulfilling.

EXPRESSIONS OF LOVE

The title of this chapter comes from a great song by the Beatles (Lennon & McCartney, 1967). You may be old enough to have heard it on the airwaves. It was easy to remember and carried a profound, timeless message. Written by John Lennon and Paul McCartney, "All You Need Is Love" repeated the title line over and over throughout the song. It addressed the listener directly as "you," reinforcing the personal message that love is both an essential and powerful force for change. This is a message that coaches often work with clients on, encouraging them to give caring and appreciation, as well as to let love into their lives.

Sometimes love scares us because it can bring hurt. Mother Teresa tried to make sense of this for a reporter who asked her how to love without being hurt. She said, "I have found the paradox that if I love until it hurts, then there is no hurt, but only more love." Martin Luther King Jr. echoed her poetic statement of this paradox: "Darkness cannot drive out darkness; only light can do that. Hate cannot drive out hate; only love can do that."

Sometimes our role as parents requires us to love until it hurts. Especially for parents of adolescents, loving until it hurts seems like a hard road. The National Longitudinal Study on Adolescent Health found that a sense of connection at home and a sense of connection at school were the two conditions most protective of children's well-being. It was the perception of connection itself that was key, not any specific program or set of actions.

For parents of adolescents—and coaches, too—Harry Palmer's definition of love offers us a hand to hold in times of frustration: "Love is an
expression of the willingness to create space in which something is
allowed to change" (1997, p. 18).

Some people resist intimacy and love because they seem confining—
a prison of sorts. Being separate feels somehow safer. As Larry Dossey
said, "We have for so long defined ourselves as separate personalities
that we have fallen into the hypnotic spell of believing that separation,
not unity, is the underlying reality" (2006, p. 72).

Yet those who truly love bring that love wherever they are, bridging
even extreme spaces of separation and distance. An example of this
ability to transform through love was told by Frida and Kate Berrigan
(2003), as they offered reflections at the funeral of their father, the
Reverend Philip Berrigan. Philip Berrigan died on December 6, 2002, at
the age of 79. A white Catholic priest whose early ministry among
African Americans opened his eyes to racism and social injustice, he
later left the priesthood but never left his commitment to justice, nonviolence, and peace. He was jailed numerous times for acts of nonviolence
and spent a total of 11 years in prison for these acts. As a writer, teacher,
and activist, he stirred the conscience of many with his call to radical
fidelity to the gospel of peace as an expression of love for all. At his
funeral, his daughter said:

> *Over the years, we had many occasions to visit our Dad in countless*
> *prisons. We have spent time with him in all these dead spaces: spaces*
> *meant to intimidate and beat down; spaces that repel and resist children,*
> *laughter, loving and family; spaces. . . .*
>
> *Some families would sit silently in the visiting rooms, some would*
> *play cards, some would fight. It seemed like those families and the loved*
> *ones they were visiting were burdened by a sense that in jail, everything*
> *was different; life does not go on as usual. You are not free to do as you*
> *please or be who you are.*
>
> *But our Dad never seemed touched by that weight. Even in prison,*
> *even in those awful spaces, he was free. In prison, as in the outside*
> *world, his work and his life were to resist violence and oppression, to*
> *understand and try to live by God's word, to build community* and help
> people learn to love one another.

> *When we visited our Dad in prison, we paid no heed to those spoken and unspoken rules; we filled those places with love, with family, with stories, with laughter. He was free in prison, thereby showing us that freedom has nothing to do with where your body is, or with who holds the keys and who makes the rules. It has everything to do with where your heart is.*

LEARNING TO LOVE OURSELVES

Most of us are taught early how to love others—that we should love others—but we don't learn how to love ourselves. Many have been taught that to love ourselves is wrong, and even that it's a sin. Consequently, many clients in midlife discover that they don't love themselves very much at all. We believe that we need to learn to love ourselves so that we have the capacity to fully love others. Think of the metaphor of a cup that, when full, has enough reserve to give to others. If all that people do is empty their cup all day—through conflict, stress, and worry—and are not having experiences that refill their cup, they have nothing left to give to others. When they arrive home, they cannot give to spouses, children, or themselves. Be aware of when your cup is empty. Consider what you can do to refill yourself.

Loving ourselves is nothing we need to feel ashamed of or embarrassed about. Loving ourselves actually makes us more loveable. In addition, loving ourselves teaches us how to love and care for someone, which means we are able to love others more richly. Sometimes this is the task of coaching—to help clients recover their capacity to love.

Before we can love someone else fully, we must care for ourselves. Before we can fall in love with someone, we must fall in love with ourselves. Loving ourselves will attract people to us. People who love themselves are a delight to be around. If you have ever been around someone who lacks self-love, you know how distressing that can be. Underneath a thin veneer of adaptation to what others expect lies a pool of self-hatred. It depletes us to be around that kind of energy. Those who love themselves naturally love others and have a respect for others and their well-being. Self-love creates positive energy that attracts more positive energy.

Until we truly create a loving relationship with ourselves, other relationships will not be as fulfilling as they could be. When we don't love ourselves, we look for others to fill the void, which drains the energy from our outside relationships. When we love ourselves, we don't have to look outside to have our needs met and, therefore, we can simply enjoy the other relationships for what they are. The outside relationships don't have to compensate for what we are missing inside—they can add to it. This can make the love of others that much sweeter because it is the extra, the icing on the cake.

Self-love is the quiet inner sense people carry that tells others that they are competent, valuable, and worthy of giving and receiving love. Self-love is critical for mental health and happiness, as well as the best insurance against mental distress and depression. A person with self-love can face and handle the shocks and setbacks that inevitably happen in life. Without self-love, the problems of life are more difficult. Something is always missing that can only come from within.

When clients lack self-love, they find it difficult to take care of themselves. As they learn to love themselves, their willingness and ability to care for themselves increases (Williams & Davis, 2002, pp. 150–169).

313

LOVE IS A CHOICE

Love is a choice . . . not simply or always a rational choice, but rather the willingness to be present to others fully without pretense. We use this statement with ILCT students and with our clients, asking them, "What does this quote mean to you?" Many reflect on the fact that being present—authentically present—makes exquisite sense and sounds simple. Yet it is very difficult to do for many of us.[1]

If love is a choice, a key coaching question becomes, "What gets in the way of choosing love for you? What do you choose instead of love?" We ask our clients to do this as a fieldwork activity, noticing over the

[1] With executive clients, Diane Menendez uses an excellent book as a resource, *Leadership and Self-Deception* (Arbinger Institute, 2000). This book, told as a story, describes the way that human beings' tendencies toward self-justification and self-deception lead us to put people "in a box," as the book describes it, and keep us feeling separate, unable to recognize our deep connectedness.

course of a week what they choose instead of love or connection. Common examples of what people choose instead of love are self-focus, anger, judgments, expectations, being right, being busy, worries, and so on. Once clients have identified what gets in the way of choosing love, we can then ask these questions: "How is it you choose these instead of love?" "How can you help yourself choose love instead?"

Sometimes clients need to begin a *practice* of some sort to begin to build their capacity to choose love. One thing we know is that many people who report feeling very fulfilled in their life have practices associated with gratitude. Keeping a journal in which the clients record daily three things they are grateful for has been found to be highly associated with increased joy and lowered incidence of depression (Seligman, 2003).

We also offer Harry Palmer's quote to clients and students as a field-work inquiry: "Love is an expression of the willingness to create space in which something is allowed to change." We then ask clients, "If you accepted this view of love, what would you do differently with yourself and with others this week?"

We use several exercises to help ILCT coaches and clients engage with the issue of love as a choice.

314

EXERCISE 15.1
The compassion exercise

The exercise is based on Palmer's (1997) belief that when people are honest with themselves, they will feel compassion with others. That is, people need to recognize that they are not special but are simply human beings, just like other human beings. Those they are angry with are human. With this humility comes compassion for themselves as well as for others. This exercise actively demonstrates the powerful role of mind-set and its impact on the clients' emotions and well-being. The client pick a specific person on which to focus for the exercise and then complete the following five steps mindfully.

Step 1. With attention on the person, repeat to yourself:
"Just like me, this person is seeking some happiness for his/her life."

Step 2. With attention on the person, repeat to yourself:
"Just like me, this person is trying to avoid suffering in his/her life."

EXERCISE 15.1 (continued)

Step 3. With attention on the person, repeat to yourself:
"Just like me, this person has known sadness, loneliness, and despair."

Step 4. With attention on the person, repeat to yourself:
"Just like me, this person is seeking to fulfill his/her needs."

Step 5. With attention on the person, repeat to yourself:
"Just like me, this person is learning about life."

We have used this exercise with clients by reading the steps to them, while they focus their attention on the person. Most clients report a shift in their emotions after the exercise, which usually brings them to a sense of compassion for the other person that may have been missing earlier. We also find it brings about the sense of connection that is the foundation for love, as we have been describing it here.

We once tried a variation of this exercise with a client who was having difficulty justifying any time she spent on her own self-care. We asked her to identify someone she respected and cared about, whose way of treating herself she admired. We then asked her to visualize herself as that person—acting as if—and to look from that friend's eyes onto her own face, repeating the five steps. This exercise resulted in a great sense of personal peace and opened up the possibility of self-care for this client.

315

EXERCISE 15.2
Expressing love

We said earlier that human beings learn better how to love others than how to love themselves. Through this exercise, we ask clients to learn from themselves how they can better love themselves. These exercises are meant to be done within a coaching session when the intention is to raise clients' awareness about choices they can make.

Step 1. Ask the client, "What do you do for a person you really love? What do you do for or with that person?"

A client might say that he does things he wouldn't do otherwise, such as scratch his wife's back without being asked or paying really close attention and listening when someone talks about their day. As the coach, take good notes on the particular words the client uses.

> EXERCISE 15.2 (continued)
>
> *Step 2.* Ask the client, "Do you do the same for yourself?"
>
> > For the client above, the coach would say, "So you do something your wife loves without being asked. How often do you do things for yourself without others asking you or prompting you to do them?"
> >
> > Or, "So you pay exquisite attention, really listening to that person. How often do you pay exquisite attention to yourself, really listening to yourself?"
> >
> > Most clients report that they do a better job with others than they do with themselves in the specific ways they show love. That leads to the next question.
>
> *Step 3.* Ask, "How can you do more of this with yourself? How can you pay more exquisite attention to yourself—really listen to yourself?"
>
> This exercises focuses on *doing*—the actions that spring out of the feeling of love. It is important to identify specific actions in Step 1 in order to get the clients to consider what actions they can create for themselves. As coaches know, actions can shift attitudes.

> EXERCISE 15.3
> Expressing care
>
> This exercise is similar to Exercise 1 in its structure and intention. It is designed to help clients focus concretely.
>
> *Step 1.* Say to the client, "Think of something—a concrete thing—that you own and really value and care about. What is it?" Then wait until the client identifies the thing.
>
> > Some client examples have included a family photograph album that goes back two generations, a piano, a Mont Blanc pen given to them as a gift, and a 1957 Chevy Corvette.
>
> *Step 2.* "How do you take care of it?" Make sure the client gives specific actions here.
>
> > The client puts the photograph album in a place close to her, protected from light, to preserve it. She also says it will be the first thing she grabs if there is ever a fire or disaster.
> >
> > The client dusts the piano every week, polishes it every other week, keeps its keys covered, and has it tuned regularly.

EXERCISE 15.3 (continued)

The client keeps the Mont Blanc pen in a special leather case so that it won't get scratched by other things in her purse.

The client keeps the 1957 Chevy Corvette in a garage and doesn't take it out when the weather is bad. He drives it carefully and has it maintained by the best mechanic he knows. He doesn't use it for everyday driving, but reserves it for special occasions and celebrations.

Step 3. Ask the client, "How could you do similar things to take exquisite care of yourself?" Treat the client's statement as an analogy, and find analogous actions by brainstorming. This can be a stretch—and a lot of fun—for both coach and client.

"So you put the photograph album in a safe place to protect it and preserve it. Are there ways you can better protect yourself and preserve yourself?" This client ended up thinking about the fact that she did nothing, really, to preserve her skin. She ended up starting a skin-care regimen for herself.

"So you keep your piano very clean, well covered, and polished, and you tune it regularly. Are there ways you can do those things for yourself?" This client thought the question was a stretch but ended up realizing that she doesn't go regularly to her doctor for check-ups (i.e., "tuning"), needs to take better care of her nails and hands ("covering the keys"), and really loves massages but doesn't regularly get one ("polishing it").

"So you keep the pen in a special leather case so that it won't get scratched. Are they ways you need to keep yourself from being hurt needlessly?" This client ended up realizing that she tended to walk and move so fast that she bumped into things and was always getting scratched or bruised. This led to a discussion about slowing down and paying attention as a way of protecting herself.

"So, you reserve your car for special occasions, keeping it out of situations that will potentially damage it and keeping its engine maintained. How can you keep yourself out of harm's way and keep your body maintained?" This client decided to have his cholesterol checked and to stop taking on a particular kind of consulting gig, one that was stressful and brought him into contact with companies whose cultures were harsh and bruising. He decided that he wasn't reserving himself enough for things that could be celebrations. Work didn't have to be so bruising.

THE POWER OF FORGIVENESS

In order to foster healthy self-love, we may need to forgive ourselves, just as healthy love of others requires us letting go of resentments, old angers, and unforgiven wounds. Forgiveness can be difficult to give when revenge seems more appropriate. Yet it grows out of love and can change the course of a life.

We offer a disclaimer here: Many cultures glorify forgiveness to the point where those who have experienced a grievance feel that they *should* easily forgive. This can bring about what Janis Abrahms Spring calls *cheap forgiveness* (Spring, 2004).[2] Those who engage in this behavior easily pardon others without really dealing with their own emotions and coming to terms with their own injury. They may make excuses for others or hold themselves at fault when someone mistreats them.

Refusing to forgive is also an unhealthy approach to forgiveness. Those who refuse to forgive stew in their own hostility, rigidly cutting themselves off from connections with life. Someone who adopts this style can be easily offended and harbor grudges. Through this reactive, rigid style, the person becomes cut off from emotions other than resentment and anger.

We don't recommend that coaches work with clients who are invested in either of the above two styles; in either case, it is likely that therapy is needed. But Spring's principles are useful for many coaching clients who are ready and willing to gain closure on hurtful experiences. Her work also offers two *healthy* options for forgiveness: *acceptance,* in which a person works toward a lasting inner resolution in the absence of the offender's availability or willingness to work on the issue, and *true forgiveness,* which is a healing process that the offender and hurt party engage in together.

In a time when many leaders are unable to say they are sorry or to offer forgiveness, this story shows the power and wisdom of forgiveness:

> *During the American Civil War, a young man named Roswell McIntyre was drafted into the New York Cavalry. The war was not going well.*

[2] Spring's Web site at www.janisabrahmsspring.com includes resources easily accessible to clients of all kinds, answering basic questions about forgiveness such as, "How can I forgive someone who has hurt me? How do I put the injury behind me?"

Soldiers were needed so desperately that he was sent into battle with very little training.

Roswell became frightened—he panicked and ran. He was later court-martialed and condemned to be shot for desertion. McIntyre's mother appealed to President Lincoln. She pleaded that he was young and inexperienced, and that he needed a second chance.

The generals, however, urged the president to enforce discipline. Exceptions, they asserted, would undermine the discipline of an already beleaguered army.

Lincoln thought and prayed. Then he wrote a famous statement. "I have observed," he said, "that it never does a boy much good to shoot him."

He then wrote this letter in his own handwriting: "This letter will certify that Roswell McIntyre is to be readmitted into the New York Cavalry. When he serves out his required enlistment, he will be freed of any charges of desertion."

That faded letter, signed by the president, is on display in the Library of Congress. Beside it there is a note that reads, "This letter was taken from the body of Roswell McIntyre, who died at the battle of Little Five Forks, Virginia."

Given another chance, McIntyre fought until the end (Goodier, 2002).

When we ask clients to consider this true story, they often realize that Lincoln's forgiveness changed the course of a life. They can consider where forgiveness—for themselves, for someone else—might be offered as wisely and generously as Lincoln's.

The Water Bearer, a Teaching Story[3]

A key task of coaching can be learning to love ourselves so that we're available to love others and to receive love. In the teaching story below, the water bearer learns how love can turn flaws into gifts through acceptance.

A water bearer in India had two large pots, which hung on each end of a pole that he carried across his neck.

---

[3] This story has been told by many, and its author is, at present, anonymous. One version of it is found at www.clergyresources.net/med3.html.

One of the pots had a crack in it, and while the other pot was perfect and always delivered a full portion of water at the end of the long walk from the stream to the master's house, the cracked pot arrived only half full.

For two years this went on daily, with the bearer delivering only one and one half pots of water to his master's house. Of course, the perfect pot was proud of its accomplishments. But the poor, cracked pot was ashamed of its own imperfection and miserable that it was able to accomplish only half of what it had been made to do. After 2 years of what it perceived to be a bitter failure, it spoke to the water bearer one day by the stream.

"I am ashamed of myself, and I want to apologize to you."

"Why?" asked the bearer. "What are you ashamed of?"

"I have been able, for these past 2 years, to deliver only half my load because this crack in my side causes water to leak out all the way back to your master's house. Because of my flaws, you have to do all of this work, and you don't get full value from your efforts," the pot said.

The water bearer felt sorry for the old cracked pot, and in his compassion he said, "As we return to the master's house, I want you to notice the beautiful flowers along the path."

Indeed, as they went up the hill, the old cracked pot took notice of the sun warming the beautiful wildflowers on the side of the path, and this cheered it some. But at the end of the trail, it still felt bad because it had leaked out half its load, and so again the pot apologized to the bearer for its failure.

The bearer said to the pot, "Did you notice that there were flowers only on your side of the path, but not on the other pot's side? That's because I have always known about your flaw, and I took advantage of it. I planted flower seeds on your side of the path, and every day while we walk back from the stream, you've watered them. For two years I have been able to pick these beautiful flowers to decorate my master's table. Without you being just the way you are, he would not have this beauty to grace his house."

We use this story with clients to help them recognize that each of us has our own unique flaws. We're all cracked pots. But if we will allow it, our flaws will be used to grace our own and others' tables. In the great connected world we live in, nothing goes to waste. We need not be afraid of our imperfections and our flaws. If we acknowledge them, we too can be the cause of beauty. In our weakness we find our strength.

REFLECTIONS ON LOVE AND SEEING ANEW

Anthony de Mello, a Jesuit priest who grew up in India, brought the benefits of being in the present—of meditative practice—to everything he did. He writes eloquently on the relationship of love and mind-set in one of his most famous books, *Awareness* (de Mello, 1992). He states how we must let go of our need for the approval and love of others in order to truly love. He uses the terms *drug* and *addiction(s)* below to refer to our attachment to fitting in, gaining others' approval, and staying busy and distracted.

We encourage you to read all of *Awareness* because the lessons he describes here often become some part of what clients bring to coaching. They are ready to understand the distinctions between love and need, and between love and attachment.

He says, for example: If you wish to love, you must learn to see again. And if you wish to see, you must learn to give up your "drug." It's as simple as that. Give up your dependency . . . *To see at last with a vision that is clear and unclouded by fear or desire.* You will know what it means to love. But to come to the land of love, you must pass through the pains of death, for to *love* persons means to die to the *need* for persons, and to be utterly alone (pages 171–173).

de Mello's reading makes an excellent fieldwork inquiry for a client who is ready to understand the paradoxical nature of love in human life. The book offers many exercises and reflections that can become a client's fieldwork on the journey to loving without neediness.

Reflections on Love for the Coach

Marilyn Gustin, a participant in a 2001–2002 ILCT training, participated in the class from which this chapter is based. She sent Pat Williams and Diane Menendez the following eloquent piece of writing based on her personal experience of losing her husband and her subsequent thoughts about love and loving, and the place of love in coaching. We liked it so well that Marilyn's writing became an integral part of the ILCT class on love. We print it on the following page, with her permission, so that you can enjoy it, too.

Our culture commonly assumes that love is a "something"—almost quantifiable—that is given by one person and received by another. We know, especially from general psychology, that love is essential to a full human life—perhaps even essential to biological survival. We almost believe it can be "poured" from one heart into another heart, like lemonade from a pitcher. We usually think that if a person does not love a child, that child is doomed to experience life as empty of love and therefore be unable to give love to others. With this assumption, we often go through life wishing for more love from others—and we seek it sometimes in very odd places.

Yet the seers, sages, and saints of the major spiritual traditions do not understand love in that way. They universally say that love is our own essential nature, pure and lasting. They say that this ultimate love is the core of every human heart, that the only reason we do not experience it all the time is that it is covered up by a mountain (or a thousand veils, or a darkness—the metaphor depends on the tradition) of lesser realities. These include all our self-centered desires and aims, our focus on the senses, and the chatter of the mind.

Love, they say, is constantly available, no matter what is going on around us, no matter how life may seem to be treating us. Love just is— flowing, spontaneous, and independent. Love sustains. Love is divine; it is God. Love is never absent. It's just that we are sometimes unaware of its presence, or we misunderstand the meaning of our experience.

This truth about love has become clear for me in the process of spiritual unfolding. But it became unmistakable soon after my beloved husband died. From that time to this, at the thought of John, love springs up, full and beautiful, in my awareness. His body, his personality, all the qualities that I associated with him are gone from this earth. Early in our marriage I would have said that he loved me, that he taught me to love by giving me his own.

Now I know better: the quality of his presence, his awareness of inner love, evoked my own awareness of Inner Love. That is why it can endure now. It was always there within me—I needed only to come to recognize it and revel in it. It is still true: I need only become aware and it is there for savoring, for resting, for delight unlimited.

Do I forget love? Yes. But not as often or as thoroughly as I used to. Is the love I experience all there is? Hardly! Love is infinite. We are pilgrims in love and pilgrims into love just as truly as we walk through air and let it fill our bodies.

These reflections are not included to demonstrate that the sages are correct in their assertion that love is our true nature and dwells equally in all. They are, rather, meant to stimulate us to ask these huge "what if" questions:

What if love is our true essence and it is therefore accessible to anyone and everyone? What if love is, in fact, always present within us and therefore always available to our perception?

Here are some thoughts in response to those questions.

- No one would be seen as helpless to discover love, because the field of inquiry would not depend on another, but rather on one's own willingness to look deep within.
- Romantic love and spousal love could be reframed as a particular expression of the essential Inner Love, thereby freeing relationships from thinking such as, "If you loved me, you would . . . " and "I want you to love me more."
- We could acknowledge that when we "feel loved" by another, what is really happening is that something in the quality of the "other's" presence stimulates our awareness of our own Inner Love. This happens, perhaps, most easily when the "other" is aware of her Inner Love. This awakens us, momentarily at least, to the reality of love in our own center.
- The experience of love is independent of circumstances; it can be accessed even in great pain. It does not require the presence of another human being—although two human beings focused on love bring immense joy to living.
- Doubts about whether one is lovable are also dispelled with the experience of inner love. In fact, the question disappears: there is Love, flowing and grand, within oneself. The experience dissolves even the question of whether I am lovable. Instead, I begin to understand that I am love.

In the modern world, a need is often felt for definitions of love. Our difficulty seems to be that English is not the best language for expressing nuances of profound subjects. It is, however, the language we have.

We use Greek (eros, agape, philios, for example) to try to define types of love. We easily say what love is not—for instance, what we feel about *our car. Some say that love and sexual involvement are equivalent, while others disagree.*

We suggest a reframing to think of love as the force or capacity that is the source of all our feelings of wonder, gratitude, beauty, affection, concern, interest, enjoyment, and fondness. As the endless capacity that makes all these experiences possible, it may well be beyond definition. Perhaps that is good!

Our society seems to believe we have confused ourselves about love, so much so that Kevin Cashman, in Leadership from the Inside Out, *says that it's a forbidden word in business circles. It seems true that we are confused, but perhaps we have only mixed in other inner states with love and are not making the necessary distinctions. We have mixed love with attachment, for example, so that we may feel we "love her/him/it so much" that we must have it in our lives to be happy. We have mixed love with sex so that many cannot tell the difference between the two. Akin to this one is the confusion between love and infatuation.*

If love is the capacity flowing beneath all our positive experiences, creating our delight in the beautiful, lovely, the precious, then love is always present within us, revealing to our perception its many-faceted nature in infinite ways, all of them quite grand. We can call it Inner Love.

324

We are reminded of a story told by Rachel Naomi Remen in her book My Grandfather's Blessings. *When she was a child, her grandfather described to her eight levels of giving and their relative worth. She promised to always "do it right," meaning to give in the highest way. Her grandfather's reply was that "some things have so much goodness in them that they are worth doing any way that you can."*

Love is like that—so utterly good that all expressions of love, no matter how mixed or how "confused" they may be, are worth including in life. If we know this, then to touch a flower tenderly, to experience a romance, to revel in a new possession, and to dedicate oneself to the Divine may all have similar value because they all spring from that deeply inward capacity called love—that capacity which is our true nature.

As long as we imagine love to be a "something" given and received, we also feel that love is limited, that it is dependent on other people, even that it can be destroyed or come to an end. Again, the seers disagree with this. They insist that love is infinite, strong, steady, constant, dynamic, and always accessible. It does not end. It does not depend on other people or on circumstances. They say that all we need to do to uncover this immense love within ourselves is to focus deep within our being.

If all this is true, what are the implications for coaching?

- *All coaches should be practitioners of some form of "entering within." The most common one is meditation, which itself has a number of forms. Just spending quiet time with a focus on the physical space of the heart can open the awareness to the great Inner Love (see below for more on this).*
- *If a coach is aware of her own Inner Love while she works with a client, the client will also experience his own Inner Love. From this can come safety, delight, trust, and eagerness to allow the coach to do her best. Aware of Inner Love, the coach creates a wonderful atmosphere in which coaching can occur with ease, with insight, and with great joy, for both the coach and the client.*
- *A coach might prepare for each session by searching for that experience of Inner Love. His own life would be immeasurably enriched by this repeated, nearly constant awareness of love.*
- *When a coach is aware of love, she is much less tempted to advise, teach, or say too much about herself. Awareness of love makes full listening the most natural of processes.*
- *When a coach is aware of her own Inner Love, her intuition flows more strongly, clearly, and easily into awareness. This might manifest as knowing the best process in any particular moment or the best timing for a particular coaching process.*
- *Once we are in touch with Inner Love, it can be directed—toward people, toward work, toward visions and goals, toward the Divine— anywhere we choose to direct it.*
- *Even if the client is not aware of this loving "soup" in which he is soaking, there will be movement and an opening. It cannot be otherwise, since awareness of our own Inner Love is the most creative force that exists.*

There are many ways of becoming aware of Inner Love. You may already know and practice methods that keep you aware of love. You also may want to experiment with the following:

- *Take a few minutes to still yourself. Focus on your chest, in the area of your heart. Just hold your attention there until your mind slows down a bit. Be aware of inner movement. Watch. Love can arise as a subtle thread or a full-flowing river. Let it be. When you notice it, let your attention rest there and watch it increase in power. Enjoy it for as long as you can.*

- *Sit comfortably and take a few deep breaths. Recall an experience during which you felt great love, or a person for whom you felt great love. Allow yourself to get in touch with that situation again as fully as you can. Now, ever so gently, shift your attention to the love you felt and let the "object" of your love or the trigger for the experience fade from your awareness. Focus on the love alone. There it is, in your own heart. Stay with it as long as you wish. Return gently when you are ready.*
- *Again, while relaxed and quiet, simply request inside to experience the love that is there. Wait. It will appear.*
- *Practice "acting as if" love is the root of your being, your anchor, your constant nourishment from within, and is always accessible. While doing this, you may wish to pause often to "check in" with your own heart.*

Once we have practiced becoming aware of our own Inner Love and have discovered that it is not so hard to access whenever we are willing to be attentive, we can direct this experience of love wherever we want. If we are with our favorite person, we can become aware of love inside and then direct it to him or her. If we are coaching, the client becomes our direction. If we are dealing with a difficult person, we can direct Inner Love to him or her. The possibilities are as infinite as love itself.

As we finish this chapter, we also complete this book. We hope that you have enjoyed the journey and will continue to revisit the skills, strategies, and techniques for launching or improving your coaching business. We chose to end this book with the Inside-Out work and conclude with a focus on love because truthfully, that is at the heart of life coaching, as life coaching is a service for our clients that comes from a deep caring for the clients' fulfillment now and in the future as total human beings. Working from the inside out and caring deeply for our clients as well as ourselves, we have the makings of becoming masterful coaches as well as masterful human beings. Better coaching brings better living.

References

Adler, A. (1998). *Understanding human nature.* Center City, MN: Hazelden.

Adrienne, C. (1998). *The purpose of your life: Finding your place in the world using synchronicity, intuition, and uncommon sense.* New York: Eagle Brook.

Albom, M. (1997). *Tuesdays with Morrie: An old man, a young man, and life's greatest lesson.* New York: Doubleday.

Alderman, R. (1997). *Managing your success.* Retrieved August 2000, from www.managingyoursuccess.com.

American heritage dictionary of the English language (4th ed.). (2000). Boston: Houghton Mifflin.

Anderson, G. (1997). *Living life on purpose.* San Francisco: Harper.

The Arbinger Institute (2000). *Leadership and self-deception: Getting out of the box.* San Francisco: Berrett-Koehler.

Assagioli, R. (1965). *Psychosynthesis: A collection of basic writings.* New York: Penguin.

Bar-On, R. (1997). *BAR-ON Emotional Quotient Inventory Technical Manual.* New York: Multi-health Systems.

Barrows, S. B. (2006). Retrieved October 2006, from www.quotationspage.com/subjects/integrity/

Belf, T.-E. & Ward, C. (1997). *Simply live it up: Brief solutions.* Bethesda, MD: Purposeful Press.

Berg, I. K., & Szabó, P. (2005). *Brief coaching for lasting solutions.* New York: W. W. Norton.

Berman-Fortgong, L. (1998). *Take yourself to the top.* New York: Warner.

Berrigan, F., & Berrigan, K. (2003). Fearless and full of hope. *Sojourners Magazine,* March–April, pp. 37–46.

Blanchard, K., & Peale, N. (1988) *The power of ethical management.* New York: William Morrow.

Block, P. (1999). *Flawless consulting: A guide to getting your expertise used.* New York: Jossey-Bass.

Bly, R. (2004). *The winged energy of delight: Selected translations.* New York: HarperCollins.

Bohm, D. (1996). *On dialogue.* New York: Routledge.

Borysenko, J. (1994). *Pocketful of miracles.* New York: Warner Books.

Braham, B. (1991). *Finding your purpose: A guide to personal fulfillment.* Los Altos, CA: Crisp Publications.

Budd, M., & Rothstein, L. (2000). *You are what you say: The proven program that uses the power of language to combat stress, anger, and depression.* New York: Three Rivers Press.

Cameron, J. (2003). *Walking in this world.* New York: Jeremy P. Tarcher.

Campbell, J. (Ed.) (1971). *The portable Jung.* New York: Viking.

Cashman, K. (1998). *Leadership from the inside out.* Provo, UT: Executive Excellence Publishers.

Chopra, D. (2005). *The seven laws of spiritual success.* Nashville, TN: Broadman & Holman Publishers.

Chrisly, M. (Sept. 10, 1986). Mayflower Madam tells all. *Boston Globe,* p. 27.

Coffey, L. M. (1997). *Simply coaching* (Audiotape series). Denver, CO: Business Coaching, Inc.

Cook-Greuter, S. R. (2004). Making the case for a developmental perspective. *Industrial and Commercial Training, 36*(7), 1–10.

Covey, S. (1989). *The 7 habits of highly effective people: Powerful lessons in personal change.* New York: Simon and Schuster.

Csikszentmihalyi, M. (1990). *Flow: The psychology of optimal experience.* New York: HarperCollins.

Dalai Lama (2002). *How to practice the way to a meaningful life.* New York: Pocket Books.

de Mello, A. (1992). *Awareness.* New York: Doubleday.

de Shazer, S., & Lipchik, E. (1984). Frames and reframing. *Family Therapy Collections, 11,* 88–97.

Dossey, L. (2006). *The extraordinary healing power of ordinary things: Fourteen natural steps to health and happiness.* New York: Harmony Books.

Drucker, P. (2003). *The essential Drucker: The best of sixty years of Peter Drucker's essential writings on management.* New York: HarperBusiness.

Ellis, D. (1997). *Life coaching: A new career for helping professionals.* Rapid City, SD: Breakthrough Enterprises.

Ellis, D. (2006). *Life coaching: A new career for helping professionals.* Norwalk, CT: Crown House Publishing.

Ellis, D., & Lankowitz, S. (1995). *Human being: A manual for health, wealth, love, and happiness.* Rapid City, SD: Breakthrough Enterprises.

Erhard, W. (2000). *Werner Erhard.* Retrieved October 7, 2002, from www.working-minds.com/werner.htm

Flaherty, J. (1998). *Coaching: Evoking excellence in others.* Burlington, MA: Butterworth-Heinemann.

Frankl, V. (2006). *Man's search for meaning.* Boston: Beacon Press.

Gallwey, W. T. (2000). *The inner game of work: Focus, learning, pleasure, and mobility in the workplace.* New York: Random House.

Gawain, S. (1997). *Meditations* (Audio CD). Novato, CA: New World Publishers.

Gladwell, M. (2005). *Blink: The power of thinking without thinking.* New York: Little, Brown and Company.

Goldberg, M. C. (1998). *The art of the question: A guide to short-term question-centered therapy.* New York: John Wiley & Sons.

Goldstein, A. (July 3, 2000). Paging all parents. *Time, 3*(47), 1.

Goleman, D. (1995). *Emotional intelligence.* New York: Bantam Books.

Goleman, D. (July 3, 2002). *Primal leadership: Realizing the power of emotional intelligence.* Boston: Harvard Business School Press.

Goodier, S. (September 27, 2002). The Friday morning story (E-newsletter).

Graham, E., & Crossen, C. (1996, March).The overloaded American: Too many things to do, too little time to do them. *Wall Street Journal, 8,* RI.

Graves, C. W. Retrieved August 6, 2006, from www.clarewgraves. com/theory_content/quotes.html

Greenstreet, K. (2004). *How to create and run a mastermind group.* Retrieved July 10, 2006, from www.passionfor business.com/articles/mastermind-group.htm.

Grove, D. (1997). *Less is more: The art of clean language.* Retrieved May 3, 2005, from www.cleanlanguage.co.uk/CleanLanguage.html

Haley, J. (1986). *Uncommon therapy: The psychiatric techniques of Milton H. Erickson, M.D.* New York: W. W. Norton.

Hargrove, R. (1995). *Masterful coaching.* San Francisco: Pfeiffer.

Hill, N. (1966). *Think and grow rich.* New York: Hawthorn Books.

Hill, H. (1976). *From goo to you by way of the zoo.* New Jersey: Logos International.

Hirshberg, J. (1998). *The creative priority: Driving innovative business in the real world.* New York: HarperBusiness.

Hoffer, E. (1951). *True believer: Thoughts on the nature of mass movements.* New York: Harper & Row.

Hudson, F. M. (1999). *The adult years: Mastering the art of self-renewal.* San Francisco: Jossey-Bass.

Hudson, F. M., & McLean, P. D. (2000). *Life launch: A passionate guide to the rest of your life.* Santa Barbara, CA: Hudson Press.

Humbert, P. E. (2001). The innovative professional (TIPS) newsletter. Retrieved December 6, 2001, from www.philiphumbert.com

International Coach Federation (2007). *What is coaching?* Retrieved January 8, 2007 from www.coachfederation.org.

James, W. (1994). *The varieties of religious experience: A study in human nature.* New York: Random House.

James, W. (1983). *The principles of psychology.* Cambridge, MA: Harvard University Press.

Johnson, B. (1992). *Polarity management: Identifying and managing unsolvable problems.* Amherst, MA: HRD Press.

329

Johnson, S. (2002). *The one-minute salesperson.* New York: William Morrow.

Johnston, R. K., & Smith, J. (2001). *Life is not work, work is not life: Simple reminders for finding balance in a 24/7 world.* Berkeley, CA: Wildcat Canyon Press.

Jones, L. B. (1996). *The path: Creating your mission statement for work and for life.* New York: Hyperion.

Jung, C. G. (1964). *Man and his symbols.* Garden City, NY: Doubleday.

Kegan, R. (1983). *The evolving self: Problem and process in human development.* Cambridge, MA: Harvard University Press.

Kunzig, R. (August, 2000). Antigravity in Pisa. *Discover, 21*(8).

Laing, R. D. (1983). *Politics of experience.* New York: Pantheon.

Laske, O. (2003). An integrated model of developmental coaching: Researching new ways of coaching and coach education. In Stein, I. & Belsten, L. (Eds.), *Proceedings of the First ICF Coaching Research Symposium* (pp. 52–61). Mooresville, NC: Paw Print Press.

Leider, R. J. (2005). *The power of purpose.* San Francisco, CA: Berrett-Koehler Publishers.

Lennon, J., & McCartney, P. (1967). *"All you need is love."* Nashville, TN: SONY/ATV Music Publishing.

Levinson, D. (1986). *Seasons of a man's life.* New York: Ballantine.

Levoy, G. (1997). *Callings: Finding and following an authentic life.* New York: Random House.

Loevinger, J. (Ed.) (1998). *Technical foundations for measuring ego development.* Mahwah, NJ: Erlbaum.

Lynch, D., & Kordis, P. (1988). *Strategy of the dolphin.* New York: William Morrow.

Marshall, J. (2006). *Types of affirmations.* Retrieved August, 2005, from www.mhmail.com.

Maslow, A. H. (1971) *The farther reaches of human nature.* New York: Penguin.

Maslow, A. H. (1998). *Toward a psychology of being.* New York: John Wiley & Sons.

May, R. (1983). *The discovery of being.* New York: W. W. Norton.

McLean, P., & Stinnett, K. (2002). *Planning on purpose: Discovery guide.* Santa Barbara, CA: The Hudson Institute. (Pamphlet available from www.hudson institute.com.)

McCraty, R., & Childre, D. (2006). The appreciative heart: The psychophysiology of positive emotions and optimal functioning (e-book). www.HeartMath.org. Boulder Creek, CA: The Institute of HeartMath.

McWilliams, J.-R., & McWilliams, P. (1992). *Wealth 101: Getting what you want—enjoying what you've got.* Los Angeles: Prelude Press.

Medical College of Wisconsin Health News (2000). *Personal values are key to physicians' job satisfaction.* Retrieved June 28, 2000, from www.healthlink. mcw.edu.

Menendez, D. (August/Sept. 2000). Coaching from spirit. *Inner Edge 3*(4), 12–13.

Menendez, D., & Lowry, S. (1999). The seamless life series. *The sideroad* (e-zine), www.sideroad.com/seamless.

Monk, G., Winslade, J., Crocket, K., & Epston, D. (Eds.) (1997). *Narrative therapy in practice: The archaeology of hope.* San Francisco: John Wiley & Sons.

Moore, M., Drake, D., Tschannen-Moran, B., Campone, F., & Kauffman, C. (2006). Relational flow: A theoretical model for the intuitive dance. In F. Campone & J. Bennett (Eds.), *Proceedings of the Third International Coach Research Symposium,* ICF, Lexington, Kentucky.

Mountain Dreamer, O. (1999). *The invitation.* New York: HarperCollins.

Murphy Jr., E. A. (September 2006). www.en.wikiquote.org/wiki/Murphy's_Law

Nadler, G., & Hibino, S. (1998). *Breakthrough thinking: The seven principles of creative problem solving.* Roseville, CA: Prima Lifestyles.

National Institute of Business Management (March 2006). 8 keys to leadership genius. *Executive Leadership,* p. 1.

Nelson, P. (1993). *There's a hole in my sidewalk: The romance of self-discovery.* Hillsboro, OR: Beyond Words Publishing.

O'Connor, J., & Seymour, J. (2000). *Introducing neuro-linguistic programming: Psychological skills for understanding and influencing people.* London: Thorsons Publishers.

O'Hanlon, B., & Hudson, P. (1995). *Stop blaming, start loving: A solution-oriented approach to improving your relationship.* New York: W. W. Norton.

O'Hanlon, B. (1998). *A guide to possibility land.* New York: W. W. Norton.

O'Hanlon, B. (2006). www.billohanlon.com.

Oliver, M. (1986). *Dream work.* New York: Atlantic Monthly Press.

Ortony, A. (1975/2001) Why metaphors are necessary and not just nice. *Educational Theory, 25,* 45–53; reprinted in Gannon, M. J. (2001), *Cultural metaphors: Readings, research translation, and commentary* (pp. 9–21). Thousand Oaks, CA: Sage Publications.

Palmer, H. (1997). *Resurfacing: Techniques for exploring consciousness.* Los Angeles: Stars End Creations.

Palmer, H. (2006). *The forgiveness option.* Retrieved from www.avatarepc.com/html/forgiveness(eng).pdf

Perls, F. S. (1969). *Gestalt therapy verbatim.* Lafayette, CA: Real People Press.

Piercy, M. (2003). *To be of use.* In C. Mauro (Ed.), *Prairie of fertile land.* Seattle, WA: Whit Press.

331

Prochaska, J. O., Norcross, J. C., & DiClemente, C. C. (1994). *Changing for good: A revolutionary six-stage program fro overcoming bad habits and moving your life forward.* New York: Harper Collins.

Proctor, B. (1997). *You were born rich: Now you can discover and develop those riches.* Phoenix, AZ: LifeSuccess Productions.

Quinn, R. (1996). *Deep change: Discovering the leader within.* San Francisco: Jossey-Bass.

Remen, R. N. (2000). *My grandfather's blessings: Stories of strength, refuge, and belonging.* New York: Riverhead Books.

Richardson, C. (1998). *Take time for your life: A personal coach's seven-step program for creating the life you want.* New York: Broadway Books.

Rilke, R. M. (1992). *Letters to a young poet.* San Rafael, CA: New World Library.

Rogers, C. (1951). *Client-centered therapy: Its current practice, implications, and theory.* Boston: Houghton Mifflin.

Roosevelt, E. (1937). Retrieved from www.quotedb.com/

Rotary International. *Four-way test.* Retrieved July 9, 2004, from www.rotary.org/aboutrotary/4way.html.

Ruiz, D. M. (1997). *The four agreements: A practical guide to personal freedom, a Toltec wisdom book.* San Rafael, CA: Amber-Allen Publishing.

Searle, J. R. (1997). *The mystery of consciousness.* New York: The New York Review of Books.

Seligman, M. E. (2002). *Authentic happiness: Using the new positive psychology to realize your potential for lasting fulfillment.* New York: Free Press.

Seligman, M. E. (2003). Teleclass on *Authentic happiness: Using the new positive psychology to realize your potential for lasting fulfillment.*

Simon, S. B. (1972). *Values clarification: A handbook of practical strategies for teachers and students.* New York: Hart Publishing Co.

Solomon, R. C., & Flores, F. (2001). *Building trust: In business, politics, relationships, and life.* New York: Oxford University Press.

Spinosa, C., Flores, F., & Dreyfus, H. L. (1997). *Disclosing new worlds: Entrepreneurship, democratic action, and the cultivation of solidarity.* Cambridge, MA: MIT Press.

Spring, J. A. (2004). *How can I forgive you? The courage to forgive, the freedom not to.* New York: HarperCollins.

Suenens, L. J. (2006). Retrieved February 7, 2006, from www.inspirational-quotes.info/

Tolle, E. (1999). *The power of now: A guide to spiritual enlightenment.* Novato, CA: New World Library.

Torbert, W., Cook-Grueter, S., Fisher, D., Foldy, E., Gauthier, A., Keely, J., et al. (2004). *Action inquiry: The secret of timely and transforming leadership.* San Francisco: Berrett-Koehler.

USA Today (October 24, 1997). *Snapshot: If I were a rich man,* p. IA.

Vuocolo, J. (2005). E-mail newsletter from www.soulbusiness.com

Warren, R. (2002). *The purpose-driven life.* New York: Zondervan.

Wells, S. (1998). *Choosing the future.* Burlington, MA: Butterworth-Heine-mann.

White, G. (December 13, 1998). Consumed by consumerism. *Atlanta Journal Constitution,* p. RI.

Whitworth, L., Kinsey-House, H., & Sandahl, P. (1998). *Co-active coaching: New skills for coaching people toward success in work and life.* Palo Alto, CA: Davies-Black Publishing.

Wilber, K. (2000). *Integral psychology: Consciousness, spirit, psychology, therapy.* Boston: Shambhala Publications.

Williams, P. (2004). Evolution and revolution of coaching in the workplace. Wellness Councils of America. Retrieved November 7, 2004, from www.welcoa.org/absoluteadvantage

Williams, P., & Davis, D. (2002). *Therapist as life coach: Transforming your practice.* New York: W. W. Norton.

Williams, P. & Thomas, L. (2005). *Total life coaching: 50+ life lessons, skills, and techniques to enhance your practice . . . and your life.* New York: W. W. Norton.

ASSESSMENT RESOURCES:
Myers-Briggs: www.knowyourtype.com
DISC: www.ttidisc.com
People Map: www.peoplemaptraining.com
Values in Action Signature Strengths Assessment: www.authentichappiness.com

Index

339

341